To Doris – my
longtime friend.

With Love,
Mom LaVera

FOUR SCORE and MORE

My memoir, history and a family legacy

LaVera Edick

LAVERA EDICK

Order this book online at www.trafford.com
or email orders@trafford.com

Most Trafford titles are also available at major online book retailers.

Printed in the United States of America.

ISBN: 978-1-4669-7396-1 (sc)
ISBN: 978-1-4669-7398-5 (hc)
ISBN: 978-1-4669-7397-8 (e)

Library of Congress Control Number: 2013900897

Trafford rev. 03/13/2013

 www.trafford.com

North America & international
toll-free: 1 888 232 4444 (USA & Canada)
phone: 250 383 6864 ♦ fax: 812 355 4082

Dedication

This book is dedicated to my parents, Ray and Minnie Woodring, my children: Sharri, Carolyn, Michael, Beckie, and Robert, and to my late husband, Robert William Edick, who gave me encouragement and financial security to pursue my endeavors in art and family genealogical research.

Foreword

These memoirs are written with the hope that they may prove not only interesting to read, but also give you, my family, a better understanding of where you came from.

I have attempted to truthfully describe life as it was over the past eighty plus years. I have tried to make our ancestors come to life as real people, experiencing the good and bad in life, as we all do. The Greeks say "The dead die when those who loved them stop talking about them—as long as they are talked about and loved—they live."

I would like to share with you one of my favorite poems, whose author is unknown:

The Weaver

My life is but a weaving,
Between my Lord and me;
I cannot choose the colors,
He worketh steadily.

Oft times He weaveth sorrow
And I in foolish pride,
Forget He sees the upper
And I, the underside.
The dark threads are as needed

In the Weaver's skillful hand,
As the threads of gold and silver
In the pattern He has planned.

Not till the loom is silent,
And the shuttles cease to fly,
Shall God unroll the canvas,
And explain the reason why.

This poem reminds me of my father's words: "God has a plan for each of us and only He knows when our life here on earth is finished." Those words have been an inspiration and a guidepost for me to follow throughout the years.

LaVera Edick

Acknowledgements

My sincere thanks go to my parents, Ray and Minnie Woodring; my older brother, Harold Woodring; my uncle Earl Woodring; and my other mother, Ruth Woodring, for sharing stories of family events that took place before I was born or old enough to remember; they, and my first teacher, Vera Connell, played a major role in helping me choose the path I followed throughout my life.

Thanks to my younger brother, Willis; my cousins, Jackie and Zilpha; my nephew, Gary; my niece, Karen; and my children: Sharri, Carolyn, Michael, Beckie, and Robert, for sharing family stories as they remembered them.

A special thanks to my daughter Carolyn, who painstakingly took all the scrawled sentences from my handwritten story, editing and copying hundreds of pages of manuscript. I couldn't have done it without her.

Thanks to Jackie for the skillful and sensitive final editing of my manuscript. I am so grateful for her help and suggestions.

This memoir is a record of events, many of them personal. In an attempt to be fair and accurate, I have cross-checked many of my memories with others to insure accuracy. I have also changed some names for the sake of identity protection. Also, I acknowledge Wikipedia, a copy left encyclopedia, as a source of help with statistics. In the end, however, this is my story. I leave it as a legacy to my family. It is my belief that one must have some understanding of the past in order to appreciate the present and look forward to the future.

My sincerest thanks to all who have gone before us including the pioneers who cut the trails and paved the roads for our journey through life.

Introduction

Life is a gift to all of us. Leaving behind a legacy of life's dreams, endeavors and lessons is the intent of this book. I was raised on a dry land farm by my parents Ray and Minnie Woodring, who were honest, hard working Nebraska farm folk. Living through the Great Depression, the Dust Bowl days and World War II, my father taught me early in life to have faith in God. His words were: "God has a plan for all of us. He helps those who help themselves."

This story of my life takes you through my adventures, determination and contributions to family and society and looks at historic world events as they occurred throughout my life. It is a memoir that reads like a novel.

I was "First Lady" of Provident Life Insurance Company for nearly twenty years, while my husband Robert William Edick was president of the company. At that time, I pursued one of my many life's endeavors, that of becoming an artist.

At the age of eighty-seven and as the matriarch of a large and loving family, I have five children, thirteen grandchildren, twenty great-grandchildren and hopes of becoming a great-great-grandmother within the next few years.

Contents

Chapter 1

THE MAN AND WOMAN
GOD CHOSE TO BE MY PARENTS

My parents were very special. I was a lucky little girl when God chose to send me to them.

Ray and Minnie Woodring were married February 11, 1914, and were blessed with three children: Harold Lowell, LaVera Mae, and Willis Wayne. Seventeen years passed between the birth of their first and last child, and I was in the middle.

Minnie Gail Forster was born in Smithfield, Nebraska, February 7, 1897, the daughter of George Forster and Anna (Tomasek) Forster. Minnie was a tiny baby when she moved, with her parents and two-year-old sister Elsie Mae, to a sod house sitting on a hill a mile north of Smithfield. In the late eighteen hundreds many of the houses in Gosper County, Nebraska, were "soddies." Lumber was scarce and expensive; sod was plentiful and cheap. The floors were dirt and soon became so packed down that they were not so dusty; however, bed bugs and sand fleas still lived in the dirt. The floors were scrubbed with milk to make them shiny. At one time, a wall of Forster's soddy caved in. They stayed with the Bartchers, across the field, while it was being rebuilt.

The Bartchers also had a baby girl, Vida Joy. Mrs. Bartcher "wet nursed" my mother. In those days there were no bottles with nipples. The mothers ran back and forth, across the field, for Vida Joy to share her mother's breast milk with my mother, Minnie. It must have bonded the two babies, as Vida and Minnie were life-long friends. Vida visited my mother in the nursing home, in Holdrege, Nebraska, not long before my mother's death from arteriosclerosis on December 26, 1976, at age 79.

As a child, Minnie had a frightening experience. While carving a face on a pumpkin, the jack-knife she was using slipped, severing an artery between the thumb and forefinger. Herman Scheels, a Forster neighbor, owned a car in the days cars were rare. Mom remembered, they wrapped a sheet around her hand and headed for town. Dr. Leese, in Smithfield, told this little girl that she was a "bleeder" and to never have surgery or she would die. My mother went through three pregnancies, afraid of dying with each one. Her babies were, no doubt, spaced years apart and all difficult births because of the words of an unthinking doctor spoken to a child.

Minnie graduated from the two years of high school offered in Smithfield at that time. It was a very special time in young Minnie's life. Her artistic talent was displayed in the calligraphy she used to sign her calling cards. Many homes had calling card tables. When a guest called and found the lady of the house not home, a calling card was left on that table. Mom must have talked to me often about those days, as I recall the name of her teacher and the story about her. Sarah Gainsforth was pregnant the last few months of school, but kept her "corset" so tightly laced, as was the style, that no one suspected she was carrying a baby until after graduation.

The girls wore smelling salts in little vials around their necks to help revive them from the fainting spells brought on as the result of tightly laced corsets. Velvet covered fainting couches were found in almost every parlor.

My mother was a beautiful young lady, with fancy dresses, bouffant hairdos and fabulous hats. The hairdo was enhanced by hair gathered from the combs and brushes, saved in celluloid hair receivers, and made into "switches" to give a bouffant look. Curls were added with a curling iron which had been heated by hanging it on the chimney of the kerosene boudoir lamp.

It was not until the Roaring Twenties, the era of the "Charleston" and the "Flapper," that girls dared cut their hair and wear dresses above their knees. Even though Minnie had been married for several years, she was reluctant for her parents to see her new "bobbed" hairdo and short dress.

Mom often told me that she weighed less than a hundred pounds until she gave birth to me, at age 28. She said, "My waistline was never the same after a nine pound baby." As a young high school girl her cinched in waistline was less than eighteen inches. At that time neighborhood invitational dances were the vogue. The boy paid admission for them, a penny an inch for the girl's waistline measurement. Minnie must have been a cheap date.

My father, christened Cyrus Raymond, but always called Ray, was born in Smithfield, Nebraska, March 19, 1894, the oldest son of Charles Wilson Woodring and Minnie Belle (Graham) Woodring.

I recall my dad saying he had croup a lot as a child, today probably called asthma. As a toddler, he was accidently scalded by boiling water, leaving his chest badly scared. In another incident, at age 10, he and his cousins were caught smoking behind a shed when the shed itself began smoking. On October 22, 1963, at 69 years of age, he died of emphysema.

Uncle Earl, my dad's brother, at age ninety told me about their childhood companion, a collie dog named Carlos. Ray made a harness for Carlos and hitched him to a wagon so little Earl could go for rides.

Dad recalled riding in a covered wagon when he was very young. His mother and her sister, Jeanette (Graham) Birt, with their two little boys, Ray and John, traveled over 100 miles to Concordia, Kansas, to visit the boys' grandmother, Lucinda (McBurney) Graham. Dad remembered that it was so cold that the wagon slid on ice and they had to unharness the oxen in order to save them. They must have been very courageous women to have attempted such an undertaking.

Ray dropped out of school when he was a sixth grader to help out at home. He never complained about leaving school but instead spent his life educating himself. He was an avid reader and a "whiz" at math.

One summer, as a teen-ager, Ray worked at an International Harvester plant for his uncle Will Woodring, who lived near Chicago, Illinois. Uncle Will bought him several outfits of clothing from his wages because he knew all of Ray's money would be given to his parents when he got home.

Ray left his sweetheart Minnie Forster in Smithfield when he and his family moved to San Diego, California, in September, 1912. Most of their courtship was by letter. After Minnie graduated from high school, Ray went back to marry her. Minnie was just seventeen, Ray was nineteen. George

Ray Woodring age 19   Minnie Forster age 17

Ray and Minnie were married in Norton Kansas
on February 11, 1914

Forster said "no" when Ray asked for his daughter's hand in marriage. Ray's cousin Ruth remembered a very unhappy young man asking her father, "What shall I do?" His Uncle Hiram Woodring answered, "Well, if you truly love one another, get a ladder and elope." That's what they did! With Ray's father as a witness they were married in Norton, Kansas. Their honeymoon was spent on a train headed back to San Diego.

Minnie went to work at a tuna canning plant (my mother never ate a tuna sandwich, or served tuna at her home; as a matter of fact, she didn't even like to watch gold fish swim.) Ray worked as a roofer, on flat roofs that were covered with tar.

Minnie's baby brother, Delmar Leo, died shortly after she left home and she missed him so much. That was probably the reason she became friends with a little neighbor boy named Lowell, and his mother. I never tired of hearing my mother tell this story when I was a child. It seemed that Lowell's mother was frying chicken and ran out of pepper. Talking to herself, as busy mothers often do, she said, "Oh darn, I'm out of pepper!" They lived on busy Imperial Avenue, across the street from Mr. Booker's little grocery store. She hadn't noticed three year old Lowell leave the house, until he tugged at her skirt saying, "Mr. Booky says to write a "peppi" on a "papi" den I get a "peppi." She panicked when she realized he had crossed a very busy street, twice, by himself. Many years later, my parents named their first child Harold Lowell.

Living with Ray's parents was not easy for Minnie; she missed her parents and wanted to go back home. They planned and saved their money. By early 1915, they had saved $300.00 dollars and bought two one way train tickets back to Nebraska. The money left over was all they had to start up housekeeping and farming. They rented the Hanlin farm between Smithfield and Elwood, in the Quakerville area. They didn't have the money for much furniture, but a Singer treadle sewing machine was one of their first purchases. (It is now proudly displayed in the home of their granddaughter Carolyn and is covered with a scarf her grandmother Minnie had embroidered with roses.) Most of their clothes were made on that machine as well as baby diapers and blankets, sheets and pillow cases, curtains, bedspreads, quilts, tablecloths, napkins and even handkerchiefs. (Disposable paper items such as these were as yet unheard of; can you imagine life without Kleenex?)

My mother told stories of her early days as a housewife. Striving to please her husband with her homemaking skills, she made a batch of chokecherry jelly. Something went wrong and it wouldn't jell. What should she do? She decided she would just feed it to the chickens so Ray wouldn't know, since that's what they did with all the kitchen food scraps. As the story goes, it was very, very sticky and the chickens got stuck in it! When Ray came in from the field, he found Minnie in tears, trying to unstick the chickens by washing their feet.

In 1918, Harold, as a little boy, knew that ducks were supposed to swim. He thought maybe he needed to teach them how, so he held them, one by one, in a tub of water and sure enough, they swam, or rather floated, on top. When his mother found him, he cried, "Look Mommy, they're swimming."

In 1920 two new amendments to the Constitution turned the nation upside down. The eighteenth amendment prohibited the manufacture and sale of alcoholic beverages. The nineteenth amendment gave women the right to vote.

Baby Harold, born July17, 1917,   CARLOS AND HIS BOY HAROLD
with his mother holding him.   Art by LaVera

DAD'S FIRST CAR
Art by LaVera
These old time photos were taken by my mother with a Kodak
Brownie camera; she also developed the film at home.

World War I had ended. Effigies of the Kaiser were being burned, and victory parades were held throughout the land. Nebraska famers were prospering, because crops were yielding well and prices were high. My parents had moved to the farm where I was born and had purchased a black (they were all black) 1914 Model T Ford touring car (a Tin Lizzie). Both my parents learned to drive. It seems Dad was a somewhat fast and reckless driver. His Uncle Wayne Hood dubbed him "Barnie," the first name of a famous race car driver of the day.

In 1925, F. Scott Fitzgerald wrote, *The Great Gatsby*. The Montmartre in Paris was a gathering place for American artists and writers.

On the other side of the world, in the tiny town of Smithfield, Nebraska, a storm raged. Flashes of lightening, claps of thunder and lashing wind and rain made the night of September 10th unforgettable. Only one light burned in the farmhouse just east of town, and that was a kerosene lamp on a nightstand next to a brass bed. There my mother lay in labor with me, her second child. Dr. Guy Clark, a country doctor with a crippled arm, had arrived hours earlier. My little Bohemian grandmother, Anna (Tomasek) Forster, and a midwife, Mrs. August Lavene, were also in the room. My father Ray and my nine-year-old brother Harold were in another part of the house, as expectant fathers were not allowed in the birthing room in those days.

Dr. Clark was worried because, as he later admitted, he was afraid of losing both mother and baby. He asked for someone to boil water to sterilize the instruments, but my grandmother was nowhere to be found. She had apparently chosen the

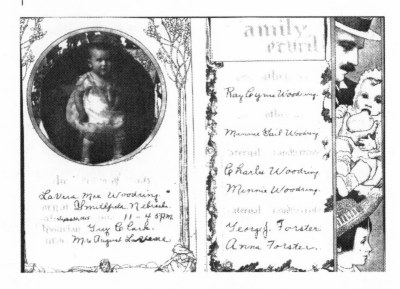

Pages from my baby book.

My mother holding me, in front of the house where I was born.

My father and my brother, Harold

stormy weather outside and was walking down the muddy lane towards the road, rather than face the stormy atmosphere inside. Mrs. Lavene boiled the water and with the aid of forceps, I was born, a nine pound baby girl, with chubby arms and legs and dark hair sticking into the creases of my neck. I had my first haircut when I was only a day old.

I was christened LaVera Mae. One of my parents wanted to name me Vera and the other didn't, so they compromised and called me La Vera. Mae was the middle name of the only sister of each of my parents and of my grandfather's sister, Clara Mae.

My mother must have been a very busy lady, with a family to care for, and a large garden to plant, hoe and harvest. She set hens, raised chickens, helped husk the corn and yet somehow still found time to record the stepping stones in the early life of her baby girl. In a baby book handed down to me many years later, I found these notations:

"First smiled at four weeks"

"Coos and laughs aloud at two months"

"Weighed sixteen and a half pounds at six months"

"Says Mama and Da Da at seven months"

"Took first steps at ten months"

"Says baby, doll and kitty at ten months"

"Hollers at Harold and tries to say his name at eleven months"

"At eleven and a half months goes on a run"

"At twenty one months, climbs up to the sewing machine, calls it a "seam-a sewmer," unwinds the thread and says, "Me working hard, Daddy," when her daddy came in from the field.

At twenty-two months says "Go milk the cow," "Go bye town buy candy" and "Don't cut Harold's overalls, Mama."

Dad was injured when his team of horses ran wild, dragging him and mangling his right arm. The doctor who made a house call to change the bandage on Dad's infected arm, at the same time performed mastoid surgery on me on the kitchen table. Mastoiditis started with a common cold; an infection from the throat spread to the inner ear, causing pain and inflammation and very often required surgery. The antibiotics today usually prevent the need of surgery for such an infection. I often had earaches and sat on my dad's lap so that he could blow cigarette smoke in my ear. I don't know if the smoke helped or if it was the comforting feeling of sitting on my dad's lap.

I recall my dad telling me I could catch that pretty bird if I put salt on its tail. He must have chuckled when he saw me running around the yard with a salt shaker in my hand. I always believed everything my dad told me!

One of my earliest memories is riding in our Model T on a windy day. I was wrapped in a blanket on my mother's lap. With one hand she held me, and with the other tried to hold the car curtain closed. On very cold winter days we used lap robes of horse and buffalo hide and hair to keep us warm.

After Dad injured his arm, he couldn't do farm work and had to hire help. Mom came to the rescue, and made extra money by proving her ability as a sales lady. I rode along when Dad drove her around the area to sell aluminum cookware and furniture polish (made by a local man and packaged in quart fruit jars). I can remember having a sliver in my finger and one of mother's customers promising me a treat if I would allow her to use a needle to remove it. The treat was a prune.

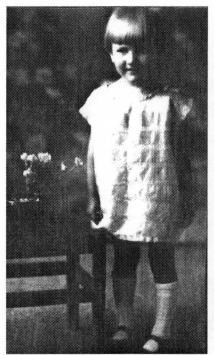

Me in the dress my mother made for me by sewing the ribbon and lace together for the fabric.

ME AND MY POOR CAT
Art by LaVera

Harold with me, his little sister.

In 1927, while our family was experiencing its own adventures on the farm, Babe Ruth, who at one time was married to a Woodring girl, hit sixty home runs.

In 1928, when I was three, my parents bought the small dry land farm where I grew up, four miles west of Smithfield in the Quakerville School District of Gosper County, Nebraska.

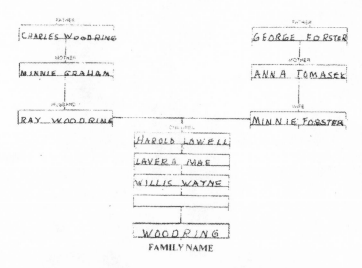

RAY AND MINNIE WOODRING FAMILY TREE

Chapter 2

QUAKERVILLE

I was three when my parents, my twelve-year-old brother Harold and I moved from the rented farm, east of Smithfield, to one owned by my parents and the Mortgage Company, in the Quakerville School District.

It was a small, dry land (non-irrigated) farm with a large house, a storm-root cellar and an outhouse. Across the yard, some distance from the house, stood a big red barn with a well, a windmill and a cistern with a hand pump. The well was made by digging a hole into the earth to reach an underground water supply then lined with cement to hold water. The windmill acted as a wind-driven water pump. The cistern was an underground water storage tank, filled from the well. The cistern pump had to be primed each time it was used; a tin drinking cup always hung nearby.

Some fifty years earlier, this area had been a Quaker settlement, known as Quakerville. Old timers told that our house was built in those years by a Quaker from the East. The first family of Quakers was soon followed by more members of the same religion. Their church, which also served as their school, was built just a mile north of our farm home. It was sod, with a roof of poles hauled from Plum Creek (later to become Lexington) and again covered with sod. The construction of this building was a neighborhood project. Two of the family names were Hibbs and Birt. The wives, Temperance Hibbs and Janette Birt were "Graham" girls and sisters of my father's mother, Minnie Belle (Graham) Woodring.

Minnie Graham went to live with her sister Janette as a young girl, and joined the Quaker church. In one of her poems she mentions "leaving the fold." She married Charles Woodring, who was non-Quaker; years later I learned that my father had been raised as a Quaker. The church disbanded in1920 and a new frame building, erected on the site, became Quakerville School. The families in the area, including my parents, attended the Christian Church in Elwood, just a few miles to the west.

It was said that the man who built our house had shot a policeman and was running from the law. He lived in fear of being caught, always afraid of strangers. He had a "peek hole" in the front door enabling him to look before he opened!

Our house was old, but well built, with wainscoting and chair rails in the kitchen, ornate woodwork and doors, twelve inch high "mop boards" and "gingerbread" embellishing the front porch.

It was a four-bedroom home with an ornate curved stairway in the dining room leading to the upper level. Two of the upstairs bedrooms were "attic-like" with just enough room for the bed. There was a "crawl in" attic off one of those rooms. Mother modernized the brass bed in my room. The posts of the bed were capped; my cousin Winona's and my imaginations turned them into ice cream containers at a soda fountain. The head of the bed was cut off and tossed; the foot became the head, creating the Hollywood style of the thirties. The downstairs had a small bedroom, dining room, parlor and a kitchen.

WOODRING FARM
Art by LaVera
Gosper County, Quakerville School District

QUAKERVILLE SCHOOL
Art by LaVera

All five students at Quakerville
School, back row, Miss Joy,
middle row, left to right—Eldora
Legott, LaVera Mae Woodring
Anna Mae Leggott, front row, left
to right-Alice Jean Leggott and
Phyllis Robb.

I remember three other small rooms: one was a walk-in pantry, one was my playroom and the other was used as a laundry room and a place where Mom hung a bucket, adapted with a hose and spray nozzle, so we could take showers on hot summer days.

Baths were a weekend affair. Water was hauled from the cistern, heated and placed in a round bath tub in the middle of the kitchen floor. The youngest bathed first and washed their hair, the oldest was last, all in the same tub and water! When it rained, we placed buckets under the eaves of the house to collect "soft water" that was used with the bar of bath soap to shampoo our hair. A vinegar water rinse cut the soap film. We brushed our teeth with Arm and Hammer baking soda and went to the dentist only when a tooth ached so persistently that it had to be extracted.

The buffet, dining room table and oak pressed back chairs were in the dining room. It was also home for a pot-bellied coal-wood heating stove. During the winter months, a large, black stovepipe was stretched across the ceiling, leading to the outdoor chimney. In the summer the stove was taken down and stored in a little cubbyhole under the stairway. On the wall of that room hung an oak cased telephone. In those days the telephone lines were only barbed wire strung on fence posts. (The first Continental Telephone line was completed in 1914. On January 25, 1915, the first call was made from Alexander Graham Bell in New York to Thomas A. Watson in San Francisco.) In rural Nebraska a dozen or more families shared the same telephone line. A "central" or telephone operator in Elwood worked at a switchboard to connect the calling parties. When the phone "twanged," you listened for your designated code number of long and short rings to see if the call was for you.

To keep up with the news in the neighborhood, you just might listen in on a neighbor's call. That was called "rubbering." A call was made by cranking the handle on the side of the phone. An extra long ring was called a "general ring" and meant everyone should listen. It was usually a crisis, or emergency call. There was a general ring when the Smithfield Bank was robbed and the banker, Mr. Mahlin, and his bulldog, had been locked in the bank vault. There was a general ring when Ruth Weber's hair was burned off. She cried, "A man in a black suit, black coat and hat, cut a hole in the screen door, poured gasoline on my head and burned my hair." The community had been looking for the criminal for days before Ruth confessed. She had made up the whole story so she could have short hair like the other girls. It was against the beliefs of her parents' church to allow women to cut their hair, or wear makeup or jewelry.

Our parlor held a green, velvet fainting couch, a pressed back oak chair and a library table groaning with family wedding and baby pictures. In one corner, a carved walnut fern stand held a Boston fern, whose fronds almost touched the floor. It was my mother's pride and joy! She often warned me, "Don't touch the ends, it will make them turn brown."

The parlor was seldom used, except maybe when company came on Sunday. Sunday was a day of rest, but cooking wasn't classified as work by my mother. (She was a very good cook and many of her recipes are still being used by her family.)

A favorite was her Pineapple Cheese Salad:

1 package lemon Jell-o

1 cup crushed pineapple (drained)

1 cup grated cheddar cheese

¼ cup whipping cream (whipped)

¼ cup salad dressing

2 tablespoons sugar

2 cups water or pineapple juice

Prepare Jell-o as usual and cool to whipping stage. Fold in pineapple and grated cheese. Combine whipped cream, salad dressing and sugar. Sprinkle grated cheese on top.

Sunday family dinners were special. The dining room table was set with an open-work embroidered white linen tablecloth and napkins to match. The table was not large enough for everyone. That may have been the reason for the men to eat first, then the children, but I believe it was custom. The mashed potatoes and gravy were cold by that time and the bony pieces were all that was left from the huge platter of fried chicken. The women, the last to eat, had to settle for the backs and necks, while the kids were given the wings and gizzards.

The women cooked, served and washed dishes. Doing the dishes was a time to catch up on neighborhood gossip. The men tossed horseshoes in the back yard. One Sunday, my Forster cousins and I got into mischief while playing upstairs and pretending we were models by wearing my mother's silk dresses, made to fit with large safety pins. Other times we jumped rope or played outside games such as "Mother May I?" or "Ring around the Rosy."

The last line of "Ring around the Rosy" back then was: "last one down is a nigger baby;" and now it is "last one down is a big fat clown." It was in the early sixties when my daughter, Beckie Jo, remembers chanting:

> Eenie, Meenie, Mienie, Mo,
> Catch a nigger by the toe,
> If he hollers, make him pay,
> Fifty dollars every day

My nephew, Kevin Schaefer, recalls a chant: "Black, White—Lets Fight" when he was a school boy in Phoenix, Arizona in the mid-seventies. Little thought was given to the derogatory terms used to refer to black people. Has verbal abuse of the blacks ended yet today? Physical abuse of the blacks supposedly ended with the freeing of the slaves after the Civil War—but did it? Segregation was alive and well. On December 1, 1955, Rosa Parks was arrested for refusing to give up her seat on the bus to a white, resulting in a U.S. District Court ruling that ended segregation on all Montgomery, Alabama public buses. Martin Luther King, Jr. organized and led marches for blacks' right to vote, desegregation, labor rights and other civil rights. Most of these rights were enacted into law with the passage of the Civil Rights Act of 1964 and the 1965 Voting Rights Act. King was assassinated on April 4, 1968, and Martin Luther King, Jr. Day was established as a U.S. Federal holiday in 1986.

Liquor was not found and never served at our house; but when we visited Uncle Ralph and Aunt Ethel Forster, there was "home brew" beer and wine that was kept in the cellar. Curious kids that we were, my two Forster cousins, Winona, Neomia and I hid in the cellar one Sunday afternoon. We found a quart fruit jar and from it served ourselves a few drinks of wine. We were mighty giggly and our mothers mighty angry when we were pulled from our hiding place. That was my first taste of an alcoholic beverage, other than just a few drops of Great-Grandma Tomasek's dandelion wine. My mother wouldn't even let me drink tea or coffee!

My maternal grandmother Anna Forster usually had "just a small glass of beer" with the boys. When the doctor suggested she drink beer as a treatment for indigestion she objected, but soon learned to enjoy it. (Beer was the favored drink in the Klatovy-Pilzen area of Bohemia where she was born.) After her glass of beer, there was always a long, drawn out, satisfying sounding "belch." (In some cultures, that was not considered rude, but just a sign of enjoying a good meal or drink.)

I remember that Uncle Ralph always had to have his pie before dinner, but, of course, the kids had to wait until after dinner for their dessert. We didn't think that was fair.

One Sunday, at Uncle Ralph's house, we three cousins found a nest of baby mice in the tool shed. We decided it would be great fun to each take a baby mouse by its tail, hold it behind our back and run into the kitchen to scare our mothers and Grandma Forster. We were rewarded by their screams before we ran back outside.

Sunday dinners were usually followed by Sunday suppers. The men did the chores at both the hosts' and the guests' farms before supper. On one occasion, a cake had been placed on the bottom shelf of our buffet to be saved for supper. My cousin Doris Holthus and I, both just toddlers, were in partnership. One climbed in the buffet and fed the cake to the other.

NEBRASKA

•GORDON

•GRAND ISLAND

• SCOTTSBLUFF

•NORTH PLATTE
•LEXINGTON •KEARNEY
• ELWOOD
•SMITHFIELD •LINCOLN
• BERTRAND •OMAHA
• HOLDREGE

OUR NEW CAR
Art by LaVera
Me, on the left, and Ana Lee, my cousin,
with our new Woodring family car, a 1929 Chevy.

I remember with shame when my playmate Floy Phillips and I, as preschoolers, stole an Angel Food Cake from the Elwood County Fair food display, sneaked it out behind the building and ate every crumb. (Were traits developed then, that taught me to hide and devour fat-making sweets in later years?) Desserts are what I seem to remember best, the pineapple "Slide Down Cake" (as I called it) the "Burnt Sugar Cake," with frosting an inch thick, and "Strawberry Shortcake" with strawberries from our garden patch and cream from our Holstein cows. For birthdays there was always "Angel Food Cake" with candles.

It was a cold day, a few months after my fourth birthday; I was wearing my little red coat and hat with white fur trim. We were on our way to Elwood to trade our old Model T for a brand new green, four-door, 1929 Chevrolet. I must have heard my dad say it would cost a lot of money, because I recall emptying my piggy bank and giving my pennies to Daddy to help pay for the new car. After the deal was closed, the nice salesman took us to a restaurant for lunch, something we didn't do often, and I remember sitting in a high chair.

Ours was a nice house, I thought, but my mother hated the old-fashioned look and the gingerbread. She was always looking for ways to modernize: by removing the kitchen wainscoting and chair rails, then the beautiful woodwork and even the gingerbread on the front porch. Using a garden rake as a tool, Mom loosened a few more boards on the porch adding to damage the wind storm had already done. Dad was upset and felt they were being dishonest by collecting insurance on it.

The kitchen was usually the center of activity, especially during the cold winter months. There was a coal-wood cook stove, with a cob box nearby, a dry sink with a bucket of water and a drinking ladle (used by all), a kitchen cupboard and a kitchen table with four chairs. They were white and decorated with prairie roses or daisies, hand painted by my mother. I didn't realize then that not every mother had that artistic ability. Another of her talents was photography. She took many photos with a "Brownie" box camera and developed her own film. Some of the paintings I have done over the years were from her photos. I treasure one of myself in my dad's hat in front of a corn crib. My favorite spot on cold days was behind the kitchen coal-wood stove with a pillow and blanket. I often had to share with our dog Snookie, or maybe even a box of new-born piglets whose mother had either died or rejected them. They were fed milk from a bottle and nipple. Blocks of wood were heated in the oven, and at bedtime we each grabbed one, wrapped in a towel, and dashed off to our unheated upstairs bedrooms. With pieced comforters weighting us down and warm feet, we slept soundly through the night. I often awakened in the morning to see small drifts of snow across my bedroom floor. In the morning, I would dash downstairs in my nightie, to dress on the corn cob box by the stove. One morning I sat on the edge of the stove! Ouch!

I was often left alone in the house when my parents and Harold worked late husking corn. One day Aunt Elsie came to visit and found me alone. Elsie left a note: Minnie, if I ever find LaVera Mae home alone again, I'm going to take her home with me. (She did take me to Uncle Walter's parents' home that day, a big old house, as I remember, with lots of cubby holes and fun places to explore.) On those occasions when I wasn't rescued, and because I couldn't light the kerosene lamp, when it got dark, I bundled up and sat on the doorstep of our farmhouse to avoid the imaginary ghosts and monsters hiding behind the doors. One evening, before dark, I decided to surprise my parents and have the table set for supper when they came in from the barn. I climbed up on the kitchen cupboard counter to get the dishes and—alas!—tipped it over. Broken dishes, flour, sugar, spices, canisters, and LaVera Mae—unhurt—all landed in the middle of the kitchen floor. They returned to the house to find a little girl in tears trying to "fix" the dishes with a bottle of glue. (There have been other times when I could have been found in tears, trying to put together the broken pieces of my life but my faith that "God has a plan for me" always helped put things in the proper perspective.)

I was a first grader at Quakerville School during the presidential election between Franklin D. Roosevelt and Herbert Hoover. Most of the farmers were Democrats and didn't believe in Hoover or his slogan, "prosperity is just around the corner, a chicken in every pot." Everyone in our school election voted for Roosevelt, except Lorene Green. I thought she was a bit strange anyway. She wore an apron to school. I wore one at home to keep my dress clean longer because I didn't have enough dresses to change every day, but not to town or school. It was also rumored that Lorene's dad sold "moonshine."

Vera Connell was my teacher, from first through fourth grades. She was short, chubby, had uneven teeth and a crooked smile, but to me she was beautiful! I wanted to look just like her when I grew up. The first day of school I rushed home to tell Mom all about my teacher. My mother asked, "Do you like her as well as Mommy?" I responded, "Well, I think just a little bit better." Wrong answer!

Our school was an all girl school, quite by accident. There just were no boys of school age living in that school district. The boys I knew either finished or dropped out of school to help with farm work, before I even started. Education didn't hold a high priority rating in the dirty thirties; better the boys learn how to farm and the girls how to sew and keep house. I particularly remember John and Howard Jones; Howard married a twelve-year-old-girl, who was a student at Quakerville for a couple of years. Doris and Helen Schroeder and their brother (who had been kicked by a horse as a child and had a horse-shoe shaped scar on his face) were all past school age. Floy and Ina Phillips had a brother who was deaf and mute and attended a special school in Omaha. My brother, Harold, had finished elementary school before my first year of school.

Six students was the highest enrollment at any time during my eight years there. The teachers had a lot of time to devote to us—or did they? A rural school teacher in those days accepted not only the role of a teacher but also that of a janitor and a nurse. I recall several times when I froze my ears, walking over a mile to school in sub-zero weather. Mrs. Connell packed ice around my ears so they thawed slowly with less pain. I often had nosebleeds and she would have me lie on the piano bench and put cold packs on my nose.

Once a week, we had "Show and Tell." I had not yet learned to read cursive when I found a bundle of letters, tied with a blue satin ribbon, in a box in our upstairs attic. I must not have shown them to Mom and Dad before I took them to school for "Show and Tell." They were my parents' love letters! I don't recall my mother's reaction but my dad let me know that I had done something wrong!

I remember the thrill of getting a new box of "Crayolas" at the beginning of the school year. I loved the smell of them. I was in awe of all the beautiful colors and I took good care of them. When my cousin Ana Lee used one to mark on my bedroom wall I was very upset. It hurt my crayon, my wall and my mother would be angry!

Mrs. Connell was a very special person in my life. Maybe she was just as special to my schoolmates, I don't know, but ours was a lasting friendship. I was ten years old the last year she taught at Quakerville. We kept in touch for more than forty years, by visits, phone calls and letters, until she passed away. I must have tried my mother's patience at times for I recall her saying, "If you don't stop being such a bad girl, they are going to come get me and take me to the funny farm." I could never erase those words from my memory. Years later, after I had children of my own, I wrote to Mrs. Connell and asked her; "What kind of a little girl was I?" Her letter of reply:

Dear Lavera Mae,

I surely remember you as a little girl. You were so pretty and neat and likeable. I think you were very happy. You smiled and laughed when it was permissible to do so. You always studied your lessons in a hurry. You got all your lessons completed so much quicker than others in your class or in the school.

You may have been reserved with other people, but not with me. You surely enjoyed coming home with me and staying overnight. I sometimes bought special candies or cookies and I would give you one.

I remember I told you as long as you had your lessons finished, you could do anything you wished with your spare time. I think the other pupils thought I was partial to you. I think I was, but I tried not to show it. Anyway, you were nice looking and easy to get along with.

Vera Connell Kunc

I think I may have been teacher's pet—and I loved it! The other girls used to tease me because they were curling their hair and mine was straight and looked like my mother put a soup bowl on my head to use as a pattern. My teacher used to say, "Don't you worry, you will be the prettiest when you grow up." I recall carving animals from bars of ivory soap in my spare time at school and doing black reverse painting on glass. I saved foil gum wrappers to put on the back of the glass. Reynolds Wrap was not yet to be found on the grocery shelves.

Winter was fun at Quakerville School. We built snowmen, made angels in the snow, and had snowball fights from snow forts. We loved recess and were never ready to see our teacher at the door ringing the brass bell. I pulled my sled up the hills to school so I could slide down them on the way home! I hated the long cotton stockings we wore in the winter, with garter belts around the waist to hold them up. On the first warm day of spring, Floy and I would take them off in the "outhouse dressing room," hide them nearby, and put them back on before we walked home. We knew if our mothers saw us bare legged we would hear something like "You're going to catch your death of foolishness." We did catch colds often and every childhood disease of the day,—mumps, measles, chicken pox and scarlatina. I brought head lice and "seven year itch" home from school. We seldom went to the doctor; home remedies were used. There was rendered skunk grease to put on the chest for colds, and one of my dad's dirty socks tied around my neck. (If the budget allowed there might be a jar of "Vicks Vapor Rub".) We drank onion tea for upset stomachs or perhaps "Pain Relief" from Watkins. Skin infections, such as boils, were poulticed with fat meat. I remember going to Dr. Clark's office in Elwood when streaks were running from my poulticed hand up my arm, a known sign of blood poisoning. The doctor took one look, and said to my mother, "Yea Gads, why didn't you add a waffle, it would have done as much good?" The seven year itch was treated with lard and sulfur applied to the whole body. All of my bedding, towels and clothing had to be boiled. I tried not to let my mother know if I was getting sick because I didn't want to miss school. Watching the "Dr. Quinn," television show recently, which takes place in Colorado Springs in the late 1800s', I was reminded of the many home remedies used in the early days. How reluctant the townspeople in that area were to accept the doctor's advice that was not a lot different from folks in the rural area of Nebraska, where chicken noodle soup (Jewish penicillin) and onion tea, were given to the sick child. Today they have both been found to have medicinal benefits.

My dad's father had two children from a former marriage. The boy lived with his mother and the girl, Marva, lived with her father and his family. I recall Dad telling me of losing his older step-sister, Marva, and his little brother Marvin, when they lived in Colorado Springs in the late 1800's. They died from scarlet fever on a Friday the thirteenth. Dad would never plan anything

Smith... Pa.
Nov. 27, 1934

Dear Lavera Mae;

Always mind your mother,
Do it with a grace,
And if your fellow kisses you,
Slap him on the face.

    Your Mother.

        Minnie Woodring.

Pages from my autograph album.

Jan. 14, 1935

Dear Lavera Mae:

Leaves may wither
Flowers may die
But forget you
Never will I

    And

Remember me, you may, you must,
As long as you can bite a crust
And when you can no longer bite
Forget me, if you think it right.

You have been a very good pupil
the past four years. I hope you will
do as well the next four years. If
all pupils were as good as you, they
wouldn't need to... such... and...
Don't forget your teacher,

        Your ...

Dear La Vera Mae:

When the words that I write
grow dim on the page
and the leaves of your album
are yellow with age,
Remember me kindly
and do not forget
that where ever I am
I remember you yet

Remember me   Your friend and
always   School Mate
                        Dibby

important on Friday the thirteenth, one of his few superstitions, unlike my mother, who was very superstitious.

A picture appears on my memory screen of a little girl, wearing a sunbonnet, a blue gingham pinafore and red stockings. She was dressed just like me and was standing beside me on a stage in front of an audience, and then I hear singing:

The two little maids stood facing one another; one shook her little index finger at the other as she threatened, "You can't slide down our cellar door or holler down our rain-barrel." The other shook her finger just as emphatically and replied, "And you can't climb our apple tree; I don't want to play in your yard if you won't be nice to me."

Even though the lyrics of this song, "Two Little Maids," were written many years ago in 1884, by Philip Wingate, they still told the story of my childhood on a Nebraska farm. We still hollered down the rain-barrel, slid down the cellar door, climbed the apple tree and told secrets down by the windmill well.

The two little girls were Floy Phillips and me. The stage was at Quakerville School and it was entertainment night, the last Friday night of the month. The monthly Parent Teachers Association meetings had developed into a social night with entertainment and refreshments such as coffee and cookies. The whole school district came, not just the families who had children attending school there. The stage was built by the men in the community, while the women added curtains, especially for such presentations as this. The students put on the show one month, and the next month folks from the community revealed their many hidden talents. We had a rhythm band where I first played the spoons, then the tambourine. One year

Santa brought me a ukulele and I learned to strum it and sing songs, such as "Red River Valley," "Birmingham Jail," "Home on the Range" and of course at Christmas time, "Santa Claus Is Coming To Town" and "Jingle Bells."

I remember only one song my mother sang to me, "Twinkle, Twinkle, Little Star" in Latin, but Dad sang a lot. Some of the songs I recall are: "When You and I Were Young, Maggie," "Silver Threads Among The Gold," "It's A Long, Long Way To Tipperary" and "Casey Jones."

Once a year, the Quakerville School community put on a three act play. I was a preschooler when I started reciting poetry during intermission time. I recall part of one of the poems:

> I fell into the pig pen,
> My new dress was just a sight,
> If mama'd made it pig color,
> T'wouldn't have showed a mite.

I continued reciting poetry though my elementary school years and was asked to do a poem as part of the Gosper County Eighth Grade Graduation ceremony.

Mom always had the leading female part in these plays and Fred Schroeder the leading male part. The title of one of the plays was "Aaron Slick from Punkin Creek." Vera Connell, the teacher, was a little girl in the play. Dressed in a short skirt with a ribbon in her hair, she was pulled from under the table by her ear when she was caught eavesdropping.

The plays were given in towns close by, and a small admission fee was charged. At the close of the season, the proceeds were used to treat the entire Quakerville School District to an Oyster Stew supper. The stew was cooked in a copper wash boiler in the school kitchen. At one such event, Mrs. Connell had filled a shaker with "Bon Ami" to clean the sink. It was mistaken as a salt shaker and used to season the stew! The cooks kept mum about the seasoning that "Hasn't Scratched Yet" and the oyster supper was enjoyed by all.

Perhaps one of the first "Hot Lunch Programs" was when we brought potatoes to school and put them on the coal furnace to bake before lunch time. It was 1930 when we saw the first sliced bread and packaged frozen food. I was jealous of my classmates who brought "store bought bread" sandwiches to school in their "Karo Syrup" lunch buckets; I would trade my "Knipp" sandwiches on home baked bread for Glenda Robb's raw onion sandwiches on "store bought bread." Was it for the bread or the raw onions? (I still love raw onion sandwiches, but how I would love once again to walk home from school smelling hot bread, fresh from the oven and watch Mom cut a thick slice for me and spread it with home churned butter and home grown strawberry preserves.) During my frequent overnight stays with my teacher, Vera Connell, at her parent's home in Elwood, I always looked forward to lunch the next day! I knew my lunch bucket would hold an apple, an orange, a banana and honest to goodness "store bought bread" on a lunch meat sandwich. I thought that teachers and people living in town had more money, since they always had "store bought bread" and fresh fruit to eat.

The only fresh fruit we had, during the depression years, were the peaches, plums and pears at canning time. There were wild plums, chokecherries and strawberries from our garden during the summer months that were made into jelly or jam. I still recall the scratches, chigger and mosquito bites from helping pick wild berries.

In the summer we looked forward to picking cherries from the tree in Grandma and Grandpa's backyard. It was the first tree I learned to climb. Uncle Ralph and Aunt Ethel had a mulberry tree, but we didn't climb it. We just put a sheet under it, shook the tree, and watched the mulberries rain down.

In the fall our whole family went to the Platte Valley fruit orchards to pick windfall apples. The bad parts were cut away from the apples before they were canned or made into apple butter; the good ones were saved. They stayed fresh for most of the winter if they were kept in the root cellar. The root cellar held a potpourri of odors during the winter months. There was a bin of potatoes, a large wooden barrel of salted whiting fish which had to be soaked overnight to make it edible and cured hams and bacon hanging from the ceiling. Large "Red Wing" crocks were filled with parsnips, carrots, beets and turnips layered in sand. Potatoes periodically grew sprouts, and one of my chores was to snip them off to keep the potatoes from spoiling. When spring arrived, the potatoes with sprouts were planted for the next year's crop. Potatoes had to be planted in the "full of the moon" according to the Farmer's Almanac. Early in the winter we would enjoy Hubbard squash, pumpkins and Christmas melons. Some of the seeds were always saved for next years' crop. We had a large melon patch that was vandalized one year. Melons were thrown, breaking them open, then only the hearts eaten. Dad discouraged this happening again by pulling a wagon near the patch and sleeping there a couple of nights with his shotgun handy. Dad would gladly have given them melons, but he couldn't see them wasted. What garden vegetables, fruits and melons we didn't use, can, sell or give away were fed to the livestock.

The root cellar was also the storm cellar. We went there often when tornado clouds were threatening. Harold and I would complain when a storm came up when we were freezing ice cream with a hand crank freezer. Mom solved that problem by taking a metal box, holding spoons and dishes, to the cellar! After that, the freezer of ice cream went with us to the storm cellar and we had a party until the storm blew over. (Maybe that is why I have never minded storms and why I taught my children not to be afraid of the wind, rain, thunder and lightning.)

The reason we were able to raise great gardens was because of the ingenuity of my father. He hand dug a six-by-ten foot reservoir, cemented the sides and bottoms and filled it with water from the nearby well. The garden was at the bottom of the hill and gravity-irrigated from the reservoir. My father also built an ice house (a basement with a roof). He froze ice in molds then stored the blocks of ice between layers of straw in the ice house. We had ice all summer to make ice cream, and to keep milk, cream, butter, eggs and other foods fresh. Before the ice house, my mother had lowered those foods in a bucket, with a rope attached, into the cistern. Dad's next project was an ice box. He built a box, lined it with tin, and equipped it with a tray for ice, a tray for food and a pan underneath to catch water from the melting ice.

Mom spent many early mornings hoeing the garden. When I awakened, I hurriedly dressed, put cereal and milk into a bowl and ran to the garden. I picked raspberries from the bushes climbing on the garden fence to add to my cereal. I remember helping pick strawberries. We ate all we could, made jam, and sold the rest to the local grocery stores. I helped pack them in pint size wooden boxes.

Over the years Dad had built a garage, a machine shop and a two story chicken house. We almost lost the garage when mice found farmers matches in the pocket of Dad's overalls that were hanging on a nail in the garage. I watched my family save the building with a five-gallon water bucket relay. Mom hand pumped the water from the cistern, Harold carried the filled buckets part way to meet Dad, who ran the rest of the way to douse the water on the fire!

I was a fifth grader when my teacher took the whole school, all six of us, to her house in Elwood for supper, a movie and to stay overnight! We had scalloped potatoes and ham for supper. I didn't know then that ham came in such perfect thin slices. Our hams were home cured and hung in the root cellar, where they collected mold that had to be trimmed off before slicing. After that lovely supper, Miss Joy took us to a movie at Elwood Theater, where I saw my first movie, "Snow White and the Seven Dwarfs."

Recently, my granddaughter Nickie gave me the angel figurine, "Angel of Learning." My angels of learning were my parents and my teacher, Vera Connell. I learned to love school and reading during my early years at Quakerville School. Each week I carried home all the books the Elwood Public Library would allow me to check out at one time. One of my favorite books was *Heidi*. I imagined climbing into the loft where she slept. The description of the melted cheese sandwich her grandpa made for her made my mouth water!

I was a lucky little girl to have loving grandparents living nearby. Grandpa Woodring and Grandma and Grandpa Forster were counted among the approximately one hundred residents of Smithfield in the late twenties.

In the middle of the main street of town stood a windmill or cistern from which water was pumped into a large tank sitting on a horse-drawn wagon. The sewer system consisted of a small building, called an outhouse, behind each home.

Main Street was the site of a grocery store, a post office, a hardware store, a doctor's office, a bank and a penny candy store. Grandma and Grandpa's house was just around the corner, handy for my Forster cousins and me to go shopping with our precious pennies clutched tightly in our little hands. There were rows and rows of jars of hard candy and black licorice: licorice cigarettes, licorice pipes and licorice nigger babies. My choice was usually pipes and nigger babies.

In the summer of 1929, we were at the free family night outdoor movies in Smithfield, when our big red barn was struck by lightning. It burned to the ground with a team of horses and hay inside. The insurance had lapsed just a few days earlier because Dad didn't have enough money to pay the premium. I watched the flames from the burning barn shooting into the sky to the west, from my Grandpa and Grandma's house in Smithfield.

Chapter 3

SMITHFIELD

My paternal grandparents, Charles and Minnie Woodring, lived in the township of Smithfield, Nebraska, in 1890, soon after it was established. Since Mr. and Mrs. E.B. Smith owned the land and built the first building, a livery stable, in the middle of a millet field, the township was named Smithfield.

Within a few years the Currier Hotel was built, soon followed by a general store called The Right Place, built in 1897 by E.E. Wood, who was also the publisher of a newspaper called Practical Farm News.

The first church was built in the late 1890's, at the cost of $3,000.00 and was debt free. A free will offering was used to purchase a church bell for the new Methodist Church, which also served as the first school. The children used benches as desks, and the teacher's desk was a tree stump. The books were locked in a trunk at night to protect them from the field mice.

In the early 1900's, Smithfield was home to several entrepreneurs and professionals. Lester Ryan invented an air cooling refrigerator and the "Easy Way Ironing Board," and built a factory for their manufacture that employed 20 people. H. K. Beisecker made cement blocks that were used to build several of the downtown store buildings. Richard Dawler built a merry-go-round, powered by a steam engine, in time for the 1899 Fourth of July celebration. In addition to a barber, the town boasted three attorneys and a physician, Dr. N.J. Leese. The first banking business was done in a small office of a lumber yard. Two grain elevators were located at the edge of town. The peak population of 229 residents of Smithfield occurred in 1902.

Ten years later, in 1912, the Smithfield's business district included Shepard's Drug Store, Biesecker's Grocery Store, and the post office. E.T. Bigelow was the postmaster. The first telephone system was installed by J.L. Biesecker when the messages were carried over barbed wire.

On May 24, 1844, Samuel Morse sent the first telegraph message, "What hath God Wrought?" from the Supreme Court chamber in Washington, D.C. to Baltimore.

It was 1860, when William Cody, a fifteen year old teenager also known as Buffalo Bill, became a rider for Pony Express. In that same year, a multiline telegraph system had been constructed alongside the route of the Transcontinental Railroad, making Pony Express obsolete.

By 1912 America had come a long way in the field of communication; however, one wonders how long it took for news, such as the "sinking of the Titanic" to reach Small Town, USA?

Across the Atlantic, on April 10, 1912, the Titanic left Southampton, England on her tragic maiden voyage toward New York City, with 2,222 souls on board. On April 15, she struck an iceberg and sank, resulting in the loss of 1,517 lives. It was one of the deadliest peacetime maritime disasters in history due to the fact that although complying with regulations of the

THE STATE OF NEBRASKA, |ss Marriage License.

GOSPER COUNTY,

OFFICE OF THE
COUNTY JUDGE

LICENSE is hereby granted to any person authorized to solemnize marriages according to the laws of said State, to join in marriage

Mr. Charles Woodring .... and Miss Minnie Graham ....

of the County aforesaid, whose ages, residence, etc., are as follows:

NAMES OF PARTIES		AGE	COLOR	PLACE OF BIRTH	RESIDENCE	FATHER'S NAME	MOTHER'S MAIDEN NAME
Charles Woodring	Groom	26	W	New Jersey	Furnas Co.	Cyrus Woodring	Mary Horn
Minnie Graham	Bride	18	W	Iowa	Gosper Co. Nebr.	.. Graham	L. McBerney

If blood relations to what degree

And the person joining them in marriage is required to make due return of the annexed Certificate to the County Judge of said County, within ninety days, of the names of the parties, time and place of marriage, and by whom solemnized.

IN TESTIMONY WHEREOF, I have hereunto set my hand and affixed the seal of said Court, at my office

in Elwood, in said County, this 4th day of June A. D. 1893

Oral C. Middleton

Judge.

CERTIFICATE OF MARRIAGE

To the County Judge of Gosper County, Nebraska:

THIS CERTIFIES, That on the 4th day of June A. D. 1893, at Elwood,

in said County, according to law and by authority, I duly joined in marriage Mr. Charles Woodring and

Miss Minnie Graham, and there were present as witnesses A. J. Simpson

Nannie Simpson

Given under my hand the 4th day of June A. D. 1893 Oral C. Middleton County Judge

for Elwood Bulletin Print

Charles Woodring and Minnine Graham were married in
Elwood Nebraska on the 4th day of June, 1863.

A 1980 photo of a deserted house in Smithfield, Nebraska.
It was the Woodring home in 1912 and earlier.

time, the ship carried lifeboats for only 1,178 people. One of the 700 survivors was the well known unsinkable Molly Brown.

Meanwhile, back in the little village of Smithfield, in September of 1912, Charles Woodring bought train tickets to San Diego for his wife Minnie Belle and their four children, Ray, Lloyd, Hazel and Earl. Charles, however, "rode the rails" as catching a free ride on a train was called in those days. They reached San Diego on Earl's fifth birthday, September 19, 1912. When little Earl saw the ocean for the first time, he said, "Whoever dug that well must have made a lot of money." Earl's father dug wells and was dubbed the "badger" because it was said he could dig a well faster than anyone else in the Smithfield, Gosper County.

One incentive for their move to California may have been the lure of a more temperate climate. Charles told his wife that it never gets cold in California; therefore, she left all their winter clothing with relatives in Nebraska. As luck would have it, that was the first winter in many years that Southern California saw frost. Another reason may have been that Charles' sister, Clara Mae, nicknamed Clate, had lived there for several years. Clate was an actress in Kansas City vaudeville before she met and married Wayne Hood in 1890. Vaudeville, a style of variety entertainment, was being performed in Kansas City, Missouri, in the early 1880's. American vaudeville began at the New York Palace Theater on Broadway in 1881 and soon spread to larger cities throughout the United States. By 1915, vaudeville began to struggle with competition from silent film, and in the following decade from radio shows. 1912 found Wayne and Clate Hood living in the fashionable Mt. Helix area of San Diego and employing a part-time maid. Hood owned the Quality Dairy during the depression years and was worth nearly a million dollars, it was said.

During the early years in Smithfield, Grandpa Charles dug wells and he was also known as a "boomer," a transient worker who followed jobs from place to place, often taking him to Kansas City and even into Canada. He obviously made good money, as his daughter Hazel remembered extravagant gifts he sent home: once an entire bolt of red velvet, and another time a piano! My grandmother was waiting at home with the children on one of his trips to Kansas City. She asked the "Ouija" board how he was, and the board replied that he was dead! That very day she received a letter from Charles stating that he was "dead on his feet!" Grandpa had the reputation of not being a good provider for his family. Perhaps it was difficult for him to find work after their move to San Diego. My dad recalled them moving a lot, often every month or so, when the rent came due. Rumor had it he spent a lot of time at the local pub. One day when he came home on the run, Grandma asked, "Why are you running?" His reply was, "Damn it, 'cause I can't fly." He had met a Mexican at the bar who was chasing him with a knife and coming close enough to slash the tail of Grandpa's coat.

Charles and Minnie Belle were divorced in the early twenties, before I was born and well before divorce was common or acceptable. Several stories have been told as to why Grandpa Charles left Minnie Belle and came back to Nebraska to live. However, none of the stories may have been the real reason he left.

I was three years old; too young to remember Grandpa giving me two shiny, new silver dollars to play with. I lost them and they were the last two dollars he had! I've been told that I stuck them in a hole in the wainscoting on the kitchen wall, and they weren't found until two years later when Mom tore the wainscoting out to modernize the kitchen. I do remember when he gave me a balloon, but he broke it when he showed me how to blow it up!

Grandpa taught me how to play "army." We put yardsticks over our shoulders and marched "Hup-one-two-three-four" the way he marched when as a young adult, he was a soldier in the U.S. Army and during the last years of World War I (1914-1918) when he was a "Camp Boss" at the Civilian Camp in Fort Kearney, Nebraska.

He often told me far-fetched stories. I was gullible as were many of the less educated "bench warmers" in the little village of Smithfield. I remember him sharpening his straight edge razor on a leather strop which always hung on the casing of the kitchen door. As he pulled the razor back and forth on the strop, he said, "See all the marks on this strop? The strop was made from the hide of a slave, and those marks and scars are where he was beaten by his master." As the story goes, Grandpa later sold that razor strop to one of the Smithfield "bench warmers" at an inflated price. Grandpa had a "gift of gab." Harold remembered when Grandpa failed to pay a debt and received a letter from a collection agency to appear in court in New York City. Grandpa wrote back, "I've never been to Niagara Falls. Could we stop there on the way to New York City when you come to pick me up?" They never answered his letter.

My two grandpas, maternal and paternal, lived in the same town of Smithfield for many years. They tolerated each other, but both were stubborn and loved to argue. One argument was about the location of "Custer's Last Stand." Grandpa Forster said, "I'll get a history book to prove it," to which Grandpa Woodring replied, "I don't give a damn, I'm still not "gonna" believe you."

Grandpa Woodring lived on the second floor of the old Currier Hotel in Smithfield. He gave me some little toy dishes, actually butter-pat dishes, that were left there from the early hotel days. I didn't have many toys and I treasured them! He invited us there one Sunday for a chicken and dumpling dinner. We argued over who could make the best dumplings. We were always arguing over who was the best cook. My mother said, "You musn't take the lid off the kettle while the dumplings are cooking or they will fall, not be light and airy." Grandpa said, "It won't hurt them to remove the lid." (I started cooking very early, as a preschooler.) A few months later a Valentine came addressed to me. I can still see it in my mind's eye. It pictured a little girl at a coal-wood stove, like the one in our kitchen, and a caption: "If I grow fat and grouch a lot, you'll be the one to blame, but, darn it all, I don't care, I love you just the same."

As a little girl growing up, I knew my grandpa "hit the bottle" a bit too much, but I never remember him being mean or disagreeable. I loved him dearly. Of my grandpa's four children, my dad was the only one who didn't have an alcohol abuse problem.

Grandpa Charles' mother, Mary Hannah was from the Horn family who had a history of alcoholism. According to a coroner's report that I found in the basement of the Hunterdon

County Court House in Flemington, New Jersey, 12 citizens made statements, signed and sealed with their thumbprints, to the effect that Elijah Horn, Mary Hannah's father, was intoxicated when he fell into the Raritan Canal of the Delaware River in Lambertville, New Jersey, and drowned. That was in 1863, shortly after he had returned home from the Civil War where he and four of his sons had served. His widow, or "relict" as widows were often referred to in those days, wrote to the War Department, seeking a pension from one of her sons. She mentioned that her husband had been "a man of drink." Mary Hannah (Horn) Woodring, my great-grandmother, had two brothers, Ben and Cornelius, who were alcoholics and a sister, Julia, who was active in the Susan B. Anthony movement. Susan B. Anthony strongly opposed the use of liquor. From 1848 until 1853, Julia took part in organizing the first "Daughters of Temperance," when the "Sons of Temperance" refused to admit women to their organization.

Mom and Grandpa Woodring had a good relationship. I recall he bought her a very fancy hat as a payoff for a bet. However, one day he was not in her good graces because he tossed the "starter". Mom baked bread several times a week, using a "starter" (fermented yeast) kept in a quart jar. Grandpa liked to help Mom in the kitchen; when he saw that jar of fermenting yeast and thought it was spoiled, he tossed it out and washed the jar. Mom was very upset, but Grandpa was forgiven when Aunt Ethel gave her a new starter.

I remember Grandpa shining his shoes and pressing his pants—"sprucing up" he called it. Indeed, a "classy old gent" he was when he donned his dark suit, white shirt and tie.

For less than a month Grandpa was married to a widowed lady, Birdie Johnson, who lived on a small farm south of Smithfield and owned a couple of Jersey milk cows. To begin with, the marriage bed was infested with bed bugs. Then when she handed him a bucket and introduced him to the Jerseys, he took one look at the cows and their full teats and said, "When I pull on one of those, it ain't gonna be on a damn cow!"

Grandpa might well have been called a "Lady's Man." I remember even in his senior years as a resident at the Odd Fellow's Home in York, Nebraska, he had his eye on the ladies. When he visited us on the farm, for a week or so in the summer, letters came from a lady friend in York.

During the time that the Woodrings lived in a house in San Diego, they discovered that mice had built a cozy nest in the wall of the bathroom. Lo and behold, there in the nest among worthless bits of glass and metal, was a diamond ring! That ring was in the possession of my grandpa when he entered the "Home" in York. He made the statement that the ring would help pay his burial expenses, but when he died it was not to be found. Was it stolen, or did he give it to one of his lady friends?

I was in high school, just a few weeks before Grandpa passed away, when a package came from him addressed to me. It held two silk dresses that fit me perfectly. I was so proud of them. They were my first "store bought" dresses!

I vividly remember the week we lost Grandpa. Since my parents and my brothers were in York at my grandpa's bedside, my friend Barb Tilson stayed at the farm with me to help do the chores. When a cow got stuck in an "A Shape" hog shed, Barb and I used a saw and hammer to tear boards loose from the "A Shape" and free the frantic cow.

Grandpa's body was brought back to the farm and placed in the family parlor for several days before burial. A nightly "watch" or "wake" was held by friends and neighbors. A quote from his obituary read, "Mr. Woodring's jovial manner will always be remembered by those who knew him." His death certificate stated that he died April 23, 1940, at age 89 of apoplexy, cerebral. Losing my grandpa left an empty space in my heart.

A few years after she divorced Charles, my grandmother Minnie Belle remarried, first a man by the name of Chittenton, and then Bennie. They lived in California and Bennie had a gold mine claim near Empire, Colorado. My parents, and my brother Harold and I visited them at their cabin in Colorado when I was less than a year old. Harold remembered that I took my first steps in that cabin. That visit was the one and only time I saw my grandmother. Harold and his son Gary found the mine site in 1947. Harold and I visited the mine site again in the early 90's but the shaft was either gone or covered over.

At the time of Minnie Belle's marriage to Bennie, she changed not only her last name but also her first name to Margaret. Her oldest granddaughter, Zilpha told me that our grandmother said, "I have never liked the name Minnie." She didn't like to be called Grandma either; she said, "Grandmother is more sophisticated."

I didn't know that my grandmother wrote poetry until a collection of her poetry was found in the bottom of her daughter Hazel's trunk after Hazel passed away. Jackie, Hazel's daughter, wrote to me telling me about the book of poems. I had always felt cheated not knowing my grandmother; I was desperate to read her poetry! Jackie and I made plans to meet in San Francisco; 40 years had passed since we had been together. She was still a little girl, with dark "Shirley Temple" curls, and I was a teenager when my parents and I spent the winter of 1939-1940 in California. We had little contact over the years as a result of miles dividing us and our busy lives and now we had grown children. I really didn't know who to look for, except that she would be wearing a white suit and a red blouse. The restaurant was very crowded and I kept thinking, "What if we can't find one another?" She would be slender, dark-haired and attractive; I was sure, though I hadn't seen a picture of her since she was eight-years-old. She was, I imagined, the "Cosmopolitan" type of girl. After all, she had grown up in California, a city girl, while I had grown up in Nebraska on a farm. By prearrangement, I too, was wearing a white suit. I was sure I was the only one who had changed in 40 years and was not feeling very attractive. My dark hair had turned "salt and pepper" and each ten years had added a few extra pounds. Funny, no one seemed to fit the picture I held in my mind's eye of Jackie; in fact, no one I saw was wearing a white suit. Then she appeared and we both knew at a glance that we had found each other. Maybe it was the searching expressions on our faces, or maybe it was the white suits. (Jackie later told me she suggested white suits because, no one, just no one who is anyone, wears a white suit in San Francisco in March.) Jackie was very attractive, but her hair was white and short, not dark and curly, and she too had gained a few pounds.

I stayed up all of one night, at the San Francisco Hilton, copying my grandmother's poetry from a spiral notebook, with tears rolling down my cheeks. Even though the poems were written at a very sad time in her life she was talking to me and I felt that I was learning to know her.

Since that memorable meeting, we have made every effort to stay in touch. By means of cards, letters, phone calls, and occasional meetings, Jackie's family and mine have kept track of one another over the years. On one of these occasions, Jackie, Harry and his wife, Eileen, my daughter, Sharllyn and I met in New York City at the Algonquin Hotel to see the sights and become further acquainted. The Algonquin opened in Midtown Manhattan in 1902, and was famous as a gathering place for a group of New York writers, actors and actresses from 1919 until about 1929, including Tallulah Bankhead, Harpo Marx, Fitzgerald, Faulkner and Hemmingway.

An interesting anecdote about the Algonquin is that in the late 1930's a white cat, with grey patches and a stubby tail, wandered into the hotel searching for food. The hotel owner welcomed the furry traveler, named him Hamlet, and a tradition was born. (Matilda, the feline resident in 2002, was given a seventh birthday party. While celebrating with 150 of her closet friends, she jumped on her cake and ran out of the room, leaving a trail of paw prints.)

It was at the Algonquin that we began planning our first Woodring reunion to be held in San Diego, California, in 1985.

My paternal grandmother, Minnie Belle Graham was born in O'Brien County, Iowa, July 25, 1875, the daughter of Calvin Graham and Lucinda (McBurney) Graham. Calvin, the son of Grove Graham and Betsy (Wood) Graham, was born in Delaware County, New York, in 1824.

Taking a train from my daughter Sharllyn's home, near Trenton, New Jersey, I traveled up the Hudson River to

Albany, New York's State Capitol, where I researched the Graham family. I was traveling very light with only my attaché case holding genealogical information, a few toiletries, and a change of clothes in a backpack. My travel agent had reserved a room for me at the Albany Hilton, within walking distance of the State Capitol. Checking in, I soon discovered I was the only Caucasian in the hotel and I quickly learned how it would feel to belong to a minority group. After a couple of days, the other guests seemed to accept me and the fact that I was different.

I rented a car and in accordance with the information I had found in Albany records—headed for the Catskill Mountain area of upper New York. I did find some Grahams as well as a land deed for Grove Graham and his wife Betsy (Wood) at the Delaware County Seat at Utica. 1830 census records for Delaware County list the Grove Graham family; however, in 1840, Betsy is listed as head of the family and Grove's name is missing. Ogle County, Illinois, 1850 census shows Betsy Graham and two sons, Calvin and Benjamin, living in the household of Betsy's married daughter, Mary (Graham) Butterfield. Betsy Graham, who died in 1856, is buried in a cemetery in that county. It remains a mystery when Grove Graham died or where he is buried.

Calvin and Lucinda (McBurney) Graham were married in Morengo County, Iowa, on December 15, 1857. Their children were all born in Iowa. My grandmother, Minnie Belle, was the youngest when they homesteaded near Concordia, Kansas. Minnie Belle grew up on the homestead and often told her daughter, Hazel, stories of her childhood. She remembered gathering prairie chicken eggs from the fields; they were small, taking several to make a meal. They lived in a "dug out" faced with logs. When wolves would try to get in, little Minnie Belle would heat the fire poker, stick it between the unchinked logs and chase them away. She was often left alone when her mother and older sibling worked the fields. Her father, Calvin Graham, died from an "abscess," according to his obituary, before the end of the five-year period required to claim the homestead. Her oldest brother Edgar was old enough to claim it. When I visited the Concordia homestead in the late 70's, one of their grandsons, son of Jennis Graham, took me to the farm where I saw my Great-Grandfather Calvin Graham's tombstone. It was of hand-poured cement, the name and dates were carved out by his older sons: b. 1824-d. 27-7-1880.

In later years, after three of her daughters, Temperance, Jeanette, and Minnie Belle had moved to Nebraska, Lucinda traveled by train to help care for new grandbabies as they came along. Grandma Lucinda put tea on her hair and it never turned gray. Was it the tea or was she part Native American as older family members claimed? She had high cheek bones, but I've been unable to prove Native American heritage. Lucinda was buried in the Elwood Nebraska Cemetery in an unmarked grave. Harold remembered that the day of her funeral in 1924 was cold and windy and that the women wrapped in blankets to keep warm at the graveside memorial service. Years later, my brother Harold and I solicited money from her many grandchildren and great-grandchildren to purchase a tombstone to mark her grave.

In 1980, I made a trip to Poweshiek County, Iowa, seeking information on Lucinda (McBurney) Graham's parents, Temperance (Clark) McBurney and James McBurney. I found not only land, church and court records, but also marriage certificates and cemetery records. My McBurney great-great-grandparents' tombstones were in a deserted cemetery in the middle of a farmer's cornfield. On that day in July, the temperature was 94 degrees and the corn was very tall. I asked the farmer's permission to walk through his corn field. My nylons and heels became increasingly more uncomfortable but I found my family's headstones, knocked down, covered with weeds, but readable: James McBurney and Temperance McBurney. I walked back to my car thinking, "Begorrah, I must have a few of those Scottish genes!" The farmer met me with a tall, cold glass of lemonade. Never has lemonade tasted so good.

As a young lady, Minnie Belle Graham went to Elwood, Nebraska area to live with her sister, Jeanette Birt. There she met and married Charles Woodring. They were married in Elwood, Nebraska on June 4, 1893, when he was 34 and she was just 18; they were divorced after more than 20 years of marriage. My brother Harold remembered seeing tears in Grandpa's eyes when he received the divorce summons in the mail.

In the twenties after their move to San Diego and two failed marriages, Minnie Belle met Bennie, the love of her life, according to her poetry. She tells of a few very happy years with her Bennie, followed by heartbreak when he found a new love. In an attempt to free himself, Bennie arranged for her to travel by car to Nebraska to visit her son and her sibling. They were to stop at the Grand Canyon where (Minnie) Margaret Belle was to "accidently" lose her balance and fall to her death. The relative, whom Bennie was no doubt paying well to implement the scheme, lost her nerve, revealed the plot to my grandmother and they returned to California. My grandmother died of a broken heart at age 62.

Older Woodring relatives have told me I resemble my grandmother in looks, mannerisms and personality. My grandmother was five feet, four inches tall, her weight fluctuating between 125 and 200 pounds. I fit that description. When her hair grayed it turned white, as mine has done.

Zilpha, (Minnie) Margaret Belle's oldest granddaughter, described our grandmother in a letter to me following my question, "What kind of a lady was our grandmother?" Zilpha's reply: She was a sweet, low-keyed kind of person, who was always busy. I don't remember her ever saying a cross word or being impatient. She was very positive; although there were difficult times in her life, she didn't let it get her down. She was very proud, had a proud way of walking and never slouched. She was a very fashionable lady, liked pretty things and nice clothes. I remember her fox boa. It was the whole fox, as was the fashion. The tail was made to fasten with a snap in the mouth. She was an excellent seamstress and made many of her own clothes, and even taught me how to quilt. She was thrifty, loved to find a bargain and she was a good cook. She was easy going, to a point, and seldom became angry. But when angry, she didn't forget easily. Grandmother had a sense of humor and laughed often. I often stopped at her house on my way home from school. One day, the dry cleaning man came running up the walk, yelling, "Open the door." He was bald and black birds were chasing him and pecking at his head. She opened the door and in he flew. After he left, she burst into laughter over his bizarre predicament.

I treasure my grandmother's Bible, a gift to me from Zilpha. One page tells where they lived in San Diego: 135 31st Street. On another page, she recorded the family names and birthdates:

Charles Woodring	April 3, 1859
Minnie Woodring	July 25, 1875
Ray Woodring	March 19, 1894
Marvin Woodring	September 9
Hazel Woodring	March 11, 1900
Earl Woodring	September 19, 1907

I remember visiting Lloyd Wilson Woodring, his wife Alene, and their three children, Zilpha, (Alene's daughter from a previous marriage, adopted and raised as a Woodring), Lloyd Jr. and Ruth when we lived in California during the winter of 1939-1940. Alene taught me to "dicker" with the Mexicans in Tijuana. Zilpha and I were about the same age. I recall Aunt Alene warning us not to walk through Balboa Park when we walked to a movie, because a girl had been raped and murdered there recently. Lloyd was a Navy man and served on a submarine during both world wars'. He was a gunner's mate on a mine sweeper during World War II and had a mascot dog named "Scuttlebutt."

Uncle Earl I remember best. He was a professional painter and during the time he lived in Nebraska, in the late forties, he refinished an old piano for me. He taught me how to refinish furniture, which was a skill I utilized over the years. I visited Uncle Earl in Lemon Grove, California, in the later years of his life. He was divorced from his first wife, Hazel, who was the mother of his three children, Barbara, Donna and John. His second wife

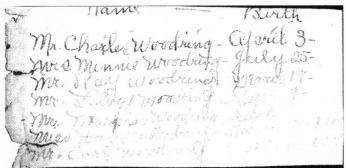

From the pages of the Charles Woodring family bible.

Charles and Minnie Woodring ca1912

A photo of me, taken in front of 1912 Woodring family home at 135 31st Street in San Diego (2012).

died after only a few years of marriage. He often talked about his parents—"My mother saw me from the window of the house on the hill in San Diego, the house, that at that time she shared with Bennie. I had just returned from a freight train trip (riding the rails) to Nebraska to visit my father and my oldest brother, Ray." A sad look came over his face and he continued, "I wish I could have really known my father. I often take his picture out of a box, look at it and wonder if I'm not a lot like him. My mother had a very hard life. She married two men who were no good; of course I can't say that about my father. He was my father." Earl was eight or nine when his father left San Diego and moved back to Nebraska. As Earl recalls, his father said, "Forget about Marvin, he is gone, start living again." (Marvin had died of scarlet fever as a young child.) That statement angered Earl's mother to the point of throwing a pot of hot coffee, grounds and all, at his father. Charles left, not to return; however, Harold remembered the year of 1926 when Grandmother and Bennie were in Nebraska. They drove down Main Street of Smithfield where Grandpa Charles was sitting on a sidewalk bench. Harold noticed his grandmother wipe a tear from her eye.

Excerpts from a letter from my cousin Jackie tell me about her mother Hazel Mae, the only girl in the Charles Woodring family. They were living in Smithfield, when one day Grandmother Minnie Belle began to experience severe abdominal pains. Thinking it was only indigestion and would soon go away, she instructed 12 year-old Hazel to warm heavy pottery plates in the oven and place them on her aching belly. The pain turned out to be an inflamed gallbladder, and she was almost dead by the time she arrived at the hospital. During that illness, Hazel incurred the wrath of the household by stashing the starched shirts and dresses away to avoid ironing them, only to discover several weeks later that everything had mildewed beyond rescue.

After several years in San Diego, Hazel became adept at climbing out of windows to attend the dances she so dearly loved and of which her parents disapproved. She was very fair, with blue eyes and blonde hair, which won her the taunt of her classmates: "Hazel fell in the flour barrel!" It could not have been easy to move from a rural community in Nebraska to the becoming metropolis of San Diego, even in 1912.

As a child Hazel was a tomboy who preferred climbing trees to playing with dolls; however, one of her prized possessions was a doll house her mother won for her. It was complete with furniture, carpet and drapes and was for her the beginning of a life-long love affair with homemaking. Years later, as a young housewife, she sat on a windy hillside, near Huntington Beach, sorting countless thousands of tomato-seedlings to pay for the wall-to-wall carpeting her heart desired. Hazel was a very beautiful woman, with a style all her own. She was a model for calendar portraits as a young lady, and at one time played the part of a blonde, marcelled Hawaiian girl in a movie.

Hazel would do battle for you, if necessary, and do it with pizzazz! If she had a motto to live by it was, "Where there is a will, there is a way." She had a mind of her own. Not easily thwarted when she wanted to have lunch at the Beverly Hills Hotel, but couldn't afford it, she and a friend packed a picnic hamper and drove in their Model T Ford to the grounds of the famous hotel, where they spread out their lunch on the front lawn and watched with enthusiasm the comings and goings of Southern California Society.

Hazel married a man by the name of Ham and had a son Harry, born in 1918. She later married Jack Incho, who adopted Harry. Jackie Lea was born October 20, 1931, to complete their family.

My grandmother died December 6, 1937. In 1982, I researched the San Diego newspaper and found notice of her death. She was 62 when she died of arteriosclerosis at the San Diego County Hospital. She is buried at the Greenwood Cemetery-Oakdale, Lot 24. The main entrance is off Imperial Avenue, the street Charles and Minnie Belle lived near in their early 1912 days in San Diego.

Less than two years after Grandmother's death; my family left the "Dust Bowl" state of Nebraska on Route 66, searching for a rainbow in Sunny California.

BLUE VELVET
Art by LaVera

CLATE'S IMAGE
Art by LaVera

Clate was a nickname for Clara Mae Woodring, sister of Charles Woodring and my great-aunt, who was an actress in Kansas City Vaudeville in the late 1800's.

Chapter 4

HE WAS GERMAN, SHE WAS BOHEMIAN

My maternal grandfather, George Forster had only one ear. My first memory of him is in his Morris chair reading the paper, his spectacles fastened around his bald head with a string. If I was really quiet, he might let me climb up and snuggle in the corner of his lap.

John George Forster, called George, was born in Lee County, Illinois on November 19, 1862, the fifth child of a family of fourteen. His parents, Henry David Forster and Elizabeth (Yetter) Forster were both German immigrants. He came to Nebraska from Iowa as a young man. He worked on the railroad and also as a hired hand on farms in the area.

At seventeen, he was a hired hand on the Olson farm near Bradshaw, in Eastern Nebraska. A storm cellar was a must in that part of the country. When a tornado cloud was sighted, the family ran to the cellar for safety. Everyone on the Olson farm was in the cellar that fateful evening, except Grandma Olson, who had been left behind! Just as George eased her wheelchair down the cellar steps, he went up with the house and came down with a heap of splintered lumber, minus one ear. The next morning he rode a horse into Bradshaw, to see a doctor. The doctor hadn't heard about the tornado and refused to believe George's story.

When George was thirty he married a little, nineteen-year-old Bohemian girl, Anna Tomasek at the bride's home, a sod house on the Tomasek tree claim north of Smithfield.

Like "Mutt and Jeff," George was six foot two and Anna measured less than five feet and wore a size 4 shoe. He towered over her in more ways than one. He was very domineering, she very shy and soft spoken. I don't think Grandma Forster had a mean bone in her body. Although he was domineering, he was also very protective of his wife. He treated her like a very fragile Dresden doll. He did all the heavy work around the house, carried water from the cistern and did the laundry.

George and Anna were the parents of four children, Elsie Mae, born July 17, 1894; Minnie Gail (my mother), born February 7, 1897; Ralph Lee, born January 12, 1903; and Delmar Leo, who was born January 21, 1913 and died as an infant.

Elsie married Walter Murphy on February 19, 1916. They didn't have children. In her early forties, she was diagnosed with multiple sclerosis. It was a little known disease in those days with no known way to control its progress and no cure. In the summer of 1937, when I was 12, I stayed with Aunt Elsie to help care for her and cook for the hired hands. When she fell, her collie "Queenie" helped her to her feet. Multiple sclerosis took Elsie's life at age 52.

Minnie Gail married Ray Woodring February 11, 1914. They were blessed with three children: Harold Lowell, born July 17, 1916; LaVera Mae, born September 10, 1925; and Willis Wayne, born May 17, 1933.

George Forster and Anna Tomasek were married
on the10th day of January 1893, at the bride's home.

MARRIAGE LICENSE.

The State of Nebraska,
GOSPER COUNTY.

OFFICE OF THE COUNTY JUDGE.

LICENSE IS HEREBY GRANTED, To any person authorized to solemnize marriages according to the laws of the State, to join in marriage Mr. _____ George J. Forster _____ and M___ _____ Annie _____ Tomasek

of the County aforesaid, whose ages, residences, etc., are as follows.

NAMES OF PARTIES	AGE	COLOR	PLACE OF BIRTH	RESIDENCE	FATHER'S NAME	MOTHER'S NAME
George J Forster	30	White	Ill.	Gosper county	J. V. Forster	E. Yother
Annie Tomasek	19	White	Bohemia	Gosper county	J. Tomasek	

And the person joining them in marriage is required to make due return of the annexed certificate to the County Judge of said County, within ninety days, of the names of the parties, time and place of marriage, and by whom solemnized.

IN TESTIMONY WHEREOF, I have hereunto set my hand and affixed the seal of said court, at my office in _____ Elwood _____

in said County, this _____ 10 _____ day of _____ January _____ A.D. 1893.

Chas L. Middleton
County Judge.

CERTIFICATE OF MARRIAGE.

TO THE COUNTY JUDGE OF GOSPER COUNTY, NEBRASKA:

THIS CERTIFIES, That on the _____ day of _____ A.D. 189_, at The Brides home

in said County, according to law and by authority, I duly joined in marriage Mr. _____ George J Forster _____

and M___ _____ Annie _____ Tomasek _____ and there were present as witnesses _____ J _____ Franklin

___ Mrs J Frahler

Given under my hand the _____ day of _____ January _____ 1893.

G B Chase
Minister

Winona Cleo, born November 29, 1925; and Norris Neal, who was born October 17, 1928 and died on September 22, 1934, in a car accident. Verlouis George was born on September 20, 1934.

Grandpa George's parents and several brothers and sisters lived in the area of Gordon, Nebraska, and in the states of Illinois, Oregon and South Dakota. They were a close-knit family and in spite of the many miles dividing them, visited one another often. In 1893 several of the brothers attended the Columbian Exposition in Chicago.

There was always a family gathering when a relative, brother, sister, niece or nephew, came to visit. I remember a Forster nephew from Hershey, Pennsylvania and the box of Hershey bars he brought. I remember a nephew "Doc" from California and his son Ralph who had a pet crocodile. Aunt Anna Pankow, from South Dakota, brought a doll for my cousin Neomia, but nothing for her sister Winona or me!

My maternal great-grandparents David and Elizabeth Forster, were in their 60s when they homesteaded in Sheridan County, Nebraska, near Gordon. Three of their children, two sons and a daughter, filed claims in Sheridan County at the same time as their father.

My family and I visited the relatives in Gordon when I was six or seven-years-old. I saw my twin cousins, Ada and Ida, for the first time and I had to touch them to make sure they were real. I recall visiting the Rosebud Indian Reservation, just across the South Dakota state border, and how impressed I was with the display of art work by the students at their school. A spark of the love of art and appreciation of Indian Art and culture was kindled.

George Forster family: back row, left to right, Minnie Gail, Elsie Mae, front row, left to right: George Forster, Ralph, Anna (Tomasek) Forster.

Minnie Gail, the little one, and her sister Elsie Mae.

My second visit to Gordon was 60 years later. I was able to locate the old homestead patent and the location of the farm at the Sheridan County Registrar of Deeds. When I found the homestead farm again after all those years, it still looked familiar. I could identify the house by a picture I had of my great-grandparents sitting on the porch on the day of their 50th wedding anniversary. Over 100 people attended the celebration, including 13 of their 14 children, and camped in the farm yard for a week. Henry gave each of his children a rocking chair and each of his grandchildren a lock of his golden, curly hair and a five dollar gold coin. My mother always regretted that she left the lock of hair in the family bible when she left home and it was lost. In their later years, Henry and Elizabeth lived with their son William on the family homestead farm.

Many stories have passed down from children to grandchildren. One of these was that Henry had a long white beard and it was habitual for him to go to the cellar after supper and return with a wine colored beard! Another was that Henry and Elizabeth conversed in German and he was upset when his children wouldn't answer him in German. He also cursed in German, "dun-heidt-ferist" was one such epithet. I'm not sure that is the correct spelling, nor do I know what it means, but probably it was something to do with flies. He was determined to get rid of the pests by sitting on the front porch in his rocker and swatting them. The same two chickens were always nearby for their treats, the dead flies.

Great Grandpa Henry died in 1917 at age 82. Great-Grandma Elizabeth died a few years later at 79. Elizabeth was a kind, soft spoken lady, devoted to her husband, family and God. Twelve of her fourteen children were at her death bedside where she asked them to lead the kind of lives that would make it possible for them to meet again in Heaven. She folded her hands and joined our Savior.

As I find and study these old family records, I feel very close to my ancestors. Whichever side I study, maternal or paternal, I find people who took pride in a day's work well done; people who were strong enough to endure the hardships of a pioneer life; people who were honest, warm, compassionate and loving. These are our ancestors!

Christmas Eve was always a special time when we gathered at Grandma and Grandpa Forster's house in Smithfield and the whole family, except Grandpa, attended the Methodist Church nearby. I could never understand why Grandpa didn't go with us, since I knew he went to church on Sundays. There was always a Christmas Story at church, a tree with lighted candles and a bag of goodies—an apple, orange, nuts and hard Christmas candy—for each child. When we got back home, Santa had been there! I guess Grandpa must have stayed home to help Santa down the chimney!

Grandpa went to bed early and was an early riser. One of his favorite expressions was, "An hour of sleep before midnight is worth two after midnight." My dad, who respected his father-in-law, often said, "I learned a lot from him." If Dad knew Grandpa was visiting that day, he got up earlier than usual.

Grandpa was a proud man. He would be waiting at the Gosper County Court House for the doors to open when real estate taxes were due, in order to be the first in the county to

Henry and Elizabeth (Yetter) Forster, parents of George Forster, celebrated their 50th wedding anniversary on the 7th day of April,1906.

Henry and Elizabeth's homestead in Sheridan County, Nebraska near Gordon. More than 100 relatives attended their anniversary celebration and many of them camped in the yard for most of a week

pay his taxes. He also was creative. I remember the doll furniture he made for me from wooden spools and I still have a handmade magazine rack he gave me as a wedding gift.

When my Forster Cousins and I stayed overnight, he had hot cakes baked for our breakfast hours before we were out of bed. He put them in a covered dish to keep them warm. They were a bit soggy, but soaked in butter and Karo syrup and with plenty of German sausage, they disappeared quickly.

I have fond memories of going to my grandparents' house as a child. I can remember every room in their house and where the furniture stood. A room off the kitchen held a white porcelain bath tub, a sink with a pump nearby, a refrigerator with a motor on top that might have been one of Lester Ryan's early inventions, and the pie safe that I loved to stand by and savor the goodies inside—the prune kolaches, the pies and rye bread. The kitchen was small, with only enough room for a table and chair set, a cupboard, and a coal-wood cook stove. The only picture on the wall, a little girl feeding chicks, was my favorite. I recall the wash boiler on the kitchen stove in the fall when it was time to make hominy. I don't have the recipe, but because they used lye, I didn't like hominy. I never stayed in the kitchen long when Grandpa ground wild horseradish, because it hurt my eyes. At butchering time, he made and stuffed country sausage for us and smoked it in his backyard smoke house. The cottage cheese I buy just isn't as good as that Grandma used to make and serve to us with sugar. A special treat was a slice of bread covered with sour cream and sprinkled with sugar. One of the earliest memories of the only Great-Grandma I knew, Great-Grandma Tereza Tomasek, is watching her make noodles in that kitchen. She could cut

Four generations: Great-Grandma Tereza Tomasek, Grandma
Anna Forster, Mother Minnie Woodring and baby Harold.

Grandpa and Grandma Forster,
left to right, Grandma, holding me,
Harold, Grandpa holding Winona,
and Neomia in front. Winona and
Neomia are Ralph's children.

My grandparents, George and
Anna Forster.

them so fine and fast, and then hung them on the chair backs to dry before they went into the chicken noodle soup.

In the dining room there was a small china closet filled with pretty Bohemian etched glass. Grandma said, "You can look, but don't open the door." The parlor held a velvet-covered fainting couch and a "wind-up" Edison Victrola. Two of the records I remember were, "Yes, We Have No Bananas" and "Oh Hel, Oh Hel, Oh Helen." My Forster cousins and I giggled when we played that one 'cause it was "naughty."

I remember a table holding a stereoscope and picture cards. Many of the cards were of the 1904 St. Louis Exposition and the 1906 San Francisco earthquake. We were too young to realize the historical value of those cards; we just had fun viewing them.

World expositions were focused on trade and were the platform where the state of the art technology from around the world was brought together. The first exposition held in the United States was the Columbian Exposition in Chicago in 1893 followed by the St. Louis Expo. in 1904.

The San Francisco earthquake and resulting fire in 1906 are remembered as one of the worst natural disasters in the history of the United States. The death toll from the earthquake was 3,000. Nearly 300,000 were left homeless out of a population of 410,000. Over 80% of the city was destroyed.

It seemed that my Grandma Forster was always cooking, piecing quilts or crocheting. As a little girl, I took my dolls to her for new booties; as a teenager planning my Hope Chest (every young girl was expected to have a Hope Chest put together before she married) I went to her to crochet lace around pillow cases and dresser scarves that I had embroidered.

Not many years ago, a box of old family photos and a scrapbook of Grandma's were found in the attic of my mother's childhood home. They had been hidden away for 70 years. When I spent hours turning the pages of that yellowed book, I may have been searching for proof that I have some of my Grandma Forster's genes. She was a tiny woman with a big heart. If any of us can claim to have patience, those genes surely came from her. I knew little about her likes or dislikes. She was a quiet lady and never talked a lot. Her scrapbook told me that she loved family, children, animals, flowers and philosophy, as I do. She saved pictures of flowers, especially pansies, and a ribbon with MOTHER written on it. Was it from her mother's casket? There were pictures of babies, a story of the Dionne Quints and cute little boys and girls, including Shirley Temple. She kept newspaper stories of the unusual, pleasant and humorous. The bizarre and bad news was obviously missing! There were stories of Franklin D. Roosevelt taking office on March 4, 1933, and of Truman's inauguration April 12, 1945. There was also an obituary for her nephew Robert Glenn, killed in action in Normandy, July 9, 1944. Scenic pictures from Oregon and a handmade Christmas card from her grandson Verlouis were included.

Grandpa celebrated his 82nd birthday by walking to his son Ralph's farm to husk corn. The farm was located a mile north of Smithfield. He filled a Karo syrup bucket with cream and by swinging it just so as he walked, he had butter when he reached his house in town. When he died at age 89, his little Bohemian girl seemed to lose interest in life. Three years later, at age 81, she very quietly slipped away to join her protector.

Jacob Tomasek my great-grandfather was on born May 1, 1852, at Widerkum (Cinov) 100, near Klatovy, Bohemia. He was the son of Mikulas Tomasek and Marie Bernardova. Jacob married Tereza Kubikova, born at Partotice 8, Bohemia, the daughter of Jan Kubik and Marie Duckkova. Tereza was orphaned early in life and was raised by a sister. In old Bohemia, now the Czech Republic, "ova" which in Latin means egg, is added to both the maiden and married female surname.

Jacob and Tereza and their six children immigrated to America on the ship "Moravia" in 1885. At that time Bohemia was a part of the Austrian Empire. Anna, who was 11 years old in 1884, was born at Widerkum (Cinov) 100, on September 6, 1873, and was the oldest of the six living children. A baby was born to Jacob and Tereza out of wedlock and died as an infant. Joe, the youngest, was only a baby and was kept warm during the trip across the Atlantic in a sheepskin lined carrier.

It was a year later, in 1886, when the Statue of Liberty, a gift to America from France, was placed on the little island of Bedloe in New York Harbor and for the many years since has welcomed immigrants to America and Ellis Island. Since all of our ancestors had arrived earlier than 1886, many in the 1700's and before the Revolutionary War, they were not greeted by the Statue of Liberty.

Although Jacob liked guns, he knew it was illegal to bring them into the United States. He solved that problem by building a special "false bottom" trunk in which he stored his firearms without detection. The trunk was used as a table in their new home in America. Jacob and Tereza settled in North Bend, Nebraska where Jacob's older brother Matej (Michael) was already established. Jacob played the coronet in a Bohemian

"The Moravia." Our Tomasek family arrived in America from Bohemia on this ship on the 2nd day of April, 1885.(From a copy of the actual ship list.) TOMASEK, Jacob36, Therese 32, Anna 12, Amalie7, Ruzena?, Wenzel 3, Joseph 11months.

The Tomasek family on their homestead ca 1885, a soddy on a tree claim located 5 miles north of Smithfield, Nebraska.

Anna Tomasek's parents before they left Bohemia in 1884.

Jacob and Tereza Tomasek ca.1920.

band which allowed him to save enough money to purchase a tree claim in Gosper County, Nebraska in 1885. The area into which Jacob and Tereza relocated was predominately German and Scandinavian. Because of the cultural and language barriers, it must have been very difficult for them to fit into the community. Their children all attended school and learned English, but neither of the parents learned to speak anything but Bohemian.

The North Bend area of Nebraska from which my great-grandparents moved was a Czech community, where their culture was kept alive, and still is, by annual Czech Festivals. The Czech people are a warm, fun loving people and love to dance. The children in Wilbur, Nebraska—home of the Czech Festival for the past 50 years—and other towns close by learn to do the polka as preschoolers. I checked one item off my bucket list when my niece, Karen Schaefer, and I attended a Wilbur Czech Festival a couple of years ago. We found the people warm and friendly, and came home proud of our Bohemian ancestry.

My mother was not proud of her Bohemian ancestry. Dad would tease her by calling her a "Bohunk." She would angrily reply, "I'm not Bohemian, I'm American; I was born in America and I'm American." Dad would grin and come back with, "If a cat has kittens in an oven, does that make them hot biscuits?"

When the Tomasek clan gathered at my Grandmother Anna (Tomasek) Forster's home in Smithfield they spoke only Bohemian. My cousins and I would hide behind a cracked bedroom door and giggle because they sounded so funny! How I wish I had learned to speak the Czech language and found out more about the Bohemian culture! Was that the source of my mother's folk art painting, acting, dancing, doing exquisite needlework and sewing?

My mother was half-German and half-Bohemian. My father was a mixture of French, German, English, Holland Dutch, Swiss and Scottish, a duke's mixture as many other Americans. My father was raised as a Quaker in a home where dancing was not allowed, nor did he allow it in our home. My mother used to tell me how much she missed dancing. My parent's ethnic backgrounds may have affected their role in life and their life together. My mother was very superstitious; perhaps it was from her Bohemian background. As a young woman, she wore a talisman around her neck to ward off evil. Work of any kind, especially sewing, was not allowed on Sunday. If an umbrella was opened in the house, there would be a death in the family. The one that bothered me the most was that the little pullet eggs had to be thrown over the roof of the hen house or bad luck would come to the gatherer of the eggs. I wanted to use those cute little eggs to make mud pies in my outdoor play house!

Four more children were born to Jacob and Tereza after they moved to the tree claim. One son, Frankie died in 1887, at three months old, from an accidental gunshot while his father was cleaning his gun.

Mom told me about the day she looked out the window of their farm house at sunrise and saw her Grandma Tereza and her Aunt Fannie, a teenager like my mother, coming down the road with a herd of cattle. It seems Tereza's cattle had gotten into Jacob's corn, which was the straw that broke the camel's back. Grandma ran away with Fannie, the only child still living at home, and her cattle, and never turned back!

According to stories handed down, Tereza was the "work horse" of the family. On the other hand, Jacob was what we might call today a "playboy." He liked his guns, wine (or perhaps it was beer), women and song, and had a large collection of records for his Victrola.

My great-grandparents weren't legally divorced, but their land was legally divided. Tereza sold her share and bought a home in Bertrand, a little town a few miles east of Smithfield. When my cousins and I visited her in Bertrand she let us drink maybe a tablespoonful of her homemade dandelion wine from beautifully etched Bohemian glasses.

Great-Grandma Tereza knew few words in English, but she used them well to impress her great-granddaughter, LaVera Mae. She would pat me on the top of the head and say, "Good girl." One day she patted me on the head with one hand and with the other hand behind her back, brought forth a small box containing a string of pearls. How I treasured that gift!

Pictures of my great-grandmother tell me she was a beautiful young lady. Eleven children and life on the "tree claim" took its toll, but even in pictures of her in later years she was very stylishly dressed, a special lady!

I was eight or nine when I visited the tree claim north of Smithfield where my great-grandparents settled in 1885. Their son Frank and his wife Beulah were living there at that time. I was fascinated by the deep window sills of the "soddy," filled with plants. Old timers recalled that "moonshine" (illegal alcohol) could be found at the Tomasek tree claim at the time of prohibition. There must have been enough trees planted to hide the "still."

The last time I saw Great-Grandma Tereza was in 1939. She was no longer able to pat me on the head and say, "Good girl," for she was senile. I remember her lying on a fold-out sofa bed at my Forster grandparents' home. Her hands were always busy, going through the motions of "sewing the quilts" on the bed. She died on February 2, 1940, at age 90.

All I know about my Great-Grandpa Jacob I learned from relatives; I never met him in person. He died on February 26, 1928, from suffocation, as a result of smoking in bed.

Both Tereza and Jacob are buried at the Bertrand Cemetery, but not together. It was during the Great Depression and, perhaps to save money; Great-Grandma Tereza was buried in whichever of her children's cemetery plots had an empty space.

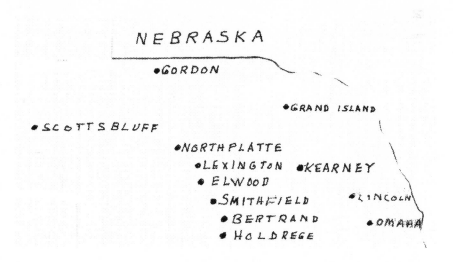

MAIN STREET OF SMITHFIELD
Art by LaVera

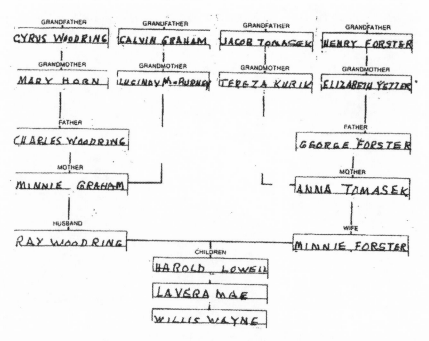

More names on the Woodring family tree.

Chapter 5

THE GREAT DEPRESSION, DUST BOWL DAYS AND MY BABY BROTHER

Stock market prices plummeted on Black Thursday, October 24, 1929, and collapsed on October 29. Banks and businesses closed and the Great Depression soon followed, to continue for the next ten years. By 1932, one out of four workers was unemployed; milk was five cents a quart and bread was six or seven cents a loaf.

Three major events helped shape the lives and attitudes of people born before 1940: the Great Depression, the Dust Bowl and World War II.

When people reminisce, they often talk about the "good times" they had during those "bad times." They didn't spend a lot of money on entertainment, but then, shivarees, card playing and P.T.A. entertainment didn't cost a lot.

I remember my mother sitting with her ear up close to the "Bakelite" horn of our R.C.A. Victor Radio listening to "John's Other Wife," sponsored by Oxydol. (The first soap opera?) Dad preferred listening to "Amos and Andy" or "Fibber Mc Gee and Molly."

Early cartoonists gave us reasons to laugh, when there wasn't much to laugh about. Among the cartoonists I remember are: "Lil Abner and Daisy Mae" in "Dogpatch," created by Al Capp from 1934 until his death in 1977 and "Little Orphan Annie," created by Harold Grey in 1924 and continued until his death in1968.

"Betty Boop" was regarded as one of the most famous sex symbols on the animated screen. She was a symbol of the Depression Era, a reminder of the more carefree days of "jazz-age-flappers." She was developed by Max Fleischer for Paramount Studios Talkatoons cartoon series, and began life as a dog. By 1930 she had evolved into a coy flapper whose innocent skirt-lifting and trademark line "boop-boop a doop" was sweetly suggestive of more than just singing and dancing. She wore short skirts, high heels, and her breasts were suggested by a low contoured bodice that showed her cleavage. She starred in cartoons from 1931 to 1939. Her design was altered several times in the 1940's in response to critics of her "hubba-hubba" look. She soon became less "saucy" and less popular. My schoolmate Barb Tilson and I used to get in trouble exchanging notes in High School Study Hall, with our own versions of Betty Boop cartoons.

A shivaree was a noisy, mock serenade by a group of people welcoming newlyweds. Usually it was after dark and the couple had gone to bed, when all heck broke loose outside with people banging spoons against pots, clanging bells or whatever would make a lot of noise. Doors were seldom locked, so usually revelers just walked right in, forcing the couple to dress in a hurry! The newlyweds were showered with gifts and money; in return they were expected to promise a party. If the bridegroom refused to promise a party, it was held against him the rest of his life; he might just as well move out

DIRTY THIRTIES
Art by LaVera

FARM AUCTION
Art by LaVera

GRANDMA BERTHA
Art by LaVera

of the neighborhood! Shivarees were dwindling by the late thirties.

I had a happy childhood. I loved both of my dolls and my "Teddy" bear. The "Teddy" bear was created in1902. A cartoon depiction reading, "Theodore (Teddy) Roosevelt refused to shoot a captured bear while hunting in Mississippi," is said to have inspired its creation.

My first doll was "Honey," a German-made "Minerva" tin head with a sock body designed by my mother. My only other doll, until much later in life when I had a collection of over 100 dolls, was a composition head doll that I named "Twinkle Toes." I planned to name my first baby after that doll!

I spent hours playing house with my dolls or playing school. My dolls and "Teddy" were the students. When we had music lessons, I played the piano. With the oven door open and my little stool as a bench, I pounded away on imaginary oven door piano keys.

Floy Phillips, a close neighbor, was my favorite playmate and a schoolmate. We stayed at one another's houses overnight once in a while. I loved the hot chocolate and spice cookies at her house. Floy was helping me with my chores when she said, "I like to sweep your floors, because you can see what you are doing." I hoped my mother didn't hear that! Some houses are so clean they seem to be for exhibit only. My mother kept her house clean enough to be healthy, but dirty enough to be happy. She was a proud lady and never used an oilcloth on our kitchen table, like most farm housewives; instead she used a cloth tablecloth that had to be washed and ironed. A sauce pan was never set on the table for convenience; food was put in bowls and served family style.

I was sitting on the steps by the storm cellar, turning the crank on a glass butter churn when I accidently tipped it over. Not only was the glass churn shattered, but little LaVera Mae was also! I gathered up what evidence I could find and hid it in the storm cellar.

My mother was nowhere in sight. Mom never punished me but she threatened a lot; best she didn't find out! I filled a jar with water, got some crackers from the cupboard, ran upstairs and hid behind a trunk in the clothes closet. I could hear Mom calling, "LaVera Mae, LaVera Mae." I didn't budge! "If she was worried about me, she wouldn't scold," I reasoned. It was getting dark and I was getting thirsty; I must have taken more soda crackers than water, so I turned myself in. I'm sure my mother felt like spanking, but she only hugged me. How many times have I followed the example she set?

I must have been six or seven when Mom became the proud owner of a washing machine, run by a Model T gasoline engine mounted on top of the tub. I was also the proud owner of a pretty, new, red silk dress. It was a chemise, or flapper style, with a ruffled skirt. I was in tears when my mother accidently dropped it on top of the new washing machine and the motor chewed it up! The hand-cranked wringer for the new machine was switched from the washer to the rinse tub. Rinse water was used to water the hollyhocks in the yard—the only flowers we had. Nothing was wasted; we followed the motto of the day: "Use it up, wear it out; make it do, do without." Prior to acquiring her "fancy" new washer, Mom washed all our clothes on a washboard, rung them out by hand, rinsed them in a tub of clean water, and again rung them by hand! The "automatic dryer" was a rope strung from tree to tree in the back yard. On freezing cold winter days the clothes were hung out and allowed to freeze, to remove part of the moisture, before being brought in and draped over chairs. The "long handled" one-piece men's underwear stood in a corner back of the kitchen stove.

Monday was always wash day. It was my Sunday evening chore to carry water, hand pumped from the cistern, to fill the copper wash boiler and the rinse water tub (the same tub we used for our weekly baths). Mom took pride in having the whitest wash on the line, just as Dad took pride in planting the straightest rows of corn. The clothes were boiled with Mom's homemade lye soap. A long wooden stick was used to stir them as they boiled in the wash boiler.

Just as Monday was always wash day, Tuesday was always ironing day. Everything was ironed, even the towels. Well before the advent of electricity, "Sad Irons" were used to iron by heating them on the coal-wood stove. Because there were two or three irons but only one handle, extra irons heated while the one with the handle clamped on was being used. If the iron was too hot, it was often dipped into water to cool it to the right temperature.

Wednesday was mending day. Mom believed that, "a stitch in time saves nine," so everything with even a tiny hole was patched before it became a big hole.

Thursday was cleaning day, just as the popular "Sunbonnet Baby" dish towels portrayed. These towels, made from flour sacks, were embroidered with "Sunbonnet Babies," depicting the chore for each day of the week. Monday she held a washboard, Tuesday an iron, Wednesday needle and thread, Thursday a broom, and Friday a mixing bowl and a big spoon.

Saturday was shopping and Sunday, church and a special dinner. These pretty towels weren't used every day, just on weekends, as they too, had to be ironed.

Friday, baking day, was a special day and I was always anxious to help. There were always pies, cakes and cookies to be baked for weekend dinners; the aroma from the kitchen filled the house. I learned to bake a cake from scratch (there were no box mixes) before I was seven.

Mom faithfully followed this schedule, except for those days when she filled in as a hired hand, put on a pair of Dad's overalls and helped husk corn.

One day my mother and I were in our farm yard, near Elwood, Nebraska, picking dandelion greens for supper, when we heard my brother Harold shouting, "Look Mom, look, gypsies are coming down the road." Bands of gypsies had been roaming the countryside that spring and summer, stealing anything and everything that wasn't fastened down. Dad had warned, "If they come here, just get to the house fast and lock the doors." They were getting close enough for us to see the tired old nags pulling a dilapidated looking spring wagon. A makeshift tarp covered one end of the wagon as well as many of their possessions; pots, pans and tubs were hanging on the sides. Gaudily dressed characters were seated at the front, one of them cracking the reins and shouting in a language of his own. "Come on, kids." Mom cried, "Get to the house quick, there's no telling what they might do to us." Clutching my kitten, I started running toward the house. Harold, not so easily intimidated, wasn't about to run and hide and let those thieves ransack our farm! "No, Mom," he said, "I'm not going. You and Sis go to the house; I'll hide in the shed and keep an eye on them." Mom reluctantly left Harold, and half pulled, half carried me to the house. Just seconds after we had pulled the bolt lock in place on the kitchen door, we saw a red-kerchiefed head appear in the little peep-hole. I could see the door knob turn and then the whole door shivered as the strange woman shook it and cried, "Let me in!" "Let me in!" I crouched on the floor under a window. I felt all goose-pimply, my mouth was dry, and I was afraid to breathe. Would the hinge hold? Was Harold all right? Mom peeked through the crack between the drawn shade and the window. Neither of us said a word. After what seemed like hours, all was quiet, and then we heard a gypsy man yell, "Giddup!" The creaking old wagon left the yard and traveled on. I think Harold had been as frightened as we were, even if he was thirteen years old and almost a man, for he hadn't stirred from his hiding place! We were lucky and happy that only a bit of grain and a few chickens disappeared the day the gypsies visited our farm.

Willis Wayne Woodring, the third child of Ray and Minnie Woodring was born May 17, 1933, in the midst of the Great Depression. Not unlike most children of my age in the early thirties, I was sure, for my mommy told me so, that babies came from the doctor's little black bag, the cabbage patch or the stork. I wasn't there at the time of my little brother's birth, but I was pretty sure the doctor had brought him. About that time I was hustled out of the house to spend the night with our neighbors, Bill and Lena White. I slept with Lena and when all three hundred pounds of Lena got into bed, I helplessly rolled right next to her!

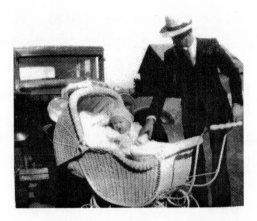

My two brothers—Harold
17 years, Willis 6 months.

Willis wearing a suit and
cap made by his mother.

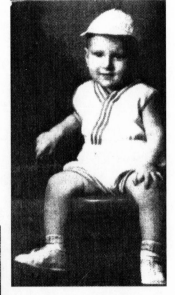

Me and Willis on his first birthday.
Harold made the table and chairs

Since I had always wanted a baby sister, I wasn't very happy to find a baby brother when I went home the next morning. Dr. Clark, hearing of my disappointment, replied: "You know what? There is a little black baby girl that I was supposed to have brought to your house. I'll take the little boy back and bring her out tomorrow." I hurriedly replied, "No, no, that's all right, we'll keep the little boy." I don't believe we children knew the meaning of prejudice. We believed what our parents told us, and had not yet learned the importance of equality and civil rights.

My mother hadn't seen a doctor during her pregnancy. I recall being upset because she cried a lot. There simply wasn't money for prenatal care, or even vitamins such as calcium. Willis's baby teeth came in black and rotten. As a result, he didn't have front teeth to properly pronounce many of the letters of the alphabet. His V's and M's came out as B's, so my name became "Bera Bay." When nieces and nephews came along, they called me "Bea Bay." I'm still Aunt Bea to many in the family, and some of my great-grandchildren call me Grambea.

When my little brother was born it was time for me to grow up. I was no longer the baby, and it was time to help my mother, who was always so busy. I was old enough to care for baby Willis, and how I loved the job! I learned to change his diapers and even to sew little sun suits for him as well as for my nephew, Harold's son, Gary, a few years younger than Willis.

We played a game, my mother and I, to see how many points I could earn as I helped her with the household chores. For each 100 points, I earned a nickel:

10 points for filling the wash boiler and the reservoir of the coal-wood cook stove with water, hand pumped from the cistern;

5 points for carrying the milk and butter to the ice-house in the summer;

10 points for washing the cream separator each morning before I walked to school;

15 points for picking up a bushel of cobs from the pig pen (corn on the cob was fed to the hogs; the cobs were then used for fuel in the cook stove.) When Mom baked an angel food cake, I earned a few extra points sitting on the cob box by the stove and stoking just a few cobs at a time to keep the oven temperature even.

10 points for a coffee can of square nails picked up from the yard. I liked that chore and was often lucky enough to find Indian arrow heads as well.

10 points for shelling popcorn (we raised enough each year so there would be plenty to fill popcorn bowls on long winter evenings around the kitchen table.)

There were points for helping clean, cook and bake. Mom made a list of chores and points and allotted a time limit for each chore. I set goals for myself. How many points did I need to order the bedspread and curtains for my room at the cost of $2.50? I could order them from my "wish book," the Montgomery Ward catalog. My shoes came from the same catalog and were often too tight. Could that be the reason I loved to go barefoot, and still do?

The catalog was kept in the outhouse, where it filled an important function. The outhouse was a place for me to take time out, to be alone, and to study my "wish book." I would hear my mother call, "LaVera Mae, LaVera Mae," and I would answer, "Just a minute."

As a child, I often sat on the back steps of our farm home, watching the clouds roll by and fanaticizing about the objects and shapes I saw. Some looked like Christmas trees, others like mountains, cities and buildings. I was always a dreamer, not only day-time dreams, but also "night-time" dreams.

I often dreamed of flying over steps and low ground and never touching the ground. It seemed so real that I would awaken wondering if I really could fly! I dreamed again and again of the same old deserted house, its rooms full of antique furniture and clothing. Twenty years later I began collecting antiques. To this day I am often lost in my dreams; (as well as in daytime reality). A mild form of dyslexia makes it difficult for me to distinguish directions. I flunked my first driver's test because the officer told me to turn right and I turned left!

When my cousin Norris Forster, six-year-old brother of Winona and Neomia, was killed in a car accident, his father, my Uncle Ralph, told us that Norris had gone to heaven to be with God. Uncle Ralph stood with his arms encircling his daughters and me, as we watched Norris's body being carried into the house on a stretcher and placed in a bedroom. His mother was in the only other bedroom in the house with Norris's two-day-old brother, Verlouis.

In those days there were no funeral homes in our part of the country. The body usually rested in the family parlor until burial. Neighbors and friends took turns in "all night wakes" each night before the funeral. After funeral parlors came into being, parlors were called "living rooms," now to be used for the living.

Probably Norris's body was placed in the bedroom rather than the parlor, as was the custom, because Aunt Ethel could see her son's body from her bed through the doorway between the two rooms. She couldn't attend the funeral, as new mothers were not allowed out of bed for at least ten days. The evening of the funeral, I sat on the steps watching the clouds and imagining I saw Norris's coffin in the sky on its way to heaven.

Norris's death brought me face to face with reality. I wondered about so many things, such as death and heaven, and whether there was a Santa Claus and an Easter Bunny. Why were my mother's hands always colored green, pink and blue at Easter time? In the car with Harold on our way to Uncle Ralph's during the week of Norris's death, I decided to ask him about the facts of life. I began by asking; "Harold, is there really a Santa Claus?" His answer, "No, your parents give you those gifts." I accepted that, (we had been discussing it at school) and replied, "And I don't suppose there's an Easter Bunny either."

Christmas was a favorite holiday. I always wrote a letter to Santa but only asked for one gift. My mother said, "If you are selfish and ask for more than one gift, you may not get a gift at all."

It was mid-December and I was playing in the unheated upstairs bedroom when I discovered little cookie sheets, animal cookie cutters and a rolling pin lying on the bed in the spare bedroom. A very excited little girl, I ran to the kitchen where my mother was cooking to tell her what I had found. My fast-thinking mother answered, "Don't touch those things. They belong to Santa. His sleigh broke down last week in a field by our house and he asked me if he could store them here for a few days." He must have picked them up, because I checked the next day and they were gone.

That year we spent Christmas Eve at Aunt Elsie and Uncle Walter's house in McCook, Nebraska. Our stockings were hung in anticipation of Santa's visit that night, when there was a knock at the door. It was Santa, with a "Ho, Ho, Ho," and "Merry Christmas!" He asked ME to help him fill the stockings from the pack on his back. Guess what he had for my stocking? Yes, there were cookie sheets, animal cookie cutters and a rolling pin. Santa set a little kitchen cupboard on the floor under my stocking. Wow! A place to put my baking supplies! There were canisters with roses painted on them, just like those in my mother's real kitchen. There were other special things for my stocking: a fancy nail file in a jeweled celluloid case, a little cobalt blue glass bear, less than an inch tall standing on his hind legs and two beautiful silk handkerchiefs, one pink and one blue.

Years later I learned that my brother Harold had built the cupboard for me from a wooden prune box, and the knobs were made from glass beads. Santa was Mr. Bruce who lived across the road from Aunt Elsie. Mr. and Mrs. Bruce had lost a little girl about my age, and I must have reminded them of her, for they were very fond of me. The nail file, bear and handkerchiefs were from them. That was one of the most wonderful Christmases of my childhood.

Another Christmas I remember, there was very little money, but a lot of love. We couldn't afford a tree, so my mother took a naked tree branch and wound green crepe paper around the twigs, decorating them with hollow eggs that had been colored with Easter egg dye. To me it was beautiful! My doll had gotten lost—my Honey, tin-headed Minerva. To my delight, she showed up on Christmas Eve with a brand new stocking body and dress. And Willis's little truck had been repainted bright red. Christmas morning I found a small table, made from an old table leaf, with two orange crate chairs (more of Santa's helper Harold's handiwork). On the table was a note that said, "My elves didn't have time to paint these. Maybe your mother will paint them for you. Thanks for the cookies and milk. Love, Santa." I don't remember Harold's gift that year, but probably it was the "gift of giving" to his little brother and sister.

I have never regretted being raised on a farm. Although money was scarce, togetherness and love were abundant commodities. I grew up with a loving big brother who adored me just as I adored my little brother. Not only did Harold build doll furniture for me, he also made doll quilts. Eighty years later, I still have two of those doll quilts.

I was a pampered little girl and never learned to work in the fields or drive horses, although I nearly gave my brother a heart attack one time when I tried to drive the tractor. I never learned to milk a cow but I remember sitting on a little milking stool in the barn, drinking milk Harold squirted from the cow's teat into my little tin cup. Yes, I drank unhomogenized milk! Mom always used whole milk, saying it was better for us. Aunt Ethel fed skim milk to her family. I'm sure neither of them had heard of cholesterol.

I was afraid of the hens and would do almost anything to avoid gathering eggs or cleaning the hen house. Our hen house sat atop a hill. Part of the house was dug into the hill, giving it two openings to the ground level. When storms threatened, we beat pans to get the chickens in before the wind blew them away or they huddled together and suffocated. I didn't learn to do outside work, but I did learn to care for my little brother, cook, clean, sew, wallpaper and paint.

Lexington, 18 miles to the north, was our trading center, where we took cream and eggs to trade for groceries. We always had a reserve credit for the months when egg production slowed down. Flour and sugar were bought in 100 pound bags before winter storms began. When we were snowed in, Dad would hitch the horses to a wagon and go to town for food. However, usually we had enough stored in the root cellar to last all winter—100 pounds of potatoes, 100 pounds of salted fish, hundreds of jars of canned fruits and vegetables, cured bacon and hams, plus the root vegetables packed in crocks of sand.

Our Saturday shopping days, were special occasions. We looked forward to finding a sack of candy in one of the bags when we got home from town and unpacked the groceries. On one memorable Saturday, however, we and our 30-dozen crate of eggs met with disaster. Dad may have been driving a bit too fast, when we hit a bump going over the Plum Creek Bridge! Scrambled eggs, complete with shells, were all over Mom, Dad, the kids and car. But there was no candy that day.

It was a big day when Dad or Harold needed a new suit or Mom's coat wouldn't last another year, because we then went to the Church Banks Mercantile to shop for those items of clothing that Mom didn't make. We never paid the price on the tag—my first lesson in "dickering." The second lesson came a few years later in Mexico.

One day at "Church Banks" there was a big sales promotion which included giving away a plate glass mirror. I was standing by my mother when the "store man" said, "Little girl, will you draw a name out of the box?" I was thrilled when I drew my mother's name! That same day, for mere pennies, Mom bought many spools of blue ribbon and lace. She and Aunt Ethel sewed the ribbon and lace together—first a row of ribbon, then a row of lace—to make fabric for dresses for me and my Forster cousins. The three of us were often dressed alike.

On our weekly shopping trips, Harold asked the merchants if he could have the large plywood boxes used for the shipment of appliances. He brought home a piece or two of plywood a week, fastened to the trunk of the car. Always resourceful, Harold turned those pieces of plywood into beautiful kitchen cabinets that were his mothers pride and joy.

It was a few years later, at the end of a shopping day in Lexington. We were in the car ready to start home, when Dad noticed a package of gum in Willis's hand and asked, "Where did you get that gum?" The gum had come from George's Grocery Store along with a few candy bars Dad found hidden under the car seat; neither the gum nor the candy had been purchased. Willis learned a lesson in honesty that day. Dad accompanied him to the store to apologize to Mr. George and to pay him for the gum and candy. There was no allowance for Willis for a whole month. Eighty years later it still bothers me that I once stole a pair of gloves. Although my conscience bothered me, I wasn't strong enough to return them. Had my dad known, I would have had to face the same music as my little brother did. One Saturday I lost my purse containing two dollars I had earned doing chores. When I cried over my loss, my mother scolded. A lady found my purse, saw me crying, and returned it to me. "See" I said, "If I hadn't cried, I wouldn't have my money back!"

I grew up loving animals, especially dogs. We had a cat, Bluey, whose kittens always died of distemper. Mama cat must have been immune. My first dog "Snooky" would sit in my doll's high chair. "Tricksie," my next dog, walked me to school then came back at four o'clock to walk home with me. One day he wasn't there! I found him dead along the road by the school, the victim of a "hit and run" driver. "Snoopy Pedro" was the stray I brought home from school. I asked my teacher if I could keep him in the school house until school was dismissed. He sniffed at the lunch buckets, which prompted Mrs. Connell to give him his name. "Snoopy Pedro" continued to sniff, and he also learned to suck eggs. Dad tried filling the eggs with red hot pepper, but he must have been part Mexican Chihuahua, because he loved the hot pepper and continued to suck eggs. One day he mysteriously disappeared!

I was sick with the flu when our neighbor boy John came to see me, bringing me a darling little puppy. I was cuddling it, but threw it down fast when Dad walked into the room and said, "That's a coyote." I remember a baby rabbit Dad rescued from the field. I tried to tame it, but it didn't live long.

Spring was a favorite time of year for me. It brought new life to every creature and all growing things on the farm. Squeaky little pigs rudely pushed one another aside as they sought a spot at their mother's dinner table. The smell of black earth as it was being turned by the plow, the first robin's song, small buds swelling in fragrance and beauty and the first wild green onions. It was time to plant a garden. I was taking care of Willis, a toddler, while my mother planted the garden. The pot-bellied heating stove had been stored for the summer in an under-stairway storage closet. Bluey, our bob-tailed cat—the result of a cow stepping on her tail—found the stove the perfect place to give birth to a litter of kittens. A curious ten-year-old, I was checking on the kittens when little Willis toddled over and slammed the door shut! Since there wasn't an inside handle, I was locked in! I tried talking to Willis to get him to open the door, but he just jabbered, rattled the handle and toddled away. I suffered from anxiety until my mother came from the garden, found Willis safe, and rescued me. I was so worried that Willis would get hurt with no one to watch over him.

It was the spring before Dad bought his first and only tractor, a 1937 Farmall. He had, just that day, become the owner of a full set of dentures. He smoked "Bull Durham" tobacco, carried in a cloth bag with a drawstring top in his denim shirt pocket, along with cigarette papers to "roll his own." He was plowing with a team of horses in the field west of the house, when he decided he needed a smoke. He pulled out a cigarette paper, filled it with tobacco and put it to his lips to "roll it." The damned dentures got in the way. Dad pulled them out of his mouth and threw them across the newly plowed field! Mom wasn't the only one with a temper! Plowing stopped for several hours while I helped Dad search for his false teeth. Spring time was also "baby chick time." Mom raised Rhode Island Reds and set hens to hatch several hundred chicks each spring. Many of them were hatched under setting hens or in an incubator that was kept in our kitchen during the hatching season. There were always young roosters for fried chicken dinners; as many as two dozen a week were sold as "fryers," and delivered to customers in Elwood. We killed the chickens by stepping on their heads and pulling them off. They were dipped in scalding hot water to remove feathers and then came the worst job of all—picking pin feathers! In the fall the hens were culled. My mother used two fingers to measure the hens and detect which ones were laying eggs. The non-layers were sold as "roasting hens" or canned.

The kitchen was the most used room in the house. Not only did rejected piglets find refuge in a box by the stove, but it also served as a hatching place for baby chicks. The kitchen had buckled linoleum on the floor and wainscoting covered the lower half of the walls. After Mom tore out the wainscoting, she covered the area below the chair rail with washable oil-cloth. All the walls were either papered or "calcimined." Calcimine was more of a whitewash than a paint and was less expensive. It was a water soluble mixture of zinc, glue and water.

After years of carrying all our water from the cistern down by the barn, the dry sink, with its white enameled water bucket and a dipper that was used by all, was replaced with a sink that drained outside the house. Water was piped from the cistern and brought into the kitchen by means of a hand pump by the sink. The water was heated in a reservoir on the coal-wood cook stove; nearby a box with a hinged lid held the pig pen cobs that were used as fuel. The stove was far enough from the wall to make the perfect spot for a little girl to hide away, with her pillow and blanket, for a nap.

The kitchen cupboard, drop leaf table and chairs were all painted white. Each time Mom repainted them she changed the floral designs on them. All by free hand, she painted beautiful wild prairie roses and daisies, and decorated canister sets and waste baskets to match. I guess I thought all mothers were like mine, but later realized how very talented she was. I had taken many art lessons as an adult before I realized that my mother was an artist.

Summers were special. Along with tending crops and livestock, raising chickens, raising gardens and canning fruits and vegetables, my parents somehow found time for family togetherness. There were picnics in the park, including a special birthday picnic on July 17, to celebrate both Harold and Aunt Elsie's birthdays. Aunt Elsie and Uncle Walter lived on a farm near McCook. When the picnic was at McCook, we traveled through the town of Indianola to get there. We stopped at a gas station where two buffalo were kept in a pen. They were killed when they escaped their pen to do battle with a freight train! A September picnic was held in Holdrege to celebrate the birthdays of Grandma Forster, mine, and, in later years, my niece Karen's.

Another summer activity was attending outdoor movies held one night a week in Smithfield. They were silent movies, projected from the upstairs window of one building onto the side of another building.

There were always Sunday dinners with fried chicken and home-made ice cream. When we went to Grandma and Grandpa Forster's for dinner, Grandpa Woodring was always invited. It must have been Grandma's idea, as my two grandpas really were not very fond of one another. The card game "Pitch" was a favorite Sunday afternoon pastime for the men. Grandpa Forster would become very angry when someone cheated, and that someone usually was Grandpa Woodring. He probably did it just to irritate Grandpa Forster. Grandpa Woodring was a character, albeit a loveable one. One of his favorite expressions was, "If you don't like my gate, don't swing on it."

We didn't have a creek or pond nearby or a swimming pool in our little town. In the summer, my cousins and I cooled off in a 50-gallon drum of water. One day we decided swimming in the slimy stock tank might be fun, when Aunt Ethel caught us skinny dipping. We tried diving into a bin of grain, but that, too, was soon forbidden for fear we would suffocate.

Our summer playhouse was an empty grain bin. We used white shoe polish, sneaked from the house, to color water for our milk. Hollyhock seeds became cereal. A poor little mouse climbed into our milk bottle one night and drowned. Willis and Verlouis, both preschoolers, butchered, quartered, and hung the mouse up like their dads did with hogs at butchering time. They must have swiped the knife from the kitchen.

My busy mother seemed to always find time to be my playmate. When she visited me at my playhouse, I made tea for her and offered her a slice of "mud pie." When I took my baby doll to visit her, she would answer my knock with, "Come in, if your nose is clean." Her favorite answer when I asked her the time was, "Half past kissin' time and time to kiss again."

We never bought soda or "pop" as we called it in Nebraska, but in the summer Mom made dozens of bottles of root beer and sealed them with a hand operated "capper." Root beer floats made with homemade ice cream were a frequent but still special treat!

My playmate, Floy, and I always managed to find ways to entertain ourselves. We didn't have bicycles, skates and certainly not cartoons on television! We made doll houses from shoe boxes, pasting furniture and appliances from a Wards catalog on the inside of the box. The people who lived there also came from Wards. One summer we decided to dig seats into the clay bank of an underpass near our homes with spoons that we had confiscated from my mother's kitchen. We would sit in our "reserved seats," watch the cars go by and maybe be lucky enough to hear the rumble of a freight train overhead.

It was the summer of 1936 when my dad's sister Hazel (Woodring) Incho, her husband Jack, and little four-year-old daughter Jackie Lea came to visit us on the farm in Nebraska. My dad was very fond of his "little sister" Hazel and always bragged that she was a beautiful lady. Jackie Lea was also a pretty little girl, with long dark curls and blue eyes. She was not a very happy little girl during the days she visited with us, because she was ill with the mumps. Grandpa Woodring promised her an ice cream cone if she would go see Dr. Clark in Elwood. She went to the doctor, but Grandpa forgot about the cone! It was a mistake he made that Jackie Lea never forgot. The California cousins never had a chance to know and love Grandpa as I did.

Jackie recalls that her mother went to the outhouse when she needed a cigarette. She didn't want her father or her big brother to know she smoked! I remember that Aunt Hazel wore shorts at a time when women wore only skirts in our conservative part of the country. After all, the Inchos were from Huntington Beach, California where they were more liberal, both in dress and lifestyle. Not long after their visit, Mom came down with the mumps, and was quite ill. She was bedfast for several days. At eleven years old, I had to help Harold and Dad in the kitchen. I learned to cut up a chicken and to bake bread that week. Using a dishtowel as make believe bread dough, Mom taught me the technique of kneading dough.

The Summer Olympics of 1936 were held in Berlin, Germany. The games had been awarded to Berlin in 1931 with no idea that Adolph Hitler was to take power in Germany two years later. By 1936 the Nazis had control over Germany and had begun to implement their racist policies. There was an international debate as to whether the 1936 Olympics should be boycotted. The United States was close to boycotting, but at the last minute decided to attend. The Nazis saw the event as a way to promote their ideology, as well as their Aryan superiority. Throughout the games the Olympic Complex was covered in Nazi banners. Leni Reifenstadt, a famous filmmaker, filmed those Olympic Games and made them into her movie "Olympia."

Jesse Owens, a black American athlete, was the star of the 1936 Olympic Games. Owens, the "Tan Cyclone," brought home four gold medals: the 100 meter dash, the long jump, which made an Olympic record; the 200 meter sprint around a turn, which made a world record; and he was part of the winning team for the 400 meter relay.

Dad was often homesick for his mother and siblings in California. He wrote a letter to one of them shortly after a "shouting match" with my mother and mailed it in our rural mailbox. I watched my mother walk down the path to the mailbox, put the flag down, and retrieve the letter before the mail carrier came by. I never learned the fate of that letter; was it re-mailed or was it destroyed?

It was 1937 when my dad received a telegram telling him that his mother had died. Because money was scarce, he couldn't afford to attend the funeral. He had visited his mother and siblings only once in the past twenty five years when he traveled by freight train as a caretaker for cattle and hogs being shipped to a West Coast market. My cousin, Zilpha, remembered her Uncle Ray's visit and said, "He was tall and thin and loved baker's bread; I guess we must have had enough bread, since it was only six or seven cents a loaf at that time."

The family took three summer excursions I'll never forget. The first was a visit to our State Capitol in Lincoln, Nebraska. It was the tallest building I had ever seen. The second was a visit to the Children's Home, an orphanage in Holdrege, Nebraska. I recall feeling sorry for the children. When my folks scolded me, I would think to myself, that I must be an orphan. They wouldn't be so mean to me if I was their real daughter. The third was a trip to the State Penitentiary in Lincoln, Nebraska in 1933. Willis was a baby wrapped in a blanket. They unwrapped him and searched him before they let us through the gate. I can still hear the "clang" of the door closing and locking as we entered the prison. We saw the electric chair, the prisoners in solitary confinement, and other inmates at the dining table. Their meal was served in large tin tubs and consisted of small, boiled, unpeeled potatoes and onions, bread and water! Were our parents trying to impress us with the importance of government, of home and of being a law-abiding citizen?

Dad was not a hunter, but he carried a gun to the fields and sometimes brought home a rabbit. Mom didn't like to feed us rabbit meat, thinking the rabbit might be diseased and the meat might make us ill. Sheep were often butchered for mutton meat, but chicken was most commonly served at our table. In the fall we butchered a hog or two. Bill White, our neighbor a mile to the west, was always on hand to help butcher and cut up the meat. A big black iron kettle was filled with water and placed over a pit fire. When the water boiled, the hog was placed in the pot, then scraped with a special tool to remove the hair. A use was found for everything but the squeal! My mother didn't make blood sausage, but many did. The head meat, ground and mixed with an equal amount of cooked oatmeal and seasoned with salt and pepper, made Knipp. The brains were scrambled with eggs; liver was the first meal, fried with onions. Hams and bacon were cured and hung in the root cellar. The scraps were made into country sausage and the feet became a delicacy known as "pickled pig's feet." Fat was rendered into lard for baking and frying. Some of the rinds from the rendered fat, "cracklings" were eaten like potato chips; the rest was used to make laundry soap. On soap making day, the iron kettle, again placed over a fire pit, held the ingredients for soap, cracklings and lye. Hating the smell of soap cooking, I often took refuge in caves in the hills back of the barn. I always returned in time to watch Mom pour the soap into flat containers to be cut into bars the size and dark tan color of Fels Naphtha soap.

It wasn't until after the first frost that the corn was ready to harvest. As a team of horses pulled the wagon down the corn rows a person on each side pitched the ears of corn into the wagon. A special tool was worn over the glove to help loosen the ear from the stalk and husk. At that same time of year, the parsnips were stored in their bed of sand. My mother believed that they were poisonous before the first hard frost, just as were the cucumbers unless they had been soaked in salt.

Two of my dad's uncles, his mother's brothers, often came from Concordia, Kansas, to help out with the corn harvest. I dreaded their coming, because I always got sick from the cigars they puffed away on when they rode in the car with us on our weekly shopping trip to Lexington.

Soon after corn harvest, a shelling crew of twelve or more men traveled from farm to farm. The corn that wasn't sold was stored in bins made of chicken wire to be fed to the hogs. Corn shelling was usually a two-day affair, which seemed to throw the housewives into competition to see who could serve the best meals. I was twelve and old enough to help serve dinner. A young crew member, Rueben Stehl, was my first teenage crush, but he didn't even know I existed! Decades later, as a friend of Rueben and his wife, I asked if he remembered me from those days. He replied, "No, I don't remember you, but I do remember the homemade chocolate ice cream at your house."

There were many homeless during the Great Depression, who traveled by foot or rail and were known as "tramps" or "hobos." One hobo "Steam Train Maury" developed a "Hobo Code"—a way of marking posts near farms:

+ Good place for handout
\# Bad bull! Stay out of the yard
= Police officer lives here
VV Poor water

Our farm must have been favorably marked, because we certainly fed a lot of hobos. Some of them made "tramp art" (jewelry boxes and picture frames ornately carved from cigar boxes) and offered them in exchange for food. I was afraid of the tramps I met on the tracks on my way home from school, but I was more afraid of the Anderson's mean bulls if I walked through their pasture. Then there was "Hamey Bearcat," a heifer who chased anyone in a skirt! My grandchildren loved to hear the story about Hamey Bearcat. Willis had broken a living room window, and when Dad asked him about it, he said, "Bera Bay broke it." Dad's reply was, "Then I'll have to spank Bera Bay." At that Willis suddenly changed his story and said, "No, Hamey Bearcat broke it." The real culprit was soon discovered. My granddaughter Amy Boehm evidently identified closely with the story, because she came home from preschool crying because her teacher wouldn't believe her name was Amy Bearcat.

I put an extra plate on the table for Willis's imaginary playmate (who must have attended the auction sales Willis held when he lined up his cars, trucks and wagon on the south side of the house and auctioned them off). Dad often took us to farm auction sales with him. I eagerly searched the 25 cent boxes of "goodies" Dad bought. One of those boxes held a cast iron waffle maker, the kind that was heated over a coal-wood cook stove. Mom "thought modern" and didn't like that "old stuff," so I learned to make waffles for Dad on that waffle iron. Today, one just like it sits on the stove at our Pick City cabin.

Many years later when Willis was in the Army and stationed at Fort Sill, Oklahoma, he learned to become an auctioneer. How much does our environment in the formative years of our lives influence who and what we will become in our adult years?

County fairs were a once-a-year adventure. We spent several days in Elwood at the fair. Indians set up their tepees, lived at the fair for a few days, and had "Pow Wow" dances. My little brother Willis joined their dance circle one night and moved to the sound of the drums, holding the hands of two little Indian girls.

Winter on the farm in Nebraska was a time of togetherness. It was not uncommon to be snowed in for days at a time during a blizzard. Long winter evenings were a time we enjoyed eating a big bowl of popcorn with lots of salt and melted butter and biting into the shiny red apples that we had stored away in the fall. It was a time for Dad to catch up on his reading and for Mom to get back to her sewing.

I remember well those cozy evenings around the kitchen table. Our lighting was either a kerosene lamp or a gasoline lantern, which gave better light. We didn't have electricity during our years on the farm. Dad usually had a book in his hand, probably a Zane Grey novel or a history book. Zane Grey, my dad's best-loved western author, was born on June 31, 1872, in Zanesville, Ohio, a town founded by his maternal ancestors.

Mom, on the other side of the table, would be sewing, embroidering or appliquéing. She made most of our clothes without a pattern, and even made sheets and pillow cases from flour sacks. I would pick out a dress I liked in the Wards Catalog and she would make it. I remember a princess-style dress with appliqué, which my mother copied down to the last detail. It was beautiful and couldn't have been more special to me if it had come from Saks. My clothes were often made from Aunt Elsie's discarded dresses and coats, turned inside out to hide the effects of fading. As clothing was outgrown, it was passed along with the remark, "It's none the worse for wear." Interestingly my mother never liked the color blue; however, her older sister Elsie loved blue dresses. They were handed down to my mother, whose favorite color was green. It must have caused some frustration for my mother as I never saw her wear blue. When woolen suits and coats were no longer wearable, they were cut into 4-or 5-inch square blocks to be made into comforters. Harold wasn't very old when he learned to help by sewing comforter pieces together on the Singer sewing machine. A few years later, as a young teenager, I made comforters for my hope chest.

We often played a card game called "Rummy." Like a lot of kids, I liked to win and cried when I didn't. Dad decided it was time I learned a lesson and went for the razor strop. I don't remember the hurt from the strop, but I do remember my dad's words, "LaVera Mae, you need to learn to be a good loser as well as a good winner; you can't win all of life's battles." Our parents taught us well to accept the bad along with the good. I loved to play Chinese Checkers; often the delivery man, who brought our fuel oil, would take time out to play a game of Checkers with me. Curiously, I always won, was that more than coincidence?

It was July 17, 1935, when I was almost ten; that Harold brought his bride Alice Clayton to live on the farm with us for a few months. I was in awe of Alice. She was so pretty, she was talented, and she was the big sister I never had. She taught me how to do my hair, manicure my nails, wear a bit of makeup and how to keep my waistline trim! She could stand on a catalog at the top of the steps and place the palms of her hands on the bottom of the next step! She could draw free hand and drew patterns for the animals that Grandpa Forster cut out of plywood and painted as lawn ornaments. We didn't have a piano, but when we were invited to Alice's family home for Sunday dinner, she played and sang, "In the Big Rock Candy Mountains" and the hymn, "In the Garden," that is still my favorite. "For He walks with me, and He talks with me, and He tells me I am His own" are lyrics that touch my heart. I have requested this hymn be sung at my "Going Away Party." I often speak of my journey through life, of death and the "dash" in between. It is all a part of God's plan.

President Franklin Delano Roosevelt fought the depression with the "New Deal" programs, WPA being the largest one of them. FDR put the nation to work. In 1935 there were 20 million persons on relief in the United States. The goal of the WPA was to employ most of them until the economy recovered. WPA was funded by Congress with the passage of the Emergency Relief Appropriations Act on April 5, 1935. Headed by Harry Hopkins, the WPA program provided almost eight million jobs between 1935 and 1939 and was the largest employer in the country. Most of the people who needed work were eligible for at least some of the jobs. The hourly wage was the prevailing wage in each area; the regulations stated that workers could not work more than thirty hours a week. Many projects included months in the field, with workers eating and sleeping on worksites. Workers' pay varied from $19.00 to $94.00 a month. The WPA was consistent with the strong belief of the time that husbands and wives should not both be working, because the second person working would take a job away from a breadwinner.

Total expenditures on WPA projects through June, 1941, totaled over 11 billion dollars. More than 4 billion dollars were spent on highway, road and street projects, a million dollars on public buildings and another million dollars on welfare projects, including sewing projects for women and school lunch programs.

The Workers Program Administration was renamed as the Workers Projects Administration in 1939. When unemployment ended with the beginning of World War II, Congress terminated the WPA in 1943.

In 1937 Harold was hired to work for the WPA project, the "Tri-County Dam." It was an engineering project to bring irrigation from the Platte River to dry land farms in three Nebraska counties. Harold drove thirty-five miles to work for five hours a day and earned thirty-five cents an hour. At that time, Harold weighed less than the hundred pound sacks of cement he was tossing around on the job.

Harold and Alice moved to the Hanlin place, where Harold had been born in 1916, and were living there when their first two children were born: Gary on October 8, 1937, and their daughter Karen on September 5, 1939. The children were born at their grandparent's home, the Woodring home place, just two miles to the west. Besides his WPA job Harold also renovated old cars to sell for a few dollars profit. By early 1942 Harold and his family were living in Wichita, Kansas. He was employed by Boeing Airplane Co. helping build war planes.

We were taught loyalty to our country and our state and respect for our parents. We learned good work ethics. I recall my mother's words, "A day with ne'er a task completed is a day wasted." Those work ethics held us in good stead when hard times hit. We had learned to appreciate the simple things in life, the satisfaction of a job well done and how to make the most of whatever was available. My father's thirst for knowledge and his life experiences educated him outside the classroom. I give him and my favorite teacher Mrs. Connell, the credit for my love of books and learning. I thank my mother for giving me the ability to speak in public, my artistic talents and for being a good speller. I entered county spelling contests for several years in which I placed second two years in a row. I have remained a good speller to this day. My mother helped me study my spelling words, and I helped her study for the three-act plays our P.T.A. gave each year.

A day at Quakerville School began with the Pledge of Allegiance to the flag and a song:

> My Nebraska, dear Nebraska
> State I love the best,
> Where pioneers first led the way,
> Now live the people blessed.
> For though the sun
> Shines hot in summer,
> And the cold winter winds may blow,
> It's always fair weather
> In Nebraska, where real folks grow.

The lyrics of this song are stored in my memory bank. I have searched in vain trying to find the author. The Nebraska State Song is "Beautiful Nebraska" written by Jim Fras and adapted in 1967 as Nebraska's official state song.

We kept abreast of what was going on in our community and our state, if not in the world, by our one and only local weekly newspaper, the Elwood Bulletin. It related such important events as Mr. and Mrs. Jones enjoyed Sunday dinner with the Smith's—as well as obituaries, weddings, and birth announcements. A magazine, Capper's Weekly which we read from cover to cover was published in Topeka, Kansas and included short stories and recipes and gave us a slightly broader perspective.

In 1937, on May 28th, the Golden Gate Bridge in San Francisco was opened to traffic. The first comic book, "Super Hero," starring "Superman" was published in 1938. CoCo Wheats, a hot cereal, was introduced in 1930 with the suggestion that hot cereal could taste good and still be good for you. The hot cereal at our house was either "cracked wheat," made from our own wheat, or oatmeal. Mom used to sliver chocolate on my cereal to coax me to eat it. I was a skinny little kid and often heard, "If you don't eat, the wind's gonna blow you away." Willis and I both loved the warm cocoa taste when we could afford to buy CoCo Wheats. In 1939, the CoCo Wheats box advertised a contest offering a prize for the most unusual animal picture sent to them. I found a picture of a giraffe getting a haircut. It won the prize. Willis was so excited when a battery operated toy train arrived complete with tracks. He didn't have a lot of toys, but he did have a tricycle that he drove, somewhat like his dad had driven the old Model T. The door casings showed the results of his reckless driving during the winter months when it was too cold to play out-doors.

It must have been a struggle raising a family in the thirties. Not only was the nation in a financial crisis, but even Mother

Nature was in an ugly mood. The farmers in the Midwest planted their crops each spring with hope and prayers, only to watch drought and grasshoppers clean them out. Wind piled dust up along the fences like snow. I walked home from school with a scarf over my face to keep from choking from the dust. Cars drove with their lights on in the middle of the day; it was like driving in a blizzard. There was no corn for the hogs, and no grain or hay for the livestock. They were forced to eat Russian thistles in order to survive. When the grain elevator burned in Smithfield, Dad went to the bank, seeking a loan to buy a few wagonloads of the burned grain to feed our starving livestock. Mr. Mahlin, the banker, said, "I'm so sorry, we just don't have money to loan, but how much do you need?" I don't know how Dad answered, but Mr. Mahlin reached into his pocket and gave my dad the money. I'm sure Dad paid him back with interest. My dad, Ray Woodring, was one of the most honest men God ever put on this earth.

A few months later, the starving cattle were sold to the government. I watched Dad and Harold drive our cattle out of the farm yard. They were met in Smithfield by government agents who shot the cattle and buried them in trenches. It was a sad end to years of hard work and devotion.

One evening during those days, the sky was darkened by a "cloud" or "colony" of bats in flight. When one landed in my hair, I screamed and ran into the house, where my dad killed it with a broom. Other than a slightly sore head, I was unharmed; however, to this day I'm still afraid of bats.

In 1938 and 1939, I remember getting canned grapefruit and powdered milk among the food commodities provided by the government. There was not enough money to buy food for the family, not enough for candy, gum or show tickets and certainly not enough for the bicycle I yearned for. In 1914, when my parents left California to make a home in Nebraska, they had managed to save $300.00 to make the trip and set up housekeeping. In 1939, 25 years later, they left Nebraska with the same amount, $300.00, to travel west and make a home in "Sunny California."

ON ROUTE 66
Art by LaVera

Chapter 6

ROUTE 66, FROM NEBRASKA TO CALIFORNIA AND BACK

In the fall of 1939, my parents gave up trying to survive on a dried up "dry land" farm in Nebraska. With no rain and no crops for several years, there was little left to hold them on the farm. Most of the hogs and chickens had been killed for food; the starving cattle had been sold to the government.

We loaded a few of our possessions in the trunk of our 1929 Chevrolet sedan—clothing, blankets, pillows, dishes and cooking utensils. The house was locked and we left Nebraska, searching for a rainbow in Sunny California, thought to be the land of opportunity and the promise of a better life. We traveled in a caravan of two vehicles. Our car was overloaded with my parents, me, my five-year-old brother Willis, my oldest brother Harold, his wife Alice, and their children, two-year-old Gary Lee and baby Karen Kay. Roy Tomasek, my mother's cousin, his wife Velma and their two boys were in the second car. Mom had $300.00 tucked safely away in her bra, to pay for food, gas and lodging, and to find a place to live in California. We bought our food at grocery stores, and carried a jug of water. Roadside cafes were tempting but too expensive. There wasn't enough money for lodging every night, so we often slept in the cars or stretched out on blankets along a ditch or by a gas station. I do remember staying at a motel in Raton, New Mexico. We were probably badly in need of a bath by that time.

My dad had two brothers, Earl and Lloyd, living in San Diego and a sister, Hazel, in Huntington Beach, California. I believe Dad had always wondered if he did the right thing when he left California and his family in 1916, shortly after he and my mother were married.

Years later, reading John Steinbeck's *Grapes of Wrath*, I could relate to his story. In 1936 John Steinbeck, a native Californian, became concerned about the plight of the "Oakies" who had been streaming across the state for several years. He began spending time with them, talking to them and hearing their stories. He then wrote a series of newspaper articles for the San Francisco News, which was later collected into a book, *Their Blood is Strong*. *Grapes of Wrath* was written and published in1939. Steinbeck was awarded the Pulitzer Prize in 1940 and the Nobel Prize for Literature in1962.

Just as the "Oakies" did, we traveled much of the way on the infamous Route 66. It was the major pathway for the migrants who went west during the Dust Bowl of the 1930's, supporting the economy of the communities through which the road passed. Route 66, built during 1926 and 1927, ran from Chicago through Missouri, Kansas, Oklahoma, Texas and New Mexico, its' entire length covering 2,448 miles.

Burma Shave signs helped brighten the day and shorten the trip. Burma Shave, an American brand of brushless shaving cream, became famous for its advertising gimmick of posting humorous rhyming poems on small sequential highway billboards from 1927 to 1963. Some of the jingles we saw in 1939:

"Good to the Last Strop"
"For Faces that Go Places"
"Shave Faster without Disaster"
"Covers a Multitude of Chins"
"Look Spiffy in a Jiffy"
"He's Nifty and Thrifty
"Looks 30 at 50"

All the jingles were followed by the words, Burma Shave.

Our exodus to California along Route 66 almost paralleled that of the "Joads" in Steinbeck's *Grapes of Wrath*. It opened up a whole new world to me. Until then I had not traveled more than 200 miles from home to South Dakota. I was allowed to wear "pants" for the first time and I was so proud of my new jodphurs. They were riding pants of green corduroy, wide across the hips and tight fitting from the knees to the ankles. I was sure everyone noticed how cute I looked. I saw huge mountains, Hoover Dam, cities, the ocean, and I met the California Woodring relatives for the first time. We went to Aunt Hazel's in Huntington Beach and started looking for housing we could afford. We found a duplex in Seal Beach, a city along the Pacific Ocean. It had one bedroom, a kitchen-living room combination with a "Murphy" bed for me. Willis slept on the couch.

Harold and Alice found an apartment in the same area. Harold found work pumping gas at a station, but Dad couldn't find a job. Mom found housework by the hour. I worked after school and evenings for a dentist and his wife most of the time we were in California. I helped cook dinner, feed their little girl while her parents ate, then washed the dishes and cleaned up the kitchen. I became fond of little Suzy and was very upset when I learned she had drowned in the ocean a short time after we returned to Nebraska.

Mom and I managed to earn enough to pay the rent and buy groceries. Many of our groceries, fruits and vegetables were bought at a Japanese-owned market. Prices were low in 1939 in that depressed economy. Anchor Hocking Glass Co. was selling water glasses two for a nickel; a first class postage stamp was 3 cents, and postcards were a penny. We could buy vegetables at the Japanese market for a nickel a bunch. Milk was 10 cents a gallon and ground beef 15 cents a pound. Shortly after the bombing of Pearl Harbor in 1941, all of the Japanese on the West Coast were rounded up and placed in internment camps.

I attended Woodrow Wilson High in Long Beach. I walked a few blocks to catch a bus, and then transferred to another bus before reaching school. It was scary for me, to say the least. Just the bus ride alone was a new adventure. The school was quite a change, from a freshman class of 8 in Elwood, Nebraska, to a class of 800 at Woodrow Wilson High. I got lost on campus and had to learn to follow classmates I recognized from class to class. I met a boy from Nebraska, who befriended me. He remarked, "If you weren't so stuck up, you might have more friends." I wasn't stuck up, I was just a shy, naïve little country girl, lost in a big city school. I met a Chinese girl in one of my classes who introduced me, by letter, to a pen pal in China. We corresponded for several months. She was part Russian, part Chinese—a pretty girl in the picture she sent me—and wrote perfect English. My last letter to her postmarked December 7, 1942, was censored and returned to me.

It was the year the Nebraska Cornhuskers played in the Rose Bowl in Pasadena. We didn't go to the game, but we did see the Rose Bowl when Mrs. Brock, our next door neighbor,

Me at Woodrow Wilson High in Long Beach, California.

Willis in a sand car built by him and his friend, Rickie, in front of our duplex

Me in front of our duplex in Seal Beach, California

took us to a restaurant in Pasadena. I was impressed by a tree growing through the ceiling of the restaurant. You paid for the meal as you chose—if you didn't have money, you ate free. Hopefully, the wealthy paid enough extra to compensate for those who didn't have a dime to their name.

Willis and little Rickie Brock were playmates. A street car track had been torn out in the middle of the road in front of our duplex, leaving a pile of sand. Willis and Rickie built a sand sculpture car large enough for them to sit in; it had gallon tin can headlights.

Willis remembers the Christmas of 1939. He had been told that Santa probably wouldn't be able to find us in our new home in California. He was so excited when he found three packages under the tree on Christmas morning. He shouted, "Look, look, Mommy, Santa did find us!" One package held a football, one a book and one a top. One of my mother's employers realized that we had no money for Christmas, and that a little five-year-old boy would be broken hearted if Santa didn't come. Her son picked out three of his gifts from under their tree, and sent them home for little Willis. Such acts of kindness have colored my life.

I could look out the window of my classroom at Woodrow Wilson and see Signal Hill, a small area completely surrounded by Long Beach. The hill was a forest of oil derricks reaching toward the sky, all drilled in the 1920's. Dad recalled that in 1912, the year he moved with his parents to Southern California, land on Signal Hill could be purchased for pennies, but pennies were scarce in those days.

I wore uniforms to school at Woodrow Wilson High, a dark skirt and white blouse, so I didn't need many clothes, just two skirts and two blouses were the extent of my wardrobe. Academically, I was doing well; Nebraska seemed to be a jump ahead of California in that respect.

A few of the girls at Woodrow Wilson smoked funny looking and smelling cigarettes in the restroom. I soon realized the "pot" they talked about wasn't the pot you sat on when it was too cold to go to the outhouse, but drugs that came from Tijuana, Mexico. The nickname "pot" comes from the Spanish word Potiguaya, which means marijuana leaves. The name became popular in the United States in the late 1930's and 1940's.

My mother gave me a dime a day for my school lunch. I ate the same thing every day, a hot dog with mustard and onions that cost 5 cents. I saved the other nickel for a licorice ice cream cone from a store that was near the bus stop, and then I walked the rest of the way home along the beach. I remember the thrill of removing my shoes and socks and walking barefoot, looking for pretty seashells, and the sand squishing between my toes.

One day I met an old man at the bus stop. Although he was probably only in his forties, he seemed old to me at the age of 15. He invited me into his house to see the photographs he had taken of the ocean waves breaking near the boardwalk in front of his house. I would panic if my 15-year-old granddaughter accepted such an invitation in our present day world; however, I was naïve and didn't hesitate to follow him into his house. He gave me several 8x10 photos which I still have in an album. We trusted people in those days and seldom locked the doors of our houses or cars.

We were visiting Aunt Hazel, Uncle Jack and their children Jackie Lea and Harry. Harry was in his first year of college and his friend Lloyd Cook was visiting him for the weekend. Lloyd asked if he could take me to the Pike, an amusement park in Long Beach. My parents obviously didn't think of it as a date, or maybe Lloyd didn't realize I was only fifteen and a bit too young to date a college-age boy. We were just leaving the yard when Lloyd heard a giggle from the back seat; Jackie was hiding on the floor but she didn't get to go along. I'll never forget that evening, especially the ride on the roller coaster out over the ocean, and the restaurant where Lloyd treated me to dinner. He left money on the table for the waitress. Until then I didn't know that waitresses could be and should be tipped. In the 1930's in Nebraska, I'm sure only the more affluent customers tipped. It was a fun evening that ended with my first goodnight kiss.

In the very early spring of 1940, we returned to the farm in Nebraska. We hadn't found the pot of gold at the end of the rainbow in California! My dad couldn't find work, and he longed to return to the land. Crops weren't the only thing he grew; he planted a love for the country and an appreciation for simple, everyday things in each of his children.

After we spent a few months on our Quakerville farm, it was either rented or sold to my dad's cousin, Robert Birt. We moved to a house on the farm that had once been the soddy home of my mother's wet nurse and the nurse's baby daughter, Vida Joy. Dad rented land and put in a crop. I traveled back and forth to Elwood High with Doris Bigelow, the Gosper County Superintendant. She lived in Smithfield and drove to Elwood, the county seat, each morning. There were a few times when she didn't make the trip, for one reason or another, and I walked the seven miles each way to school and back; on one trip, in subzero weather, I froze my ankles.

I began my freshman year of high school in Elwood. After attending Quakerville, an all girls' school for eight years, Elwood High was an awakening for me, an awakening to boys. I matured early. At 125 pounds, I was quite voluptuous, and embarrassed to wear sweaters. The boys loved to tease me by tying my dress sashes to my desk, dipping my long hair in ink and putting bubble gum on the seat of my desk. I wasn't used to being around boys my own age; however, I soon learned that they were really trying to just get my attention. I maintained good grades, mostly A's, but I was also learning a few nonacademic activities, such as playing hooky with my closest girlfriend, Barb Tilson. I avoided getting caught by forging my dad's name on excuses. Because of his injured arm, Dad used a lot of pressure to sign his name on letters he wrote on 100-page tablets. His signature, Ray Woodring, left a perfect replica for me to copy!

I remember Halloween in Elwood. Trick or treating was not what we did in those years; we just played tricks, mean tricks like soaping windows, letting air out of the high school principal's car tires, and piling Russian thistles in the entry way of the schoolhouse door. The boys tipped over outhouses and even hauled a piece of farm machinery into town and left it in the middle of Main Street. Today that would probably be classed as a misdemeanor; then it was chalked up as a bunch of boys having fun.

December 7, 1941, on a Sunday morning at 7:55 a.m. 183 Japanese war planes swooped out of a cloudless sky and demolished the United States Pacific fleet, docked at Pearl Harbor. Many citizens and military personnel were killed or injured. One thousand are still entombed in the hull of the U.S.S. Arizona.

Harry Hines Woodring, a distant cousin of my father, served as U.S. Secretary of War under President Roosevelt during the pre-war years from 1936 to 1940. He followed the recommendations of his predecessors for increasing the strength of the Regular Army, National Guard and Reserve Corps. During his tenure he directed a revision of mobilization plans to bring personnel and procurement into balance and stressed the need to protect the initial (peacetime) protective force. He resigned in 1940 after disagreeing with the administration's policy of shipping war materials to Britain. He was married to Helen Coolidge and served as governor of Kansas from 1931 to 1933.

The beginning of my sophomore year found me enrolled at Huntley, Nebraska Consolidated School. I was not popular with the sophomore girls there when I was given the leading female part in the class play, "Good Night, Ladies." My mother's acting ability talents may have rubbed off on me.

I was a cheerleader for the Huntley Football Team that fall and enjoyed it. Sports definitely weren't my priority, even though I could outrun and out high-jump most of the boys at "County Play Day" when I was a student at Quakerville.

I grew up covering my ears when I heard swear words. My mother had a temper and used them often. She gave me the excuse that she learned them from my dad. I told my fourth grade teacher, Mrs. Connell, "If I can't find a man who doesn't smoke, drink or swear, I'm not going to get married." She assured me, "Then, honey, you will probably never get married."

Two boys at Huntley learned how very much I disliked foul language and swear words. They, no doubt, considered me a "square," prompting them to hold me between them in a car and verbally abuse me by quoting every bad word they could think of.

Harold and his family had moved to a house near Huntley, on the main road into town. He built a small structure there, installed two pumps, and opened a gas station. He also helped my father open another station a mile east of Elwood. My dad's farming days were over. Harold's wife Alice needed help; not only were their two children Gary and Karen both preschoolers, but Alice also managed the gas station much of the time. I lived with them that school year to help pump gas and baby sit after school and weekends.

Dating was easy without my parents to supervise me, and with the exposure I got by working at the Huntley gas station. I still remember the two boys I dated that year. Gaylord David was several years my senior and out of high school. He called me "Honey Bea," and he liked to sing the song "Hut Sut," which was popular at the time and one of my favorites. He painted "Hut Sut" on the mud flaps of his old Chevy. I felt he was becoming too serious, asking me to attend family gatherings and to meet his parents. One evening, waiting for him to pick me up, I remarked to my sister-in-law, Alice, "I really should stop seeing Gaylord. I'm too young for a serious relationship." When Gaylord drove into the yard, little Gary Lee, who had been eavesdropping, ran to tell him, "My Aunt Bea ain't gonna go with you anymore." Gaylord spun his tires in the gravel and left, not to return. He was drafted, went to war, stepped on a land mine and was left a paraplegic. I was to meet him again four years later, in Holdrege, Nebraska, when he answered my ad: "Puppies for Sale." The puppy he purchased from me for five dollars grew up to be a big white dog that resembled an Alaskan Husky. He became Gaylord's constant companion and pulled him around the house in his wheelchair. Gaylord was employed by a local photographer as an artist coloring black and white photos. It was before the days of color photography. Gaylord and his wife lived just a few blocks from my parent's home in Holdrege, Nebraska. I visited them one day to give them a letter I had found in an antique secretary I was refinishing. The letter was dated 1908 and was from his great aunt to his grandmother telling of plans to attend the St. Louis Exposition.

In 1941 the world was clawing its way out of the Great Depression, only to come face to face with three dictators hell-bent on world domination.

In his State of the Union address on January 5, 1941, President Roosevelt identified the four essential human rights—freedom of speech; freedom of worship; freedom from want; and freedom from fear—that should be universally protected. In his words, "In the future days which we seek to make secure, we look forward to a world founded upon these essential human freedoms."

In 1943, Norman Rockwell produced four oil paintings—Freedom of Speech; Freedom of Worship; Freedom from Want; and Freedom from Fear. These four paintings appeared in the Saturday Evening Post over four consecutive weeks in 1943, alongside essays by prominent thinkers of the day. Later they were the highlight of a touring exhibition sponsored by the Saturday Evening Post and the United States Department of Treasury. This exhibition and accompanying War Bond sales drive raised over 132 million U.S. dollars.

Willis Grant, a sailor home on leave from Tallahassee, Florida, came into the station and into my life soon after I stopped seeing Gaylord. We were together every evening of his leave. We were in love. I stopped dating and started corresponding with Willis when he returned to base, exchanging several letters a week. Among the gifts that he sent me was a watch and an 8x10 photo of him in his Navy uniform. He asked me to come to Florida and marry him. Spur of the moment marriages in those pre-World War II days were common. The future seemed so uncertain, and there might not be time to wait; but, I was afraid. Tallahassee, Florida, was a long way from home. If I had been a male, I would no doubt have been drafted and overseas with many, many of my classmates and friends.

In September of 1941, I returned to Elwood for the beginning of my junior year. I was maintaining an excellent grade average, but those nonacademic activities, such as playing "hooky," still took up much of my time. We were living at the gas station near Elwood. A classmate, Bob McKenzie, often stopped by the station and gave me a ride to school in his old Model A, that had a rumble seat.

We didn't have drugs in our part of the country; however, we teenagers found other ways to boost our adrenaline. One was an aspirin in a bottle of Coca-Cola. I am revealing the "devilish" side of me that I chose not to talk about when my children were growing up. "Riding the rails," was another dangerous thrill. A train track running between Smithfield and Elwood did not have regularly scheduled runs, but it was not abandoned; a freight train passed through now and then. The boys let part of the air out of Bob's old Model A tires and lifted the car onto the tracks. They climbed in front, we girls in the rumble seat, and away we went on our "joy ride." We were flirting with danger.

In the spring of my junior year our whole class, all eight of us, played "hooky" to attend the farm auction of the parents of our classmate, Lloyd Weber. The school principal sent a Highway Patrolman, who had given a talk at assembly that day, after us. We heard the sirens as we left the farm yard on our way back to town. The drivers of the cars, one of them being Bob McKenzie, and their passengers were not arrested; but we were given a thought-provoking lecture by the Patrol Officer, reminding us of how selfish we were. It was during gas rationing, and we were hurting our parents and even our country by wasting gas and skipping school. It was a quiet ride back to town!

Our punishment was to stay after school an hour every day, until we could type with no errors, a thousand-word essay on the sale. Principal Peterson, who was also the typing and shorthand teacher, supervised us. I had to stay after school longer than most of the others, since I was not a fast typist. At the beginning of my first typing class at Huntley School, I had scalded my hand trying to cool a flat iron by dipping it into cold water; it was too hot to iron my white satin blouse and I was in a hurry! Of course, I was unable to type with a bandaged right hand.

The entire junior class at Elwood High.
I am second from the right in the front row.

Me the "goil" down at the Woodring Oil with Frosty.

Frosty drove a motorcycle and often stopped at the Elwood Station. I rode with him on his cycle, just a mile or so down the road, several times and he wrote in my autograph album:

> One day I met a girl
> Down at the Woodring Oil
> I'd rather have a smile from her,
> Than a kiss from any other "goil"
>
> Frosty

I didn't think of Frosty as a boyfriend, just a friend. I don't know how old he was, but he must have been of legal age to gamble. He returned from a trip to Las Vegas and brought me twenty-five silver dollars from his winning jackpot. Later those dollars were to save the day and a car.

My dad never really approved of any of my boyfriends. I realize now that he was only trying to protect me, his only little girl, from making a mistake.

I met a nice looking boy at the Elwood County Fair that fall by the name of Tom George. His family was of Syrian descent and ran "George's Grocery" in Lexington, Nebraska, where we did most of our shopping. Tom and I rode on the Ferris wheel, drank Cokes, ate cotton candy and I consented for him to give me a ride home in their family car. The car was really a school bus converted to hold a family of fourteen; Tom had eleven siblings. My dad was furious and warned me never to see him again. It may have been because he was Syrian. Dad also warned me that if I married a Catholic, he would disown me. He didn't know of our ancestry, as I do now, and was unaware that the Vautrin-Woodrings were French Huguenots, persecuted by the Catholics in France in the 1600s. Had a dislike of Catholics been passed down through the generations without questioning why?

I didn't go back to school for my senior year in September of 1942. I have often asked myself why not. With my grades, I could have been Valedictorian of my class. Changing schools may have contributed to my loss of interest in school. I had thought about college, but it would cost money and of that we had barely enough to feed the family. Besides, college was not a high priority in our Midwest environment, especially for girls; it would be best to learn to keep house, and find a good husband with whom to have babies. Perhaps it was just that I was impatient to get on with my life. Willis still wanted me to come to Tallahassee and marry him.

I asked my dad if I could apply for a job as a waitress at a café in Lexington, Nebraska, and live with my cousin Winona, who already worked there. Dad said, "No, I'll pay you for helping out here at the station." So I pumped gas, washed windshields, checked oil and helped Mom in the kitchen. She baked pies several times a week, pineapple sweet rolls by the dozen, and always had a large pot of coffee brewing to serve the customers sitting around our big round kitchen table.

And then, one day this tall, dark haired, handsome man, named Elmer Miles, drove up to the gas pumps in a fancy new car. He was wearing a black pin striped suit, white shirt and tie. I pumped gas to fill his car tank and he asked me if I would like to go roller skating. I replied, "You will have to ask my mother," feeling sure she would say no. First of all, I didn't know how to skate and then he seemed so much older. Mom amazed me by saying that I could go! Against my better judgment, I agreed to go skating with him! It was a disaster from start to finish. Not only was I unable to stay on my feet on those dumb skates, I ran him into a brick wall. Apparently my awkwardness didn't discourage him, however, because he came back.

Elmer swept me off my feet. Our courtship was rather like Irving Berlin's popular song, "Doin' What Comes Natur'lly." I lost my virginity to Elmer and when he asked, "Will you marry me?" I said, "Yes." I was committed; I had given myself to him and in the society of those days that meant marriage.

I wrote a "Dear John" letter to my sailor boy, Willis Grant, and broke his heart. Two of his friends wrote to me asking me to change my mind. I met Willis again several years later, after I was married, living in Holdrege, Nebraska. When I called a garage one bitter cold morning to start our truck, Willis, a mechanic, came to my door. We were both speechless, then he started the truck and he was on his way. We didn't see one another again, but I heard that he and his wife had moved to California.

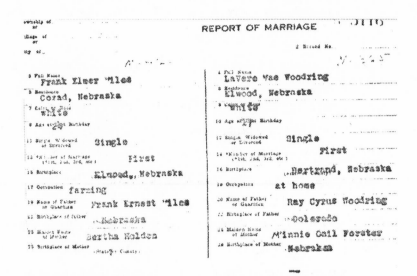

Frank Elmer Miles and LaVera Mae Woodring were married in Lexington, Nebraska on the 24th day of December, 1942.

Photo taken at Woodring Oil near Elwood.
My mother baked our cake.

Chapter 7

MARRIED AT 17
DURING WORLD WAR II

On December 24, 1942, my mother accompanied me and Frank Elmer Miles, without my dad's knowledge, to the office of the Justice of Peace in Lexington, Nebraska, where we were married! Since I was only seventeen, I needed a parent's signature of approval. Elmer was twenty-seven. We spent our honeymoon night at the Dale Hotel in Holdrege and returned to my parents' home at the Elwood Station the next morning. My dad was understandably angry and very, very hurt. My mother had baked a three-tier wedding cake; the family and a few friends gave us gifts. Our wedding pictures weren't taken until months later.

I gathered up what few things I had collected in my hope chest—a couple of pieced wool comforters, two sets of pillow cases and dresser scarves, a set of "Sunbonnet Baby" dish towels I had embroidered—and, of course, my twenty-five silver dollars.

We went to live with Elmer's parents near Cozad. Their home was a two-room tenant house, one room a kitchen, the other a bedroom with four feather-tick mattresses on the floor. The beds, divided by curtains, slept seven of us:

his dad, Frank Ernest Miles, his mother, Bertha (Holden) Miles, his three brothers, Floyd, George and Homer, and the newlyweds. Frank Ernest, 25 years older than his wife, was too old to work in the fields husking corn. He and his wife had lost twins, a girl and a boy, as infants, and a son Dale, two years younger than Elmer was accidently shot when the two boys were hunting near their home. Homer was still in school, while Floyd, George and their mother husked corn.

I was well entertained by the stories Elmer's dad related to me and by the "hoe down" music from his fiddle. He had once played for the barn dances that were popular in those days. His wife Bertha played the pump organ. He showed me his small coin collection, including a very rare "half dime."

Elmer's dad had a long white beard, often stained from the tobacco he chewed. He was quite adept at hitting the brass spittoon when he spit tobacco juice across the room. He often told me of his great-grandfather who had worked in the Queen's stables in London, before he stowed away on a ship and came to America, never to see his English family again. His grandfather Miles served in the Civil War as a volunteer from the State of Wisconsin. After the war he homesteaded in Gosper County, Nebraska. Elmer's father remembered that his parents wanted a little girl, so they dressed him in dresses until he was a big kid.

Less than a month after we were married, a man came to repossess Elmer's car. My twenty-five silver dollars saved the day and the car! It was the first and only car of the Frank Ernest Miles family. Before that they had driven a team of horses hitched to a wagon. Frank was often too intoxicated, after a night at the saloon, to drive home. "The horses were

Our wedding picture, taken six months
after we were married.

Our first home, a tenant house on the German farm
near Cozad, Nebraska.

well trained," the boys said "When dad passed out at the saloon in Elwood, his buddies loaded him in the wagon, untied the team, and the horses knew the way home."

Corn husking completed, Elmer found employment, at $100.00 a month and a tenant house to live in. His employer was Al German, a cattle feeder, who lived near Cozad. Our first home was a two-story, two-room building. The upper floor had once held storage tanks for a gravity water system, and the main floor had held batteries to furnish electrical power for the German household before the days of electricity. The house had bare wooden floors, and a bedroom with our new blonde bedroom set where I proudly displayed the embroidered scarves from my hope chest. The kitchen was furnished with a table and chair set, a cupboard and a gasoline stove that had to be "pumped up" and seemed to work for only a few days after each cleaning of the gas line. We had a kitchen sink, but carried our water; I put a nail in the wall over the hole that should have housed a faucet. One morning when I grabbed the wet dish cloth hanging on the nail, a mouse came with it. The building had been a home for mice and still was. When we went to bed and all was quiet, we heard the snap, snap, snap of the mouse traps we had set.

The outhouse in back, guarded by a turkey gobbler who loved to peck at my heels, was infested with bed bugs, who tried to hitch a ride on my clothing and shoes and go home with me. I found nerve enough somehow to tell Mrs. German my sad story and ask, "Could I use your bathroom until the outhouse is fumigated?" She answered "Yes."

Mrs. German liked me and was like a mother to me. I missed my mother, and she missed her girls who were married to service men and living far from home. I worked for her, helping clean house and paint, for ten cents an hour. I helped her plant a large garden and she shared the vegetables with me. I canned many quarts of vegetables, fruits and pickles that year. Raising a garden and canning the produce was a necessity. It was during World War II, when rationing and doing without was a way of life.

The Japanese attack on Pearl Harbor had dramatically ended the debate over America's entrance into the war that was raging around the world. Citizens flooded the local draft board. Elmer was not drafted due to a handicap. Ordinary citizens felt the impact of the war as the economy shifted to military production and consumer goods took a back seat. In May of 1942, the U.S. Office of Price Administration froze the prices on practically all everyday goods, starting with sugar and coffee. Soon after that ration books were issued to every adult and child of school age, dictating how much gasoline, sugar, meat, silk, shoes, nylons and other items could be purchased. Production of cars and trucks had been stopped in 1941, and new car and truck sales were banned in 1942. Farm equipment and even chicken wire was rationed.

Sears Roebuck listed which farm equipment was rationed and who was eligible to buy it. In 1943, a quote from Sears read:

"You also serve; you who stand behind the plow, pledged to feed the soldiers, the ally and with God's help, all the hungry victims of the war! You also serve; you who pray and sacrifice. You'll feed the world even if it means plowing by lantern light and harvesting by hand—even children's hands—even if it means putting up the trucks and going back, once again, to covered wagons. Farmers must win the "Battle of the Land" with the machinery they already have."

By 1943, half of U.S. automobiles were issued an "A" sticker which entitled their owners to four gallons of gasoline per week. You couldn't fill your car with gasoline whenever you liked, even if you could afford it. We handed the gas pump jockey our ration book and cash and she (yes, female gas station attendants; the boys were fighting the war) tore the appropriate coupons from the ration book and sold you three to four gallons of gas—no more. We used to buy white gasoline to do our dry cleaning, but during war days we needed it to go that extra mile.

You couldn't just walk into a store and buy as many groceries as you wanted or needed. Almost every product, with the exception of eggs and dairy products, was rationed. Stamp #30 was good for five pounds of sugar that had to last from January 5th to March 31st. If you had sugar on hand at the time of using your first coupon, you were allowed to keep it, but coupons for that amount were taken from your book. All canned foods, such as vegetables, fruits and soups, were evaluated by points. Each coupon holder was allowed 48 points per month—a can of peas was 16 points, a can of peaches 21 points and a can of spinach 11 points.

Airplane stamp #1 in Book Three was good for one pair of shoes, meant to last indefinitely. Shoes could be bought from Sears Roebuck by mail, because of a shoe rationing order that allowed the holder of Ration Book #1 to tear out coupon #17 and attach it to the order. Servicemen were allotted 30% of all cigarettes produced, making them scarce on the home-front. Never before had gas been rationed, even during the Great Depression. Many people couldn't afford a car then, let alone gas. A gas curfew as early as 1941 closed gas stations from 7 p.m. to 7a.m. "Victory Speed" was 35 miles an hour to help conserve rubber tires. Even in popular Warner Brother cartoons, Daffy Duck urges his readers to "Keep it Under Forty." Bugs Bunny's plunging airplane halts just before impact, out of gas as a consequence of the "A" sticker on its windshield.

Any person holding a gasoline ration book had to have his tires inspected every three months before the gasoline ration book would be renewed, or a certificate for a new tire or tube issued. One family could own no more than five tires.

An "Emergency Statement to the People of the United States" was published on April 20, 1942, in the Des Moines Register. Part of the statement read:

"The steel industry has been rapidly stepping up its' production, but we need to get production up to the industry's full capacity of 90,000,000 tons—a total equal to the rest of the world combined. We cannot do this unless an additional 6,000,000 tons of scrap metal is obtained promptly. We are faced with the fact that some steel furnaces have been allowed to cool down and that many are operating from day to day due only to the lack of scrap metal, iron and steel.

The rubber situation is also critical. We are collecting every possible pound from factories, stockyards, automobile graveyards and even tearing up abandoned railroad tracks and bridges, but unless we dig out an additional 6,000,000 tons of steel and great quantities of rubber, brass, copper, zinc and tin, our boys may not get all the fighting weapons they need in time. Even one old shovel will help make 4 hand grenades." The first nonfood item rationed was rubber. The Japanese had seized plantations in the Dutch East Indies that produced 90% of raw rubber used in America. F.D. R. urged citizens to contribute scrap rubber to be recycled, such as garden hoses, bathing caps and rubber boots.

In 1943 Sears Roebuck urged shoppers to buy War Bonds every month. A picture in their catalog showed a mom, dad and little sister huddled together reading a letter from their Johnny on the South Pacific War Front. An excerpt from the letter read:

"Last night the Japanese "Zero" planes came again in a nightmare of bombs and shells. I knew my family was with me—praying for my safety, pinching pennies, sacrificing and doing without to send us guns, bombs and planes."

A popular slogan was: "Don't Stop Buying—They're Still Dying." War Bond dollars were life-saving dollars for our boys on the front. School children were urged to save their allowance to buy War Bonds and stamps and even to save the foil wrappers from sticks of gum. The American Women's Cook Book revised recipes in a special wartime issue to help deal with food shortages. A quote from Life Magazine, April 20, 1943, read:

"Uncle Sam last week assumed the role of "Fashion Designer." Restrictions will save 15% of yardage used on women's and girl's apparel, through restricting hems and belts to two inches and eliminating cuffs on sleeves." Bridal gowns, maternity clothes, and religious orders were exempt. Patches were sewn on the elbows of jumpers, cardigans and jackets and on the knees of trousers and jeans to make them last longer. Silk stockings were rare; women put tea or a thin mixture of gravy coloring on their legs with a pencil-line seam down the back to make themselves look as if they were wearing stockings.

In 1945 the U.S. dropped atom bombs on Japan, thus abruptly ending World War II. Of the 16,596,639 Americans who served in the armed forces during World War II, 416,837 lost their lives. World War II, a global military conflict involving most of the world's nations, was the most destructive war in history. It is estimated that 16,000,000 military personnel and 45,000,000 civilians, throughout the world, died during World War II.

During the war millions of women left the homemaker role to become factory workers, taking the place of the men who were fighting in Europe and the Pacific. The women made up more than one-third of the work force. By 1946 and the end of the war the boys came home and the "Baby Boomer" era began. Forty million babies were born between 1946 and 1960. My Carolyn was born during that era.

I was pregnant with my first baby, Sharllyn. My only visit to a doctor was made after my weight dropped from 125 to 104, due to persistent morning sickness. The doctor prescribed Coke syrup and soda crackers to control the nausea.

I was so thrilled to learn that I was going to be a mother, but so naïve about pregnancy, fetal development and childbirth. At least I had discovered that babies didn't come from the cabbage patch. Mrs. German gave me a book to study about the stages of a baby's development and the birth process. In my family sex and babies were never discussed.

I bought fabric and started sewing and with Mrs. German's help I hemmed diapers, blankets and "belly bands." Belly bands were 4 inch wide strips of cloth, sterilized by heating, and worn over the baby's umbilical cord until it dropped off. I made little dresses and slips, embroidered with tiny pink flowers and trimmed with lace. The blankets and nighties were trimmed in pink as well. Not once did I doubt that my baby was a little girl, even though ultrasound images were not available at that time.

The four gallons of gasoline a week that we were allowed didn't permit us to do much driving. As a result, my parents never came to see us, and it was seldom that we could afford the fifty mile round trip to see them. I missed my family. A trip to Cozad once a week used up most of our gas. On our way home from shopping one evening we came to a sudden halt when we encountered large trees blocking the road. A tornado had ripped through the area near the German farm. We left the car, climbed over the fallen trees, and walked quite a distance home, carrying our groceries. Our houses were still there, however, the barn and some of the other buildings had been moved partly off their foundations.

Elmer's parents left the tenant farm and Bertha, his mother, who was an excellent cook, found employment at the Dale Hotel in Holdrege as a pastry cook. Late in the year of 1943, Elmer left his job at Germans and we moved our furniture to Holdrege, hoping to find a house and employment. Before we had completed the move, however, Elmer met with disaster. As he was trying to start the car one very cold morning by pouring gas into the carburetor, he spilled gas on his woolen trouser leg which somehow ignited. I remember him pulling his trousers off along with flesh from the calf of his leg. It was a fourth degree burn that kept him in the Holdrege Hospital for several weeks and unable to work for months.

We went to my parent's home at the gas station near Elwood shortly before my due date. Sharllyn has fun telling people that she was born in a gas station.

Chapter 8

SHARLLYN AND HER LITTLE SISTER CAROLYN

The small oak rocker, with a cane seat, had belonged to my maternal grandmother, Anna Forster. My mother and her siblings had been rocked in it, as were my two brothers and me. As I prepared for the birth of my first baby I was determined to have the rocker sanded and refinished in time to rock her. My dad warned me, "LaVera Mae, you shouldn't be doing that; you're going to make your baby come early," but of course I didn't listen. It was snowing the very next morning, two weeks before my due date, when I went into labor and my mother decided it was time to call Dr. George Clark. The snow was piling up between the glass and the screen, shutting off the view of the outside world through a window of my parents' living quarters in back of the Elwood gas station.

At the far end of the room, I could hear Doc Clark and my husband visiting. Doc was an elderly man, white haired, and bespectacled. He was known throughout the area. Not only had he delivered all of the babies in our family, but, in fact, all of the babies for miles around Elwood, Nebraska. His brother Dr. Guy Clark, from Bertrand, had delivered me. Doc Clarks' fee for delivering a baby was twenty-five dollars, but he never sent a bill. "Folks will pay when they sell their grain or some hogs," he said. If they didn't, well, that was the life of a country doctor.

"Lucky I made it," Doc said. "Those drifts are getting so bad that no one will be traveling in another hour." My father came in from waiting on a customer at the gas pumps out in front and joined in the conversation. "Snow's really comin' down; it's been a rough winter." "Yeah, you got that right," Doc answered. "Say did you hear 'bout Johnsons' boy, Jerry? Sure feel sorry for his folks; his plane was shot down and he's reported missing in action." It was the midst of World War II.

At the foot of my iron rail bed, supported by two kitchen chairs, was an oblong wicker basket painted white. In it was a tiny seven-and-a-half pound, eighteen-inch long baby girl, my beautiful little daughter.

I watched my mother in the adjoining kitchen. At 12:55 p.m. she had helped Doc bring her new grandchild into the world, and now she was preparing tea and lunch. I smiled as she absent-mindedly poured water through a sieve onto the floor, missing the cup. I wondered why she was so nervous. I felt very calm, secure and happy.

"We are going to name our baby Sharllyn Faye," I told Doc. "Ye Gads," he sputtered, "she'll hate you the rest of her life for hangin' a name like that on her." Maybe it was a bit unusual, I thought, as I looked down at her; but she was an extra special baby and I wanted an extra special name for her—not Bertha, not Minnie, not Annie.

I was eighteen when Sharllyn was born. I was playing house and Sharllyn was my doll. I dressed her in ruffled dresses and bonnets that I spent hours designing and sewing. Scraps from Grandma's sewing basket worked fine for little ten-inch-long pinafores. My baby's bright eyes and ready smile indicated she was doing well on mother's milk and an abundance of love.

Sharllyn was only a few weeks old when we rented an old five-bedroom house in Holdrege for $25.00 a month. The landlord, Sam Bunson, agreed to furnish paper and paint to cover the red woodwork and bright floral wallpaper, if I would do the work. I was able to convince him to have natural gas piped into the house so that I could put two-burner gas plates in three of the five bedrooms. Perhaps he agreed because he had a weakness for pretty girls, and I was a pretty girl. As the story goes, years later, when he was an old man in a nursing home, his son took power of attorney over his finances when he bought a new Cadillac for a checkout girl at Safeway. I sublet one-room apartments to the families of soldiers stationed at the German prisoner of war camp just a few miles from Holdrege. I bought used beds, dressers, tables and chairs at a second hand store, and painted them to furnish three one-room apartments. I also rented out one small bedroom to a single mother and took care of her little girl, Rosalea, while her mother worked. She was Sharllyn's age and had long blond finger curls like Sharllyn's that I combed every morning.

I was kept very busy, but I still missed my mom and dad and my little brother Willis. They were only twenty miles away, but we had used our last gas ration stamp for the month and the tires on our car were bald.

Sharllyn Faye

My mother and 10-year-old brother moved in with us in late spring of 1944, when my parents temporarily separated. It was while they were staying with us in the old house across from the grain elevator that a tramp came to our house late one night, and banged on the door. He had been hiding in the yard and saw Elmer leave for work. Willis grabbed an iron skillet from the kitchen and was on his way out the back door to "do that guy in" when Mom grabbed him. I called the police, who soon arrived, handcuffed him and hauled him away. He was carrying a long knife. Willis was indeed a brave little boy.

Willis used to stand on a stool to pump gas at the Elwood station. When they moved to Holdrege, he got a job at a gas station. He had filled Mr. Good's car with gas and was standing on a stool to wash the windshield, when Mr. Good, owner of Pelz Hardware, asked, "Why don't you come to work for me at my hardware store?" Willis replied, "How much will you pay me?" "I'll give you 15 cents more an hour than you are making here." Willis thought for a moment and said; "When do I come to work?" Willis started working at Pelz Hardware for 40 cents an hour as a clean-up boy. He was obviously born an entrepreneur with big plans for the future, for he memorized the names of all the tools as he dusted them. That was the beginning of a very successful wholesale tool business.

Willis must have been a good driver, even though he had to sit on a book to see out the window, for Mr. Good bought a pickup truck for him to use. Loaded with an electric stove and a refrigerator, he visited the farmers whose homes had just been wired for electricity and demonstrated how handy these appliances were. Sometimes the farmer bought, but if they were reluctant, he would say, "Well, just take them for a week

and try them out. If you don't like them, I'll take them back."
Usually after a week of using these time-saving devices, the
farm folks felt they couldn't live without them. Oftentimes he
traded for older appliances, and on at least one occasion
he accepted a couple of pigs in trade. He took the pigs to
his brother Harold's farm to raise them, then sold them at a
nice profit. Mr. Good generously gave Willis 50% of the profit
on the used appliances he sold! Within a short time he had
his own resale appliance business in the basement of Pelz
Hardware Store, and was making more money than the adult
employees. He worked there until he was drafted into the
army at age eighteen.

Mom and Willis stayed with us for a few weeks until Willis
was making enough money to pay $10.00 a month to rent
a small house south of the tracks. Willis traded his power
scooter for a kerosene refrigerator for their new home.

Mom started working at a local hotel, which provided a little
income. Since there was not a laundry in town and service men
stationed at the POW camp nearby needed uniforms washed
and ironed, I took the job and at 25 cents a garment, picked
up a few badly needed extra dollars. One hot summer day a
lady came into the hotel carrying a tiny puppy, almost dead
from heat and neglect. The puppy's mother was a show dog
in the circus at the edge of town. The lady offered to give the
puppy to my mother, saying, "Maybe you can keep it alive."
The little black and white baby was accepted at our house
with open arms and was named "Spotty." Thirteen years later
she was still a loved family member.

Mom worked at the Zephyr Café for a few months. I also
worked there for a whole day, until I dropped a tray of food

and my wages didn't cover the damages! Later, Mom rented space on Main Street and started a café of her own called "Dew Drop Inn." She sold sandwiches, rolls, pie and coffee; her specialty was "Coney Islands," hot dogs in a bun with chili sauce.

While Mom and Willis were living in Holdrege, Dad left the Elwood station and for a short time worked as a railroad section hand until he was injured, resulting in his inability to work and his receiving a small disability check. The Smithfield gas station, located on the corner of Main Street, was his next venture. A hardware store was located in back, where he sold tools that he bought from a Hastings manufacturing company; he also kept minnows and worms to sell to the local fishermen. Harold and Alice and their family were living in Smithfield at that time. Their daughter Karen remembers digging fishing worms from the yard and her brother Gary remembers selling them at Grandpa's station, but Karen doesn't remember getting her share of the money!

I watched Sharllyn from the kitchen window as I washed dishes. Her long blond curls were flying in the breeze as she clutched Tiger, her kitten, tightly in her arms. Spotty, our Fox Terrier-Alaskan Husky mix breed, was at her heels, as usual. We lived on a busy street; if Sharllyn crossed the sidewalk, Spotty grabbed her by the seat of her panties, pulling her back into the safety zone. Pat and Mike—yes, Pat and Mike Murphy, whose daddy was a guard at the POW Camp, came from the upstairs apartment to play. They sat on the porch, Pat on one side of Sharllyn, Mike on the other. "I don't like your old kitty," Pat teased. "Me neither," Mike joined in as he pulled Tiger's tail. With a very determined "I won't cry" look on her little

SHARLLYN AND SPOTTY
Art by LaVera

Sharllyn with her mommy and daddy.

face, Sharllyn warned, "You boys musn't tease Sharllyn; that makes Sharllyn mean."

Two German prisoners worked at the grain elevator across the alley from our house. Although they were supposed to be our enemies, they were Sharllyn's friends. Sharllyn spoke English, while they spoke German, but their waves and smiles to one another was a universal language. Sharllyn pulled green onions from our garden to share with them. During the summer, I earned over $100.00 selling produce from my garden to the local grocery stores, as well as filling hundreds of fruit jars with peas, beans, corn, tomatoes and pickles. I didn't want to run out of food ration stamps.

One thing I had going for me was determination: to make a go of my marriage, and somehow, someway, to make the pennies stretch. I was not going to ask my parents for help. The product of hardy, pioneer stock, I learned the satisfaction of a hard day's work well done at an early age. I was reared to believe in the old adage, "You made your bed, now lie in it." I was trying to be a good wife and mother and to never, never waste time crying about what might have been. Although it had been a happy few years, trying to find ways to pay the rent and buy the groceries without an education was a challenge. I needed to find a more profitable way of supporting our family. Elmer's job at the creamery paid 25 cents an hour, which wasn't enough to pay the bills. We bought a used ton-and-a-half Ford truck on the Black Market, paying an inflated price via monthly payments. New car and truck sales had been banned in 1942. The new truck would enable us to sell and deliver salt to the ranchers. I was on my way to becoming a twenty year old female entrepreneur. I wrote letters quoting salt prices to general stores and grain elevators in several of the sand hill towns from Elm Creek to Taylor. The response was good. We were in the salt business. To keep the trucks busy, however, we hauled anything and everything: cattle to the Omaha stockyards, corn and grain to the elevators and even horses to the glue factory in McCook. By the 1940's, the faithful old work horses were being replaced by "iron horses." We also hauled antiques to the "Pioneer Village" in Minden, a museum built by Harold Warp, a well known Minden businessman. Some of my Grandma Forster's former possessions can be found there.

We hauled a double deck load of sheep to Rapid City, South Dakota. When our truck broke down and was being repaired in Rapid City, I bought and sold a load of lumber to haul back to Nebraska.

"Now I've seen everything," were the exact words of Mr. Beers, manager of the Elmcreek Farmer's Elevator. The words were addressed to me, a young, attractive, very pregnant lady, dressed in faded blue jeans, boots and a plaid mackinaw. I was holding a harnessed two-year-old, blond curly haired girl in one hand, with another little girl of about the same age holding my other hand. It was an era when women just didn't do that sort of thing in Small Town, Nebraska, U.S.A.—especially not pregnant women! Nor did they put their children in harnesses! I had just announced, "My name is LaVera Miles, I represent Morton Salt Company of Lyons, Kansas. How is your salt supply today?" Maybe it was the attractive prices I quoted or perhaps Mr. Beers felt a bit sorry for me; anyway, he gave me an order for several tons of salt and continued buying from me as long as we were in business.

"I made enough for both of us," Georgia drawled, as she handed me a pan filled with something that smelled "yummy." "Gee thanks, what is it?" I asked. "Banana pudding," she said. I was learning what southern dialect and southern hospitality were all about. I loved to listen to her talk. Her name was Georgia Bowling, she was a year or so older than I and a native of Nashville, Tennessee. Georgia's husband was a guard at the prisoner of war camp and the couple rented my downstairs one-room apartment. Just a door separated our apartments, and it was usually open. Because I missed the companionship of girls my own age I suppose Georgia was just the medicine I needed. I was twenty, my little girl Sharllyn was a toddler, and we were expecting our second baby in just a few months. Georgia had a baby girl named Carolyn, a little sweetheart, dark haired just like her mother. We spent many hours together—Georgia, Carolyn, Sharllyn and I. "I'm going to name the baby Carolyn," I told Georgia. I didn't even have a boy's name picked out. Just as before Sharllyn's birth, I was so sure my new baby would be a girl. The little embroidered dresses, gowns and blankets that I had made for my first baby would now be used by my second baby. Sharllyn knew she was going to have a little sister soon; and she was right beside me as I painted a little crib that I had bought at a second hand store. My mother, Grandma Woodring, whom Sharllyn loved very much, was with us to care for Sharllyn while Mommy was in the hospital.

It was a very warm summer evening, almost midnight, and although I had been having labor pains for awhile, I finished ironing half a dozen shirts for soldiers at the POW camp before I picked up the phone. "Please send a cab to 1200 Main

Street—and hurry." I was feeling a bit sorry for myself as I climbed the steps of the hospital and admitted myself. My husband was traveling with a combine crew in Kansas. In spite of the troubled world into which she was born, Carolyn was very anxious to make her entry. It took less than an hour, and when the nurse finally answered my call, she found Carolyn lying beside me on the bed. A very frustrated nurse and a doctor in his suit coat and tie wheeled me and Carolyn into the delivery room. Fortunately, there were no complications. She was a beautiful baby, just as beautiful as her namesake, Carolyn Bowling, with lots of dark hair covering her pretty little head. A week later Elmer called to say "hello" to his new baby daughter.

Willis borrowed a car from Pelz Hardware to take us home from the hospital. Sharllyn's first words upon seeing her little sister were, "Sure a good thing we got that bed painted."

Grandma Woodring and Uncle Willis gave the new baby a buggy. I didn't know how to drive a car, so that buggy was a necessity. It served as both a baby carrier and a shopping cart. Both baby Carolyn and Sharllyn could ride the half mile to the nearest grocery store. On the return trip, Sharllyn and Rosalea and our dog "Spotty" tagged along behind. Spotty sat by the buggy and guarded it while we were in the store shopping. We often stopped at the ice house to pick up a ten-pound block of ice for the ice box. I carried a pillow to put between baby Carolyn and the ice to keep from freezing her. We would have made an interesting Norman Rockwell painting. Later that year I bought my first car. When Elmer's youngest brother, Homer joined the Army he said, "Sis, if you could drive I would leave you my car." I replied, "I'll learn to drive," and gave him $75.00 for his 1937 Ford coupe.

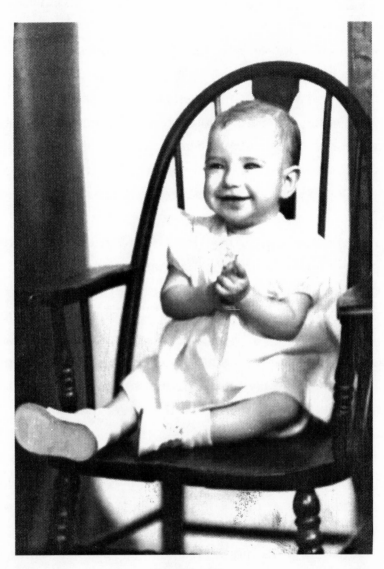

Carolyn Kaye

Grandma Miles was so very proud of her little granddaughters. She loved to buy the prettiest dresses she could find for them. She was a very firm, rather cold person who rarely laughed or smiled. She had never cut her hair, wearing it in a bun at the back of her head. Her love for her granddaughters revealed the warm, soft side of her.

It was June, 1945, when the armistice was signed and World War II was over! In our little town of Holdrege, Nebraska horns were honking, bells were ringing, people were shouting and firecrackers were exploding. Our boys would be coming home, prisoners would be released—both our prisoners over there and the prisoners held here! The prisoners in the Nazi Concentration Camps would be freed!

From 1940 until the end of the war in 1945, more than 400,000 prisoners of war were shipped to the U.S. and detained in rural areas across the country. Close to 12,000 POWs were held in camps in Nebraska. Construction of the POW camp at Atlanta, Nebraska, began in 1943. The entire population of Atlanta was only 130 people, while the POW camp there housed 3,000 German POW's over a period of three years.

Many of the POWs were hired out to local farmers to help harvest crops. Some worked at the grain elevators, picked vegetables, stacked hay and worked in the beet fields or just about any place else that required minimum security. There was a critical shortage of labor; however, at first authorities were afraid of mass escapes that would endanger the American people. Eventually, they relented and tens of thousands of POWs were put to work in our part of the country.

My brother Willis remembers that our older brother Harold farmed near the Atlanta POW Camp. Harold picked up prisoners from the camp every morning during the corn harvest season to help husk corn. Willis, eleven or twelve at the time, drove a tractor pulling a wagon down the corn row with six of the prisoners husking corn. Harold worked in another field with the other six prisoners. The prisoners shared their thick sliced lunch meat sandwiches with my brothers, and Willis remembers that they gave him cigarettes.

Many of the POWs gave the impression that they were glad to be out of the war. When they returned to Germany after the war, they took with them news and views of America that spoke well of our country, the land of their former enemies. Early in the year of 1946, some German soldiers returned to live in Atlanta, applied for U.S. citizenship and married Nebraska girls.

A good friend of mine, Vidette (Rubidow) Freir, tells me of her marriage to Carl Freir, who was a POW at the Fort Lincoln POW Camp near Bismarck, North Dakota. "He was a POW working at the Schultz Creamery in Bismarck when I met him in 1943. We were married in 1945, as soon as the war ended and he could apply for and become a U.S. citizen. Although he had a mother and two sisters living near Hamburg, Germany, he never went back."

German legislation to remove the Jews from civil society, "The Nuremberg Laws," was enacted long before the outbreak of World War II. The Nuremberg Laws, for the protection of German Blood and German Honor, were drawn up on September 15, 1935, and signed by:

The Fuehrer Reich Chancellor
  Adolph Hitler
Reich Minister of Interior
  Frick
Reich Minister of Justice
  Dr. Guertner
The Deputy of the Fuehrer
  Rudolph Hess

These laws consisted of seven articles and included forbidding marriages between Jews and Germans; forbidding Jews to employ female Germans under age 45 as household help and forbidding Jews to fly the Reich flag. Any violators were to be punished by a prison sentence, hard labor or both.

Hitler and the Nazi Party began training and brainwashing German children, both boys and girls, at a very young age. The Nazi plan, "The Perfect Solution," was to form the "Perfect Nation" by exterminating all who were not considered perfect—the Jewish population, Romani gypsies, homosexuals, mentally or physically handicapped, and Jehovah Witnesses. Two-thirds of the population of nine million Jews who resided in Europe before the Holocaust were killed.

The German Nazis required many of the Jews and Romanis to be confined in overcrowded ghettos before being transported to extermination camps. More than 10 million innocent people were moved by freight cars or herded by foot into the Auschwitz extermination camp.

Auschwitz, in Poland, occupied a chilling and disturbing place in the history of mankind. It began as a Nazi labor camp to terrorize the local Polish population and evolved into the site of the largest mass murder ever recorded. The Commandant of Auschwitz was Rudolph Hess. Joseph Mengele who performed inhumane and unthinkable experiments on the prisoners, was known as the camp doctor; and the SS Commander was Heinrich Himmler.

As the prisoners arrived at Auschwitz, their belongings were confiscated and sorted; those of any value were sent to Germany. The victims were classified by their usefulness. Able-bodied men, women and older children were sent to the right as slave laborers until they died of exhaustion or disease. Those sent to the left, older men and women and children under fifteen, were sent to the gas chambers. Before going to the gas chambers, they were ordered to remove all of their clothing and enter the "showers," otherwise known as the gas chambers.

World War II ended in June of 1945, when the Allies were victorious and Nazi Germany was defeated. A plan for the trial of European war criminals was drafted by the U.S. Secretary of War, Henry L. Stimson in cooperation with the War Department. The initial trials, from November 20, 1945 to October 1, 1946, known as the Nuremberg trials, were held for the prosecution of members of the political, military and economic leadership of the defeated Nazi Germany.

The trials were held in Nuremberg, Bavaria, Germany, because that city was considered the birthplace of the Nazi party with the drafting of the Nuremberg Laws in 1935. Nuremberg was also the site of Hitler's annual propaganda rallies, which made it a fitting place to mark the party's symbolic demise.

The first and best known of the trials was the "Trial of the Major War Criminals," which tried twenty-two of the most important captured leaders of Nazi Germany. Several of these prominent Nazis including Adolf Hitler and Heinrich Himmler, had committed suicide before the trials began. Along with others, Rudolph Hess was sentenced to life imprisonment.

Shortly before the German annexation of Austria the Von Trapp family, who were descendants of Austria for generations and fiercely patriotic, traveled to the United States for a concert tour. In their absence, the Nazis confiscated their home and modified it to meet their needs. Heinrich Himmler made it his headquarters for the duration of the war. The chapel was turned into a beer parlor, and one room was designated as Hitler's quarters when he came to Salzburg.

Maria Von Trapp was the guiding force behind a family of singers who won world renown when their story was portrayed in the play and film, "The Sound of Music." After the war, they founded the "Trapp Family Austrian Relief Fund," which sent tons of food and clothing to the impoverished in Austria.

Opinions differ on how much the civilian population of Germany knew about the Nazi government's victimization of the Jews. Some believe that an unwilling population just looked the other way in fear of punishment or death. It is difficult to understand how a cultured nation like Germany could be a party to such acts of inhumanity.

By early 1945, Sam Bunson realized his mistake in making it possible for me to turn his house, rented to me for $25.00 a month, into an apartment house bringing in over $100.00 a month. He couldn't evict us during wartime, since regulations made that illegal! He could, however, move the house, and that is just what he proposed to do by digging a basement just a few feet away to move the house onto. Before the basement was finished, the United States dropped atom bombs on Japan and World War II ended.

Chapter 9

A POW BARRACKS BECOMES OUR DREAM HOME

Carolyn was less than a year old when we moved from Sam Bunson's house, with a partially dug basement beside it, to our new home on Morton Street in Holdrege, Nebraska.

At the end of the war and the closing of the German Prisoner of War Camp near Atlanta, Nebraska, we bought two deserted barracks buildings. We poured a concrete slab as an "L" shaped foundation on our newly purchased lot and the buildings were moved onto it.

It was the first home we owned, our "dream home" come true! As a young girl, I used to dream of someday having a house with a white picket fence, ruffled curtains at the windows and flower beds.

Our dream home was built with love and plenty of elbow grease! I helped my husband and his brothers by learning to pound nails, put up partitions and siding, shingle a roof, and hang a door, as well as how to paint, paper, and lay carpet and linoleum.

The bathroom was the last room finished. We couldn't just go to a store and buy the needed pipes and fixtures; in fact, we traveled to many towns in the area picking up the supplies we needed to do our own plumbing.

The carpet in the bedroom Sharllyn and Carolyn shared was a piece of used green indoor-outdoor carpet, large enough to glue down wall-to-wall, that I bought for a ten dollar bill. Their room was special! I made ruffled green and white curtains for the corner windows and a bedspread to match. Yes, it was truly our "dream house." No, it didn't have shutters or a white picket fence, but it did have ruffled curtains at the windows and many flower beds around the house. There were blue morning glories, red oriental poppies and one bed of lavender phlox under a dining room window. The window housed an evaporative water cooler that not only cooled the house but also watered the flowers. More than sixty years later and after undergoing several "facelifts," our dream home is still being lived in.

My girls loved their room and kept it neat. There were shelves for their toys and books and they seldom needed to be reminded to put their things away at bedtime.

We lived across the street from Dr. Smith, a pediatrician, his talented wife Maxine, and their three boys, Donald, David and Tommy, who were my girls' constant playmates. Carrying their daddy's discarded doctor bag, holding an old stethoscope and some safety pins, they took good care of Sharllyn and Carolyn's sick dollies. They used the safety pins as needles to give the sick dolls shots. I hope they had good malpractice insurance, because after a few months those "rubber armed babies" lost their arms! Tommy was the youngest of the boys, just old enough to ride a tricycle. He often came to our house early in the morning on his tricycle, wearing only his birthday

Sharllyn and Carolyn in their room.

Sharllyn and Carolyn with their mommy.

Carolyn and Snowball

suit. Mommy soon followed with his clothes that he had hidden behind a bush.

Maxine composed music, had a beautiful voice and often sang as she worked in the yard. She was a good mother, planning outings, activities and projects for her children, many times including me and my girls. One summer she bought baby chicks and put them in a pen in the back yard. It was the children's responsibility to give them food and water, for which they were to receive some of the profit when the chickens were sold. Our dog Spotty hated birds of any kind. One night she got into the pen and killed all two dozen of the baby chicks! The children all loved Spotty. We didn't want them to know what had happened, so I replaced the chicks early the next morning before the kids were out of bed.

Morton Street was a young community with many children. When Sharllyn saw me mixing batter, with animal cookie cutters near-by, she ran out the front door and shouted to her playmates up and down Morton Street, "Come to my house, kids, my mommy's bakin' cookies!" By the time the first pan of animal sugar cookies came out of the oven, our kitchen table was crowded with wide-eyed, open-mouthed little boys and girls. "I want a dog!" Donnie yelled. "I bit off the elephant's head," said Dave. Whoops! "Mommy, Suzy spilled her milk." I ran for a cloth. No need to scold or cry over spilled milk.

Sharllyn was the more outgoing of our two girls. She often visited older ladies in the neighborhood and just sat and talked. Mrs. Smith commented, "She's just like a Dresden dolly." With her long blond curls, fair complexion and frilly dresses, she was every bit a little lady, but sometimes a very determined little lady. One day we disagreed and she ran to her room. She closed—not slammed, just closed—the door. Checking on her a few minutes later, I found her sitting at their little table. I can still see her; her new color book was torn in shreds in front of her. I scolded, "Why did you do that?" The corners of her pretty little mouth turned down as she looked me straight in the eye and very emphatically answered, "It's my color book, and I can tear it up if I want to." Should I have spanked her? An old Chinese proverb says, "To understand your parent's love, you must raise children of your own." I remembered the time I broke the churn.

"Mommy, this is Ronnie, may he stay and play?" Ronnie was a new friend from Sharllyn's kindergarten class. He stayed and played. He picked her up for school the next morning and walked her home at noon. On Valentine's Day he brought her a heart-shaped box of candy, Woolworth's best! Ronnie was the first of many boys to share my opinion that Sharllyn was extra special.

Carolyn was small for her age, wiry, active and curious. She climbed onto the kitchen countertop, tumbled over the back of the couch and wore her hair off standing on her head so often. I panicked when she fell head first into a galvanized tub of rinse water, but she emerged unharmed. Carolyn was always up early; Sharllyn liked to sleep late. At family gatherings, Sharllyn stayed up late with the adults; Carolyn would find a spot among the coats on Grandma Minnie's bed and go to sleep when it was her bedtime. Carolyn wasn't very old when I began to notice a gift she had, a concern for others.

My girls shared with me a love of animals. We always had pets. Grandma Woodring's dog Brownie became a real live doll, dressed in doll clothes and riding in their doll buggy. Our Spotty had many male suitors. They brought her bones as gifts, which she buried in our garden. Since she had not been spayed, she often had a litter of puppies. I found it better to sell the puppies for a few dollars than to give them away, since people tend to value possessions more if they have an investment in them. They were cute puppies of "Heinz Variety." The girls spent hours playing with them and didn't want to give them up when I ran an ad and the puppies found new homes. When the last puppy of one litter was sold, Sharllyn ran away—away downtown to Pelz Hardware—to tell her Uncle Willis what a mean mommy she had. Willis brought her home; our truck driver, Lucky Gannin, gave her a dime to stop crying, and eventually she forgave me.

And then we adopted Snowball. One very cold, wintry morning I opened the front door to get the milk from the box, and there sat a beautiful, white Angora cat. She must have been waiting for me to open the door. She looked up at me, her saucer-like baby blue eyes pleading, "Please give me a home." She ran past me when she saw Sharllyn and rubbed up against her legs. Both girls began begging, "Please, Mommy, please, can we keep her?" A closer look made me realize this orphan certainly did need a home. Bit by bit, the story unfolded. The girls had been feeding the cat in an old shed in the back yard, afraid to ask if we could keep her. Snowball had become a loving and much loved member of our family. One day the girls found her in their underwear drawer, where she proudly presented them with three fluffy white balls of fur. Spotty and Snowball became good friends when several years later they both had litters of babies at the same time. Snowball disappeared, leaving three hungry kittens. Spotty adopted them, washing and nursing them with her own puppies.

I made most of my girls' clothing on the old Singer sewing machine Mom and Dad bought when they started keeping house. I equipped it with an electric motor, which left the foot treadle a perfect place for little Carolyn to sit and watch me sew. I often dressed the girls alike. They had matching blue silk dresses and "imitation leopard-skin" coats trimmed in red; however, most of their clothes, as well as sheets and pillow cases, were made from flour sacks. When flour and seed suppliers found women were making dresses, curtains and sheets out of hundred-pound sacks, they began turning out sacks in all sorts of flowered and pastel prints. Ten cents would buy a sack at the elevator. Six sacks made a sheet, two made a pair of pillow cases. Twenty cents made a dress for each of my girls with panties to match. I have been given Valentine gifts of diamonds and pearls over the years, but the one gift I remember and treasure most was a gift from my mother, a set of sheets and pillow cases purchased at a store, not made from flour sacks.

I learned to "make do." What clothes I didn't sew, I bought at thrift stores. We needed a couch and chair for the living room, but couldn't afford new ones. I went to a household auction, not really understanding the rules of the game. I didn't realize that scratching my head could mean a signal of a bid; thus, I bought a living room set, badly in need of upholstery. But, if I was handed lemons, I made lemonade. I bought Naugahyde, a vinyl coated fabric, at the Army surplus store and learned to do the first of many upholstery jobs.

We splurged on a new dining room table, chairs and buffet that had been sun damaged by sitting in the store window too long, and we put new carpeting in the living room and dining room area. I bought a used piano, Uncle Earl helped me refinish it and the girls started taking piano lessons.

Learning to drive the car I had bought from Elmer's brother Homer when he went into the service proved a challenge. I once hit the side of our house and pushed the piano into the center of the living room! However, with my new-found skill behind the wheel, I parked the baby buggy and drove to the grocery store. In addition, I was able to travel into the sand hills and sell truck loads of salt to the cattle feeding ranchers in the area. It became a common sight to see me visiting with the grocers, elevator managers and ranchers from Elm Creek to Taylor and asking, "Would a straight job of salt be enough or could you use a semi-load?"

I had learned that trucks couldn't "dead-head" (run empty one way) and realize much of a profit. I started dealing in the hay and grain market and became quite adept at buying those commodities locally and selling them to grain elevators and farmers in Kansas, Oklahoma and Texas. I must have had an honest looking twenty-year-old face, because the elevator sold to me on 30-day credit. We hauled Morton Salt from Lyons, Kansas to Nebraska; the company gave me a small commission for handling their brand of salt.

Our business was doing well. We had a little extra money to work with, allowing us to purchase three more trucks, two straight jobs, (one and a half-ton trucks) and a semi. We hired three drivers, one of whom was Lucky Gannin. He had drifted into town, following the wheat harvest, before he went to work for us. Not only was he a very dependable employee, but he seemed to be such a nice person. My girls loved him and he seemed to like kids; the girls sat on his lap when he read to them. He was dating a local girl and talking marriage. He had worked for us for several years when—one day—Lucky's luck ran out. The Phelps County Sheriff knocked on my door with a warrant for his arrest. He was being charged with bigamy and delinquent child support payments. He had a legal wife and family in Ohio and an illegal wife and family in another state. Lucky was sentenced to Ohio State Penitentiary. Five years later I received a letter from Ohio State Penitentiary Parole Board, asking if I would, as a former employer, recommend he be granted parole. What could I say? I gave them a good report on his character and dependability as an employee.

On April 19, 1948, I lost my big sister and best friend. Harold's wife Alice passed away from a blood clot traveling to her heart, following surgery. She left four young children; the youngest, Sheila, was just six months old.

After their mother's death the children lived on a farm near Atlanta, Nebraska. A woman named Sue became their caretaker; and, shortly after that, their step-mother when Harold married her.

Karen remembers Sue burning all of her toys, including a little cabinet with toy dishes. Sue was like "Jekyll and Hyde." She was on her best behavior when the children's father Harold was home; however, he was on the road a great deal of the time and that was when she turned into a monster! She threatened the two older children, Gary, 11, and Karen, 9, "If you breathe a word of this to your dad, I'll let you have it twice as hard next time." The two youngest children were little more than babies. I recall Sheila being spanked for lifting her little dress so her panties showed and Gordon being punished for spilling a glass of milk. She inflicted physical and emotional abuse on all of them. Gary and Karen tried running away several times to escape her wrath. Sue must have been a very sick woman to have abused the children as she did. I have asked God to help me forgive her for hurting my loved ones.

I remember one day when I was watching Gordon and Sheila at my house. Gordon climbed upon the counter of the kitchen cabinets and knocked my favorite cookie jar to the floor, shattering it. I was about to scold, when he said, "That's all right ain't it Aunt Bea?" I just hugged him and said, "Yes, that's all right, it was an accident, wasn't it?"

A couple of years passed; Harold was in Kansas combining and had not yet sold his own wheat. Before he returned, Sue collected for the wheat, cleaned out his bank account and floated a few bad checks. She bought a house in town, furniture, and a car and moved out!

Funny, how destiny plays a part in our lives. My parents had been separated; however, when their grandchildren needed a home and caretakers, they came to the rescue and reunited. Harold bought a house on Nobes Street in Holdrege and they moved in with his children. Sharllyn and Carolyn spent a lot of time at Grandma and Grandpa's house with their cousins and remember it as a large house with an attached storm cellar. They can still smell the "earthy" scent of the dirt floors and dirt shelves in the cellar. The shelves were lined with rows of preserved food in glass jars.

One day Sharllyn and Carolyn were meowing like cats and were quite proud of sounding so realistic, when Grandpa yelled, "Get that damn cat out of here!" It was about the same time that Grandpa went to the refrigerator, found some meat

Harold's family
Back row from left: Harold holding Sheila, Great Grandma Forster,
Great Grandpa Forster holding Gordon, Grandma Woodring.
Front row from left, Karen and Gary.

Spotty and her puppies.

Sharllyn and Carolyn

in a dish and made a sandwich. Grandma came in and asked, "What are you eating?" He answered, "I don't know, but it made a really good sandwich." Grandma replied, "That's dog food." The half-eaten sandwich hit the opposite wall!

It was Halloween when Grandma made gypsy skirts for the girls from the old floral, living room drapes she had replaced. They wore fruit jar lid rings as earrings. The girls still remember the dresses she made for them with doll dresses to match.

God must have had a hand in leading Harold to a convenience store in Kansas, where he met an angel named Dee. He asked her for a date the following week, but he didn't show up until a year to the day later, after his divorce from Sue was final. Harold married Dee and she became a wonderful mother to his children. Harold had four children, Gary, Karen, Gordon and Sheila. Dee had two little boys, Dennis and Dallas. When Terry Lowell was born a couple of years later, their family was complete.

It was November 17, 1948. My mother, my brother Willis and his wife Dee Dee, Harold and Sue and his children had been invited to my house for a fish dinner and to see Sharllyn starring as "Goldilocks" in a school play. We returned to the house early in the evening to play cards, paying little attention to the weather until it was time for them to go home. It was three days later when they were able to leave the house! One of us managed to get across the street to borrow blankets, pillows and night clothes from my neighbor Maxine.

Our small house was filled with wall to wall sleepers. The kids thought it was great—all six of them slept crossways on one bed. I don't remember who was lucky enough to sleep on the other bed, probably Harold and Sue. Sharllyn and Carolyn recall how shocked the kids were when Sue showed up in a very revealing black negligee that she must have found among the night clothes Maxine sent over. I didn't own such a luxury, and I'm sure Sue hadn't brought it with her!

The storm continued through the next day and well into the following day, the 19th. I ran out of food, but still had flour, water and baking powder. We ate a lot of biscuits and pancakes! Harold's wife Sue ventured out to a grocery store nearby on the third day when we ran out of coffee.

The winter of 1948-1949 became known as the hardest Nebraska winter in the history of the state. Blizzard after blizzard pounded Nebraska and the Great Plains from November to April. Drifts 30-to 40-feet tall melted, froze and re-drifted for five months.

Army pilots in Piper Cubs airlifted medicine, hay, food, and coal, and transported the sick and the infirmed across the frozen land. Air Patrol pilots with planes from Kearney Air Base participated in what was known as "Operation Hay Lift". They picked up hay in Kansas to drop off to cattle in the sand hills.

A rotary plow was used to cut tunnels through the drifts on sand hill roads. Our trucks hauled food, flour, sugar and potatoes to the farmers in that area. They met us at the main roads with their tractors.

In spite of "Operation Hay Lift," thousands of cattle either froze or starved to death. Our trucks helped haul them to rendering plants.

Along with helping run a trucking business, I found time to be a Camp Fire Girl leader. One Christmas we visited the children's orphanage, west of Holdrege (the same one I visited as a child). We made fudge, packaged and sold it, using the

THE NATIONAL COUNCIL
OF
CAMP FIRE GIRLS

APPOINTS

LA VERA MILES

AS A GROUP LEADER

THOU ART THE LEADER. It shall be thy task
To keep the newly kindled fire alight;
To know the earth, the sea, the stars above;
Hold happiness; seek beauty; follow right;
Offer a friendly hand to all who ask.
And, day by day,
Lead sister feet along the golden way —
The road that leads to work and health and love.

National President

National Director

The Busy Bluebirds
c/o Mrs. Elmer Miles
824 Morton
Holdrege, Nebraska

Dear Friends:

Just a note of appreciation for the Christmas gifts
left for our boys and girls when you visited our Home in
December. The children were very happy to receive them,
and we do appreciate your thinking of them.

We were happy to have you visit our Home...we trust
you enjoyed your visit!

Sincerely yours,

CHRISTIAN CHILDREN'S HOME

Ivan L. Larson, Superintendent

ca.—1953 My Campfire girls made and sold candy
to buy the gifts.

proceeds to buy, wrap and deliver Christmas gifts to all the orphans. I tried to teach my girls to help others, especially those less fortunate. It was always a Christmas time project to make candy and cookies for special people in the neighborhood, the shut-ins, the poor and the elderly.

I continued to raise a garden, sell to grocers and can the surplus. Sharllyn still liked to pull green onions from the garden and sell them to the street workers in front of the house for a dime. Who wouldn't pay a dime just to see her smile?

I went to garage sales often and remember buying a manual typewriter and an electric phonograph with a few Country Western records. I had scalded my right hand at the beginning of my high school typing class and was never a good typist—now I could practice! Since the days of strumming my ukulele at Quakerville PTA, I loved to sing. My girls got used to my singing in the kitchen, imitating "Texas Mary" on a local radio station and singing special bedtime songs to them.

When we lost Lucky, we lost our best truck driver. Not all drivers were as dependable as Lucky in making sure the cash I sent with them got into the right hands. For one reason or another, my health being one of them, our trucking business failed. I had been told by Holdrege doctors that I needed a hysterectomy. I borrowed a dependable car from my brother Harold, and drove to Rochester to go through the Mayo Clinic for a second opinion. They diagnosed my problem as spastic colitis and assured me I didn't need a hysterectomy. Today I have three more beautiful children.

Elmer and I were divorced after ten years of marriage. Although traveling down the road of life with Elmer for those years was oft-times a bit bumpy, he holds a very special place in my heart. He was a kind, gentle, soft spoken person. Without him and those years I wouldn't have our very special daughters. Without him, I may not have found the recipe for "Lemonade."

Chapter 10

STANLEY VERSUS IKE

Elmer and I divorced in 1952, after our trucking business failed. I found myself praying for God's help; and, at the same time also remembering Dad's philosophy, "God helps those who help themselves." The divorce court granted me $12.50 a month child support for our two girls and half of all the debts.

I began doing day housecleaning for the more prominent and affluent families in town—the doctors, lawyers and business owners. It was when Mrs. Berry, whose husband owned a car dealership, wanted me to wear a uniform to serve a luncheon to some of the same ladies I had worked with in Camp Fire Girls that my pride got in the way!

I had recently held a Stanley party in my home. Winnie Watson, the dealer, told me about the wonderful future I could have with Stanley. Stanley Home Products was the first of the party plan companies. Frank Stanley Beveridge was the Director of Sales for Fuller Brush Company when Foster Goodrich went to work for him. Mr. Goodrich was selling brushes door-to-door to earn his way through college when he hit upon the idea of the party plan. Why not sell to a group of ladies rather than just one at a time? The party plan was born! Mr. Beveridge was founder of the Stanley Home Products

Company in 1931. When I started working for them, in 1952, Foster Goodrich was President of the company.

I decided Stanley might be a good part time-hobby, a way to earn a few extra dollars. I also applied for full-time work and was hired by Dutton Lainson Manufacturing in Hastings, Nebraska, at the minimum wage of 75 cents an hour. I was to begin work there on Monday. Two days before, on a Saturday, I attended a Stanley sales assembly in Grand Island, Nebraska, and told George Irwin, the Branch Manager, my plans to go to work full-time at a factory. He said, "I will guarantee you $30.00 a day, if you will hold three parties a day." It sounded too good to be true. I hadn't stopped to think that I had to book three parties a day in order to hold them! With new goals in mind, I didn't show up for work at the factory on Monday morning.

The first of each month, I wrote checks for all the bills I needed to pay that month, then I calculated how many parties I needed to book and hold at ten dollars profit per party, before I could mail the checks. (The early experience Mom gave me doing chores for points and figuring how many points I needed to buy a new bedspread paid off.) I seemed to have a knack for that type of work (after all, I recited poetry to groups of ladies when I was a preschooler), and very soon I was realizing more than ten dollars profit per party.

I had been a Stanley employee for only a few weeks when I rolled my car—totaling it! I was traveling on a gravel road, on my way to a Stanley Breakfast Party in Juiniata, Nebraska, when I lost control on an unmarked curve at the bottom of a hill. (Although a man had been killed there a month before, it was still unmarked.) As I came to my senses, I realized that a middle-aged couple was trying to pry the door open on the driver's side with a crow-bar. I was on the floor with a gash in my lower back from having been jabbed by the ignition key.

The back seat of the car was filled with boxes of Stanley merchandise to be delivered to the hostess of a party held the previous week. All the liquids were packaged in glass bottles—broken glass, germtrol, degreaser and aquilaun covered me and the car! The hostess gift, a table lamp with a "bird cage" base, had been thrown from the car. (For months that "caged bird" sat on a fence post near the site of my accident.)

Someone called a wrecker and I rode in it to tow my wrecked vehicle into town. I bought a "beater" for $25.00, loaded what merchandise I could salvage and went to the home of the lady, Mary Osborn, who was to have been my hostess that morning. When I didn't show up, she held the party anyway and sold quite a few dollars' worth of Stanley products! She loaned me a dress and took me to a doctor for stitches in my back. The previous week I had also scheduled a 2:00 p.m. party and a 7:00 evening party on that same day. I swallowed a few Aspirin and held the parties as planned!

When I delivered merchandise the following week, I said to Mary, "You should be a Stanley dealer—you would be a natural!" A few days later I called my branch manager, Mr. Irwin, and told him I had hired a new dealer and needed a sample case to issue to her. I didn't realize that dealers weren't supposed to hire new dealers and issue sample cases; that was the job of the Unit Sales Leader. However, my misunderstanding is probably what gave Mr. Irwin the idea that I should be a Unit Sales Leader and I was promoted.

My co-worker, Vi Jones, and I had traveled together to a training class for new Stanley Unit Sales Leaders, being held in Hebron, Nebraska. When we left Hebron at midday the sky was so black that we had to turn on our headlights. Minutes later a tornado struck and nearly wiped out the town. Strong winds and torrential rain, with dark clouds hovering over us made us stop at a service station to wait out the storm. Vi's boyfriend just happened to be there with his best friend, introduced to me as Ike Massey. He was cute, young and "cocky;" "Where have you been all my life?" was his response to the introduction. Before we left the station, he asked me for a date the next week and I accepted. On the night of our first date, I held a party for Mrs. Swede Garrison (Sally), a neighbor of my mother. I had just hired my mother as a new dealer. Sally remembered years later that I left early that night to get ready for my date with Ike. (Ironically, Sally and Ike celebrated their fiftieth wedding anniversary in 2010, and I sent them a card.)

Ike and I had been seeing one another for a couple of months when the rods went through the block of my $25.00 "beater," which had lasted longer than I thought possible. Again, the car was full of merchandise to be delivered! What should I do? I called a tow truck, delivered the "beater" to a salvage yard, where I sold it for the purchase price of $25.00. Then I indebted myself to Ike, when I called and said, "Help!"

My "dream house" in Holdrege was sold to help clear up debts before the girls and I moved to Grand Island in the fall of 1952, when Sharllyn was 8 and Carolyn a first-grader. I recall that when I answered an ad for a duplex for rent, I had to use my sales ability to convince the owner that a single mother could pay the rent! We moved into the duplex, and I began fulfilling my dream of becoming a teacher by hiring and training new dealers for my fast growing unit.

My girls were both in school, but I needed help to care for them. I hired a high school girl, Sara Thompson, from the rural area to live with us and help with the girls. Their school in Holdrege had been very close to our house, but in Grand Island it was several blocks away and across busy streets. I paid cab fare every school day for Sara to go from high school to their school and walk home with them, teaching them the way, and how to cross busy streets safely.

Ike served in the occupational forces following World War II and was stationed in Korea from October of 1945 until he was honorably discharged on February 9, 1947, with a World War II Victory Medal and the Army of Occupation Medal. The Korean war claimed the lives of more than 50,000 U.S. and other United Nation's forces.

Ike returned from Korea to find his fiancé pregnant with another man's child. I was recovering from a divorce after a 10 year marriage. Maybe we should have taken a "breather!" We were, no doubt, both lonesome souls and a friendship soon developed that led to marriage. I don't remember a romantic marriage proposal; I think we just mutually agreed that we were in love. I had a professional photograph taken and gave it to him as an engagement gift.

I became very angry the night before the wedding when Ike pushed me against a wall during an argument. I was tempted to call the whole thing off! Perhaps, he was too. We may both have had cold feet, however, gifts had been sent and out-of-town guests were there for the big day, so what could we do?

Floyd Le Roy Massey, aka Ike and I were married at the Methodist Church in Grand Island, Nebraska, on January 10, 1954. I wore a blue formal, that I had worn to a Stanley banquet, and made a blue net veil to match. Vi Jones and her boyfriend were our attendants. We spent our honeymoon night in a motel at Alma, Nebraska. Someone had found our suitcase and filled all the empty space with rice, an annoying prank of the times.

Soon after our marriage, we bought a "fixer up" house at 114 S. Sycamore Street, near the downtown area of Grand Island. Ike found a job driving a cement truck. It was his first real job, other than working as a janitor and an assistant rural mail carrier during his high school days. He had also worked in his dad's repair shop for an allowance. I was kept busy also; in fact, Stanley took up most of my time. Thinking back, I realize that Stanley and Ike were in competition for my time and attention. We were, however, trying to make a new life for ourselves as a family.

We had new green siding put on the house, Ike put a brick facing below the front porch and I started painting walls. The girls were making friends and busy with school and piano lessons. Carolyn joined a ceramics class, where she made pink and black roosters and a pair of black panthers for our new pink and black decor. One of those panthers has lived for more than sixty years and today is guarding the bathroom of Carolyn's California home.

The girls recall the open field in back of our new home, and the fun they had using fallen autumn leaves to mark off

1. PLACE OF MARRIAGE	STATE OF NEBRASKA	54 005391
County of Hall	DEPARTMENT OF HEALTH	Charles Bossert
Township of	BUREAU OF VITAL STATISTICS	County Judge
or Village of		Hall
City of Grand Island	Record of Marriage	County of
	Personal and Statistical Particulars	

GROOM *A-200*

BRIDE *A-420*

3. Full Name	4. Full Name
Floyd LeRoy Massey	LaVera Mae Miles
5. Residence	6. Residence
Republican City, Nebraska	Grand Island, Nebraska
7. Color or Race	8. Color or Race
White	White
9. Age at Last Birthday (Years)	10. Age at Last Birthday (Years)
26	28
11. Single, Widowed or Divorced	12. Single, Widowed or Divorced
Single	Divorced
13. Number of Previous Marriages— 1 2 3 4 5	14. Number of Previous Marriages— 1 2 3 4 5
1st	2nd time
15. Birthplace (State or Country)	16. Birthplace (State or Country)
Harlan, Kansas	Smithfield, Nebraska
17. Occupation	18. Occupation
Mechanic	Stanley Unit Manager
19. Name of Father	20. Name of Father
Francis L. Massey	Raymond G. Woodring
21. Birthplace of Father (State or Country)	22. Birthplace of Father (State or Country)
Republican City, Nebraska	Smithfield, Nebraska
23. Maiden Name of Mother	24. Maiden Name of Mother
Hazel Baker	Minnie G. Forster
26. Birthplace of Mother (State or Country)	25. Birthplace of Mother (State or Country)
Franklin, Nebraska	Smithfield, Nebraska
27. If a minor, name of person consenting	28. If a minor, name of person consenting

29. Maiden Name of Bride if she was previously married LaVera Mae Woodring,

31. License Record Number 35 — Page 461

33. By Whom the Marriage Ceremony was Performed and Official Title

30. Date of License January 9th, 1954

32. Date of Marriage January 10th, 1954

Rev. J. Alan Justed, Methodist Minister

Witness Mrs. Violet Larry
Address Hastings, Nebraska

Witness Mr. Lee Smith
Address Beaver City, Nebraska

LaVera Miles and Floyd Massey January 10, 1954

rooms in their play home and barn, where they kept their imaginary horses. There was even a "fireplace" in the "kitchen," in reality an old grill, where they built a fire and boiled water. Their piano teacher, who lived nearby, saw the smoke and ended their fantasy world. (Why did they have horses in their fantasy world? Why did Sharllyn's daughter, Cindy, love horses and become a Junior Olympic rider? Why did Carolyn's granddaughter, Elissa, love horses and choose to live on a horse ranch, work in a tack shop and care for horses through her college years? Was it a legacy left by their fraternal Grandfather Miles who cared for horses for the Queen of England before stowing away on a ship and coming to America?)

Grandma Woodring sometimes came to visit and stayed overnight. Sharllyn was having a slumber party and remembers that her grandma was quite shocked and upset when she heard them talking "girl talk" about a forbidden subject, SEX!

I depended upon Ike to stay with the girls when I held evening parties and got upset when he quite frequently called to say, "I'm going to have a few drinks with the boys." At this time in my life I had never been in a bar and did not drink, (well, other than the wine my cousins and I sipped in the cellar). My "I'll get even" attitude took over! I bought a six-pack of beer and drank a can and a half. I must have been feeling the effects when Ike came home a few hours later. He was furious and said to my girls, "Look at your mom, she's drunk."

Ike and I obviously found some time to spend together. He had awakened a sexual awareness I had not realized during my first marriage. We decided that we wanted a baby, and nine months later, Michael Ray was born at the St. Francis Hospital

CINDY AND TALK OF THE TOWN
Art by LaVera

ELISSA AND PRINCESS
Art by LaVera

in Grand Island, Nebraska. We named him Michael, but planned to call him Mike, something like his daddy's name, Ike. His middle name was for my daddy, Ray. When Michael was born, I had a letter from my Branch Manager, George Irwin, urging me to take some time off to get acquainted with the new ruler of our house. Good advice, because I realized at that point that I needed either day time or live-in help. I tried hiring a lady from job service and planned to stay home for a few days to help her become accustomed to caring for a baby. The first time I saw her face turn "beet red" when little Michael cried, I sent her home!

I held only evening parties for just a short time, and discovered that a Stanley party was the perfect place to advertise for help. A Mrs. Stephens applied for the job, and when I interviewed her in her home the next morning, I hired her on the spot. She was a god-send, for she was a substitute Grandma as well as a housekeeper and cook. The girls loved her; she was always there when they came home from school to give them a hug, hear about their day at school and fix their supper. One day when Sharllyn wanted to shave her legs Grandma Stephens said, "If God wouldn't have wanted you to have hair on your legs he wouldn't have put it there." She took good care of the baby and even took him to doctor's appointments when I was not available.

Michael was six-months-old when we happily discovered that we were to be parents again. I planned my work and parties in order to have two weeks to stay home with our new baby, but she was late in arriving. I used the two free weeks to finish painting the living room and dining room walls in what my girls remember as "wild colors," burgundy and forest green. I turned my back one day long enough for Michael to pick up a 10-inch brush, loaded with paint, and decorate the back of the couch!

Beckie Jo arrived two weeks late, at the same hospital, St. Francis, where her brother was born. Little fifteen-month-old Michael, climbed up on the bed the day we came home and gave each of us a big kiss. He loved his little sister and tried to help care for her.

We didn't discover until after we had named her that she had a great aunt a few generations ago named Rebecca Jane. Another name we considered was "Vickie," but we never regretted the name we selected.

Beckie was only a few days old when I went back to work. I was not a happy new mommy when I left the house that evening to drive to a party in another town. Tears were making it difficult to drive; I pulled off the road and took time out for a "good cry." Ike was good help with the babies, but by the time I got home from an evening party he was ready for bed.

Diapers were still a square of cloth fabric that had to be washed. We had a combination washer and dryer. I put a batch of diapers in when I put the babies to bed and folded them when I awakened for Beckie's 2:00 a.m. feeding.

In 1954, I lost a couple of good dealers due to "Race Track Fever." They tried but failed to double their proceeds from parties by betting on the horses at the new Fonner Park Horserace Track.

Then in the mid-fifties during the years of peace and prosperity, television became popular. Ike and the girls kept reminding me, "Everyone but us has a TV." I weakened, and in 1956 we bought our first black and white TV. It was a Zenith, blond wood, a console with a phonograph in the top half of the cabinet.

F. STANLEY BEVERIDGE, *Chairman of the Board*   CATHERINE L. O'BRIEN, *President*

Stanley Home Products, Inc.

WESTFIELD, MASSACHUSETTS

2702 Y Street
Lincoln 3, Nebraska
April 25, 1955

Mrs. LaVera Massey
114 S. Sycamore
Grand Island, Nebraska

Dear LaVera:

It was lot of fun to get to know the new ruler of your
house, and everything looked fine and I was awfully proud
of your bright and cheerful attitude.

Your sleeping room in Omaha has been canceled simply
because the meeting is not timed properly to fit Michael
Rae's entrance in this world. As far as the information that
will be given our people, I'll try very hard to carry the
message to you.

You probably at this time are very anxious to go to
work and I'm not going to tell you how to live your personal
life but I'd rather you'd take a little longer to recuperate
than to start back too soon.

Send Ike on those two parties this week or dovetail them
or do something. I just don't want to take any chances
about your going to work too soon.

You see, LaVera, you're a mighty important person in the
Lincoln Branch and I'd much rather you'd wait a week or two
longer and be absolutely sure than to regret a quick return
later. There's only one place for the Massey Unit and that's
at the top of the flagpole and when you're physically able
there'll still be plenty of time in '55 to get the job done.
Believe me.

                    Best wishes,

                    STANLEY HOME PRODUCTS, INC.

                    George F. Irwin, Jr.

GFI:lh

*Stanley Hostess Parties-Better Stanley Hostess Parties
Bigger Stanley Hostess Parties-Will Make
The Fifth Magnificent*

A letter from my boss.

My engagement gift to Ike

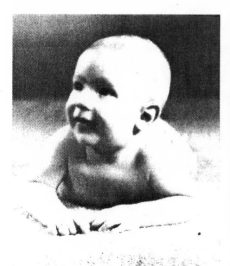

Michael Ray

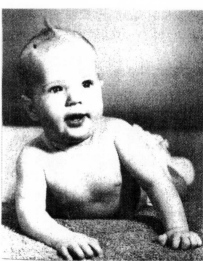

Beckie Jo

Television was a problem for me. My hostesses and their guests preferred watching "Elvis" to hearing about "lightening their household chores with my mops and brooms!" I solved the problem by explaining "why" to the hostess before I covered the TV screen, with 3 yards of a 36 inch piece of blue satin, and my sample suitcase sitting in front. It was a perfect place to display my Stanley products and available hostess gifts!

I enjoyed my first boat ride when Ike and I bought a small boat to use on the Harlan County Dam Reservoir near his parents' home in Republican City, Nebraska. Their house had been moved from the site of the dam to that newly incorporated small town. Perhaps it was lack of money, but for some reason several of the walls of their home were only lath rather than plaster, and mice were a big problem. I had a phobia about mice; that house was not my choice of a place for my babies to crawl.

Sunday was my only free day, and we often visited Ike's parents and siblings. He had a married older brother, Raymond and his wife Marquerite, a little brother Bob, and two sisters Donna and Clara Mae. One Sunday, our boat was missing from Ike's parents' back yard. It had been stolen, given away or sold. If it was sold, we never saw the money.

Ike and his dad had the same initials, (F.L.)—Floyd Le Roy Massey and Francis Le Roy Massey. Our checks started bouncing when we discovered too many counter checks had been written on our account, signed F.L. Massey. Ike always signed his checks Ike Massey and not F.L. Massey.

Ike's dad, "Shorty" walked with a limp, resulting from an injury as a young boy. It seems he went through life with the attitude of "life owes me a living." Ike's mother was a sweet, hard working woman who enjoyed few luxuries in life. She loved her first two grandchildren, Michael Ray and Beckie Jo.

As a Unit Sales Leader in Grand Island, I began seeing and appreciating a world I had not seen before. I was leading not only in personal sales, but also in Massey Unit Sales. My mother did very well as one of the dealers in my unit. She attended a banquet in Kansas City, where she was presented with a "gold cup" for personal sales. The Massey Unit won a trophy that same quarter. Because we had led the Kansas City area in sales for the past three months, I was the winner of an all-expense trip to Washington, D.C. to attend the Stanley International Convention. It was a Western theme and Ike and I dressed the part, complete with cowboy shirts, hats, boots and play-gun holsters hanging at our sides.

I give my branch manager, George Irwin, a lot of credit for my success in Stanley. He was constantly encouraging me with notes on post cards such as:

> Good, Better, Best,
> Never let it Rest.
> Until the Good is Better,
> And the Better Best.
> Or
> Make the Plan,
> Work the Plan,
> And let the Plan
> Work you.

Norma Nielson, to the left.
my Stanley co-worker and
life-long friend.

My mother to the right, the first
and one of the best dealers in the
Massey Unit. She won a trophy and
a trip to the Kansas banquet.

George Irwin
My Stanley boss—
and special friend.

Mr. Stanley Beveridge, founder of Stanley Home Products, encouraged us to say this prayer at the beginning of each new day:

Oh, Lord, grant that each one who has to do with me today may be the happier for it. Let it be given me each hour today what I shall say, and grant me the wisdom of a loving heart that I may say the right thing rightly. Help me to enter into the mind of everyone who talks with me, and keep me alive to the feelings of each one present. Give me a quick eye for little kindnesses that I may be ready in doing them and gracious in receiving them. Give me a quick perception of the feelings and needs of others, and make me eager hearted in helping them.

Amen

Author Unknown

That prayer helped me appreciate and understand not only my customers and co-workers during the years I spent with Stanley, but also my family, friends and fellowmen, then and now.

I devoted more and more time to my work and less and less time to Ike and my family. "Stanley" was winning the battle! Because I was leading the Kansas City area in Unit Sales I was offered and accepted a promotion to a Branch Office in Bismarck, North Dakota.

To LaVera Massey on April 25, 1957 — one to whom the future holds no limit other than those self-set. Sincerely Geo F Irving

INITIATIVE

THE world bestows its big prizes, both in money and honors, for but one thing, and that is Initiative. ¶ What is Initiative? I'll tell you: It is doing the right thing without being told. ¶ But next to doing the thing without being told is to do it when you are told once. That is to say, carry the Message to Garcia; those who can carry a message get high honors, but their pay is not always in proportion. ¶ Next there are those who never do a thing until they are told twice: such get no honors and small pay. ¶ Next, there are those who do the right thing only when Necessity kicks them from behind, and these get indifference instead of honors, and a pittance for pay. This kind spends most of its time polishing a bench with a hard luck story. ¶ Then, still lower down in the scale than this, we have the fellow who will not do the right thing even when some one goes along to show him how and stays to see that he does it: he is always out of a job, and receives the contempt that he deserves, unless he happens to have a rich Pa, in which case Destiny patiently awaits around the corner with a stuffed club. ¶ To which class do you belong?

—*Elbert Hubbard*

I was presented with the book Message to Garcia by Elbert Hubbard for leading the area with the Massey Unit for three consecutive months.

To LaVera, Continued success to you. Best wishes, J. E. Foster

From the president of Stanley Home Products.

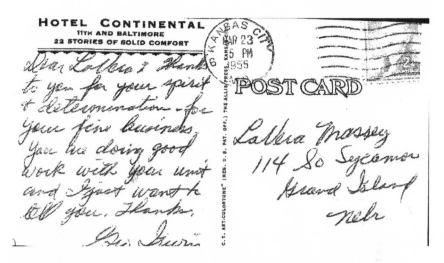

January 11, 1957

Mrs. Lavera Massey
114 So. Sycamore
Grand Island, Nebr.

Dear Lavera:

You are the winner of the all expense paid
trip to Washington, D. C. to the big
International Convention, which starts
January 27 through February 1, Congratu-
lations!

The Southwest Region is going to go western.
The more western the better. A big hat,
pistol and the works. Let's make it a
convention to remember always-put Southwest out in front.

I will be looking forward to seeing you
there.

Sincerely,

Dorris Steward
Stanley Home Products, Inc.
Kansas City Area
Sales Manager

Ike and I attended this convention before our move to Bismarck.

Chapter 11

MICHAEL RAY, BECKIE JO
AND A PROMOTION

It was a very cold, sub-zero day in mid-January. I had driven from the South Dakota border on icy roads. As I entered Bismarck city limits, I started searching for the "Beacon Light" on top of the Provident Life Insurance building. My company, Stanley Home Products, had rented an office for me in that building. I was their new Bismarck Branch Manager.

I checked into the Prince Hotel and met my area manager, Doris Stewart, who worked with me for a few days, introducing me to the branch dealers and recruiting new dealers. I rented an apartment on 21st Street and Avenue C in Bismarck, and would move my family when Ike and I returned from the Stanley International Convention in Washington, D.C.

I had been refused a loan to buy a house, or to own a gas credit card in my name, because I was a woman. I was a married woman; however, the bank loan officer said, "You might get pregnant." Although we have come a long way, statistics show that even today females are still not on an equal pay scale with men.

It was another frigid night, when the children and I arrived in Bismarck. Sharllyn was 13, Carolyn was 10, Michael was not quite two and Beckie Jo only six months old. I recall she threw her last bottle out of the car window and I took her off a bottle. Mistake! (She always claimed that was why she sucked her thumb, and I'm sure she was right!) It was several days before our furniture arrived; however, we managed with the blankets and pillows we had carried with us in the car.

Ike had chosen to stay behind and put our house in Grand Island on the market. He came to Bismarck a couple of months later and found a job driving a cement truck. In early July he returned to Nebraska to follow the harvest. In the fall of that year our marriage ended. Ike and I were together less than five years. I know he loved our babies, because he helped care for them, giving me time to pursue my career with Stanley. In retrospect, however, I realize that Stanley received more of my attention than Ike did. But God surely does have a plan for each of us; without our marriage we wouldn't have Michael Ray and Beckie Jo.

Ike did not inherit his dad's philosophy of "the world owes me a living." He became a very successful business man and a well-liked, caring and responsible individual. After our marriage ended, Ike became acquainted with my friend, Sally, and had been married to her for more than fifty years, when he passed away on April 19, 2011.

For many years Ike was a Master Mason of the Masonic Lodge and a "Shriner Clown." These clowns, in their red fez hats at mini-scooter parades, are the funny side to their serious support of the Shriners' Hospitals for Children, which were founded in 1922 and treat orthopedic conditions, burn injuries, spinal cord injuries and cleft lip and palates. Twenty Shriners' Hospitals are located in the U.S., one in Canada and one in

Mexico. These hospitals, supported by fund raising events arranged by members of the organization, allow children under the age of 18, if in the opinion of surgeons they can be helped, to be treated even though their family may not be able to pay. Shriners Clown Association is composed of Master Masons in the "Freemasonry" fraternity.

My first year as Bismarck Branch Manager was a busy and hectic year, both at home and at work. Our monthly board meetings weren't all work, however. As a group we sometimes found time to "bar hop," where I learned the popular dances of the day, the "Twist," the "Bunnyhop" and the "Jitterbug." On one occasion we were snowbound for several days at the President Hotel, our usual meeting place. The kitchen staff joined us in dancing and singing around the piano, and we helped out in the kitchen. I found it very difficult to find reliable live-in help and I missed our Grandma Stephens. Beckie was less than a year old and Mike not yet two. I couldn't have managed without my two older girls!

I inherited 125 dealers, many with little or no training. I hired a part-time secretary, a college girl, to enable me to spend more time in the field, training and recruiting new dealers. I soon discovered that the former manager had left unpaid bills and unhappy dealers. I had a lot of bridges to rebuild!

I was given a $500.00 bonus with my promotion, barely enough to cover my moving expenses. I was expected to look, act and dress the part of a prosperous Stanley Branch Manager; that meant driving a newer model car, living in a good neighborhood and dressing in a suit, nylons and heels. Until I could pull my branch out of the red, I pinched a lot of pennies. I tried not to be seen when I picked up pop bottles along the roadside, using the rebate to buy a loaf of bread or a bottle of milk. My older girls used to say, "We have fruit and orange juice at the first of the month when Mom gets her check, and by the middle of the month we are living on peanut butter sandwiches, macaroni and cheese and lots of Mulligan stew."

I recall a phone call from George Irwin on January 28, 1958, asking me not to leave town and to please be careful. "A nineteen year old mass murderer named Starkweather and his accomplice, Caril Ann Fugate, have fled Nebraska and are believed to be headed north," George said. He was concerned for my safety. The fugitives were captured in Douglas, Wyoming, the next day, January 29, after murdering a Montana salesman for his car. Starkweather was executed in the electric chair at the Nebraska State Penitentiary in Lincoln, on June 25, 1959. Fugate, at 14, was the youngest female ever charged with first degree murder. She served 17 years at a Correctional Center for Women before being paroled from her life sentence in 1976.

George Irwin and I had a very special friendship that lasted through the years. At one time he said, "Since the first time I met you, I just wanted to put my arms around you and protect you." I missed George when I left Nebraska and I missed Nebraska. It will always be "home." Strong family roots of our heritage are embedded there. I have always been proud to say, "I'm from Nebraska." The 37th state to be admitted to the union on March 1st, 1867, it is known as the "Cornhusker State." The state flower is the Goldenrod, the state bird, the Western Meadowlark and the state tree, the Bur Oak.

I chose to use the Bur Oak tree on the cover of this book because it reminds me of my Nebraska ancestors. It is a pioneer, a long-living tree that invaded the prairie grass lands years ago. Bur Oaks have lived up to an age of 400 years. They have the largest acorns of all native oaks that provide much of the food for red squirrels, wood ducks and deer.

J. Sterling Morton was the founder of Arbor Day, which originated in Nebraska City, on April 10, 1872. An estimated one million trees were planted in Nebraska that day. By the 1920's, each state had passed public laws that stipulated a certain day to be Arbor Day.

Unicameral Legislature was established in 1934; Nebraska has the only one-branch legislation in the nation. At the time I moved to Bismarck, Nebraskans were not paying state income tax.

Nicholas Sparks, author of *The Notebook,* was born in Omaha and raised in Norfolk; former talk show host Johnny Carson came from Norfolk; Henry Fonda claims Grand Island as his hometown; Willa Cather, a Nebraska native, was the author of *My Antonio*, the story of a little Bohemian girl. Marie Sandoz, author of *Old Jules,* tells the story of her father in early Gordon, Nebraska, and of the fruit orchards successfully planted and maintained by Old Jules when his neighbors said fruit trees wouldn't grow in the native sod. The Pine Ridge Indian Reservation, just 13 miles from Gordon, was the site of the Wounded Knee Massacre in 1890. My maternal great-grandparents, Henry and Elizabeth Forster, were living in Gordon at that time.

Mammoths have been discovered in 90% of Nebraska's 93 counties. A Nebraskan, Joyce Hall, moved his card company from Norfolk to Kansas City, Missouri, to become "Hallmark," the largest producer of greeting cards in the world. Kool-Aid is Nebraska's official soft drink, invented in Hastings in 1927 by Edwin Perkins.

During World War II the nation's largest naval ammunition depot was built just outside of Hastings, Nebraska. With 11,000 new jobs, it revived the area after the Great Depression. The 911 emergency communications system was developed and first used in Lincoln, Nebraska.

I return to Nebraska often to visit my brother, Willis Woodring, founder and owner of Omaha Distributing Co. I relive my salt selling days when I drive through Norfolk in the sand hills. I also remember my early days as a child when I visit Smithfield and the park which is now home to the old Main Street windmill.

Our family has always been a close-knit family; and when the children and I moved to Bismarck, we missed the special times together, especially Christmas. The older girls remember walking on the crumpled Christmas paper on the living room floor at Grandma's house as being almost as much fun as unwrapping the gifts. We still remember Grandma's advice, "Save the bows." Over the years we built our own Christmas traditions. We always had a big tree and all the gifts we could afford piled under it. A big bowl of Grandma's Pineapple Cheese Salad was part of our Christmas dinner.

It was a difficult time for my Sharllyn and Carolyn. They weren't happy changing schools and leaving their friends. Bobby socks, saddle shoes and "poodle skirts" were the fad of the day. Sharllyn had been dropped in favor of "Sharri." Doc Clark would have chuckled, saying "I told you so."

My girls learned to do laundry, cook, babysit and change diapers. Although we had a live-in housekeeper, it was Sharri and Carolyn who kept the household running smoothly.

I was assigned a car parking space at Provident Life, next to the Vice President, Robert W. Edick. He came to my office a few days later to check on the rental status of my office. It was a nice gesture, but totally unnecessary as Stanley Home Products rented the space for me and paid the rent each month. Several of us were invited to Mr. Edick's home one evening. It was a beautiful new ranch-style, brick home at 1100 N. First Street, and much too large for a bachelor! I recall noticing the pull-down lamp over the kitchen table and his remark, "That's for the kids to do their homework." "What kids?" I thought. I have often said Bob married me six years later for my kids. He loved children.

I was working long, long hours trying to build my branch. The company had offered me a 10 day, all expense paid trip for two to Hawaii if I doubled my business in the following year of 1959. I told myself, "I can do it!"

Some of my most successful Stanley parties were in the Strasburg, North Dakota area with kinfolk of Lawrence Welk. They called the parties "Name's Day Parties" and included both husband and wife. They served "Red Eye," a very potent liquor, by passing a glass around the circle of guests. I participated with just a sip of "Red Eye," just enough to make them feel that I was one of them, and sales were great! During the same years, Bob Edick and Lawrence played golf together.

Gradually, my family adjusted to their new surroundings; they were doing well and growing up so fast. Sharri joined a pot-luck group with friends at school who got together in their homes once a month. Carolyn became a "Candy Striper" at the hospital. Both of the girls were Rainbow Girls. Carolyn made friends with those who needed a friend. She met the "love of her life," Richard, early in her teen years. They always went to the Carnival when it was in town on her birthday and driving through the "Big Boy" for a "hot 'n tot" and "pizza burger" (flying saucer style) was an often enjoyed treat.

Every Thursday was TV night at our house. Tom, Jim, Dave, May and Jan sat in front of the TV set in our small shabby living room munching popcorn—spilling more than a little of it on the worn green carpeting and watching their favorite detective show. Often they scrambled eggs or made a pizza. "But, Mother, they aren't boyfriends, they are just friends," Sharri explained. Often just one of the kids sat with Sharri at our kitchen table, drinking hot chocolate or coke, and telling her their problems. She was a friend, counselor and psychiatrist. Dave had just found out who his biological father was and wanted to take his name—should he? Tim's older sister wasn't married and was going to have a baby—what would everyone think? May's parents didn't trust her because her sister had gotten into trouble. "My folks don't understand me," May said. But Sharri did.

Sharri was popular with both boys and girls. She sang in the Presbyterian Choir and was a candidate for DeMolay sweetheart in Rainbow Girls. She was also my friend. After a date she often sat on the edge of my bed and told me all about it. "Don wants to run away and get married," she confided. "I just laughed at him, and told him if we put our allowances together we wouldn't have enough money to buy gas to get us to the state line." I don't have to worry about her, I thought.

Then in the very next sentence, I heard, "Mother, the gang's going to the Plamoor Club tomorrow night, may I go?" I reasoned, "Sharri, I don't believe it's the place for teenagers." "But, Mother, (using the age-old argument) everyone else is going," she said. Reluctantly, I agreed, "If you really want to go, O.K. I don't approve, but I won't forbid you from going." Next evening the gang arrived and off they went for a few hours of fun. Half an hour later, the phone rang and there was a tiny voice on the other end of the line. "Mother, please come and get me." "I know now what you mean," she said as she climbed in the car beside me, "This just isn't the place for this teenager."

After graduating from high school and entering college, Sharri's goal was to become a psychiatrist. "I want to help people," she said. So many she knew needed help, even her mother! Sharri was enrolled at the University of North Dakota; however, a graduation gift from her uncles, Harold and Willis, changed her mind. They gave her a plane ticket to Phoenix, Arizona, to housesit Harold's home there for the summer while he was in Nebraska. A friend of Sharri's, Jan Morris, joined her. They loved Arizona and started taking summer classes at Arizona State University in Tempe. Somehow, I managed to hold enough extra parties to pay her out-of-state tuition for the next few years.

I have always believed in God and that He has a plan for me, but I was not a regular churchgoer until after our move to Bismarck. The girls started attending the First Presbyterian Church with some of their friends, and I followed. After receiving some religious training, I became a member. I sought Reverend Butler's help in trying to straighten out my life; I was troubled by my two failed marriages. "Why?" I asked myself. In trying to analyze why I chose to marry the men I did, I realized one thing: I felt they both needed me, and I needed to be needed. And now, a very special man had come into my life. No, he didn't need me, since he already had a wife; but, in spite of the fact that I knew it was morally wrong, I became very fond of him. He had come home from the service, unannounced, to find his wife living with another man, which prompted their separation.

We went for boat rides on the Missouri River, where he wrote "I love you" on the beach of a sand bar; he put pheasants in my mailbox after a successful hunting trip; he brought roses to me after "Ladies Day" at the car dealership where he worked. He called me "Boss Lady" and sold me a new car at "cost plus ten." I had letters waiting for me when I arrived in Dallas, Oklahoma City, Kansas City, wherever my work took me. We realized our relationship was involving a lot of lives and with counseling from his father and my minister, we said a tearful goodbye. He reconciled with his wife, and they had two more children. His children were not yet raised when he was killed in an accident. Years later, one very sad day in my life when I couldn't keep tears from my eyes, my dog Czar and I went for a long walk. I aimlessly walked up a hill to the cemetery. Someone or something led me to the grave of this very special man. I stood there as a message came to me, "Cheer up, Boss Lady."

Stanley took me away from home for days at a time. Mike was still a preschooler and missed me. He put push-pins on maps to keep track of where I was. One day he climbed under my car with a wrench. He was going to tear the car apart so

From left Carolyn, Beckie, Mike and Sharllyn

This is to Certify that

Mrs. LaVera Massey

was received _by Confession of_

Faith and Baptism

_____ into full membership in the

First Presbyterian Church

of _Bismarch, North Dakota_

on the _7th_ day of _February_ 19 _60_

Wm R Lindsay
Pastor

_____
Clerk

his mommy couldn't leave home! More than once, after I had been gone for a few days, I would awaken at 5:00 in the morning with little hands pulling the blanket off my face. "Upsy Daisy, Mommy, it's time for breakfast." Mike had made French toast! One day he was scolded for using the baby crib he and his little sister Beckie had slept in—as a coloring book. His reaction shocked me! "Mommy, I don't know why you are upset; you know there won't be another baby as long as there isn't a man around the house." And, this profound statement from the mouth of a five-year-old! When Mike was going to be held back in first grade because of his poor reading skills, his sisters took it upon themselves to tutor him in reading during the summer. The result was that he wasn't held back and today he is an avid reader. He tried to learn to drive at the tender age of three, when he climbed in my car sitting in the driveway, took it out of gear and rolled it down hill! Luckily, he was stopped when he hit the curb. I was upset enough to spank him, but instead I only hugged him and thanked God he wasn't hurt.

Beckie was also a very active little one. We have pictures of her dancing on the coffee table. She loved to play office, like mommy, and always had a paper and pencil in her hand. Before she could write or print, she drew picture stories for me, telling me of her activities during the days I was away from home.

It was 1959 and Beckie was three when Mattel invented the first Barbie doll. Although she had not seemed to like to play with dolls, she loved her Barbie dolls. I carried a suitcase containing a Barbie doll, fabric and pattern with me when I was working out of town, and made Barbie clothes to help shorten the long nights away from home and my kids. The new doll clothes always put a smile on Beckie's face.

One day a neighbor lady came to my door carrying a bottle of Stanley perfume. She said, "Your little girl brought this to me and I'm not sure she was supposed to do that." Beckie, a preschooler, sometimes went with me to a Stanley party. She saw me giving away samples, and apparently didn't think it would be wrong to give away a few bottles of perfume!

I did double the business in my branch in 1959, as I had vowed to do. Early 1960 found my mother and me on our way to Hawaii. It was my mother's first ride on an airplane. Our ten days together gave us the opportunity to become acquainted as adults. I had left home when I married at seventeen.

We bought muumuus, coconut straw hats and sandals. We toured the island of Oahu in a rented jeep with a pink-striped top and even visited a night club or two. We ate all the papaya and pineapple we could hold. It was August 21, 1959, when Hawaii became a state, and so in 1960 it was still very native, not yet westernized in dress or living style. There was only one big hotel, the Royal Hawaiian. "Diamond Head" was clearly visible in the distance. Though I returned to Hawaii several times in later years, my first trip with my mother was extra special.

Stanley Home Products was a great company to work for; it opened up a world of opportunity for me. I studied under Professor Elmer Nyberg, who formerly taught Norman Vincent Peale's "Power of Positive Thinking;" but at that time he was holding training workshops for Stanley Branch Managers. Much that I learned about how to get along with people I still use today.

In 1949, Mr. Beveridge, the founder of Stanley Home Products, established the Stanley Park of Westfield, Inc. on 25 acres of land in Westfield, Massachusetts. Mr. Beveridge said, "This park was made possible because thousands were interested in doing something worthwhile for their fellow man." Today, Stanley Park consists of nearly 300 acres of trails, woods, picnic areas, recreational facilities and gardens. An all-American Rose Garden; an Asian Garden; a Wildflower Garden and an Herb Display Garden are among the many gardens included in the park. Other attractions are a Wildlife Sanctuary, The Carillon Towers, a working mill and waterwheel, an old town meeting house, a carriage shop, a blacksmith shop and arched bridges, all with a backdrop of flowering azaleas and rhododendrons.

In 1962 the children of the branch managers, were invited to attend the Stanley Convention in Westfield. The company provided entertainment, such as bowling and movies, as well as caretakers for them. Mike was seven and Beckie six that year. Beckie remembers going to Plymouth Rock with me, while Mike remembers how disappointed he was that he didn't go along on that side trip and chose instead to stay at Stanley Park and go horseback riding.

In 1971 a plaque was placed in a part of Stanley Park, dedicated to Foster E. Goodrich, Chairman of the Board of Stanley Home Products, Inc: "In recognition of his progressive leadership and his devotion to the Stanley Ideals." (Presented by A.W. Elzerman, President)

New York, the "Big Apple," is a city like no other! My first visit there was in1960 with a group of Stanley Branch Managers. Six of us left the convention in Westfield a couple of days early to

The beginning of a wonderful ten day vacation
in Hawaii for me and my mother.

We toured the island in a jeep with a pink striped top,
wearing our muumuus and woven cocoanut straw hats.

Westfield, MA. Stanley Convention
Beckie is in front of me in the center, Mike is to the left.

Mike

Beckie Jo

see New York, as if one could see New York in such a short time. We squeezed in all the tours possible before the rest of the branch managers met us for a night at the Latin Quarter, a well-known nightclub opened in1942 by Lou Walters, father of Barbara Walters, and featuring big name acts like Frank Sinatra, Ella Fitzgerald, Sophie Tucker, Mae West and Milton Berle.

My first jet plane ride was the next day. My enthusiasm for the trip was somewhat dampened by the fact that a jet had crashed off the runway at La Guardia Airport hours before our scheduled departure!

On May 5, 1961, the first American astronaut, Alan Shepard, was launched into space from Cape Canaveral, Florida.

There was a lot of talk about UFO's in those years. I held a Stanley party in Hastings, Nebraska, for a lady whose nephew was admitted to the State Mental Hospital for claiming he saw a UFO land in a field. On that same day, cars had mysteriously stopped running and then started again along a certain stretch of road in Nebraska.

Norma Nielsen and I had become Stanley Unit Sales Leaders at about the same time, and both of us were subsequently promoted to branch managers. She had the South Dakota Branch and lived in Rapid City. We traveled by car to the area meetings in Kansas City in all kinds of weather. We were the "babies" of the ten branch managers on the Kansas City Area Board. On one memorable occasion we decided to be "different" by wearing our new "chemise" dresses and tinting our hair red. The dye job was, to say the least, more than a bit unprofessional. We were dubbed the "hue it yourself twins" by the older, more sophisticated, board members. I claimed Norma as the sister I had always longed for, and we became life-long friends.

Since Bob and I had offices in the same building, we saw one another often. He found excuses to come to my house during lunch hour when I was home, probably to see the kids. He picked Beckie Jo up from her high chair more than once when she wiped her grimy little hands on his white shirt, necessitating a trip to his house to change clothes before he went back to work. This may have been the beginning of the bonding between Beckie Jo and her "Daddy Bob."

Beckie learned to love Siamese cats when she was just a few years old and now, nearly fifty years later she still loves them. Her first Siamese kitty was "Candy," a name acquired because she stole all the candy she could get her little paws on. She was a very curious baby kitten managing to climb through a broken grate on a floor register and sliding down the duct right into the furnace. Luckily, only the pilot light was on—again, I called my boyfriend Bob for help. He came to the kitty's rescue by cutting a hole in the wall. It was in the wee hours of the morning, and he didn't even complain about my disturbing his sleep!

For three years, Bob kept company with both me and Miss J, however, he assured me that their relationship was currently platonic. He had fathered her child, who was given up for adoption, during the five years he was legally separated from his first wife of 17 years. I tried to understand. He asked me to marry him and in order to simplify things, we arranged for Carolyn to attend Hughes Junior High, near his home, that fall. The engagement was not formal, and I had not been given a ring. One day he showed me a beautiful diamond solitaire and asked me if I thought Miss J would like it! Not many days later, I opened the Bismarck Tribune to the "Nubs of the News" section to learn of their marriage in another state! I was in shock, but I remembered that Bob once confided in me, "Since I fathered her child, I should have given her my name." I rationalized that their marriage was the honorable thing for him to do. I dried my tears, made lemonade, and held the previously scheduled training assembly for 100 plus dealers in the Provident Auditorium.

When Bob and his new wife returned to town, I called, congratulating the newlyweds, and wishing them a long and happy life together. Within a few months, Bob was knocking on my door asking me to give him another chance.

I had started dating a lawyer during those months; however, when Bob saw Mr. B's car at my house, he slid nasty notes under my door. I stopped seeing Mr. B.

A short time later, Bob came into my office one day and said, "My wife wants me to have a vasectomy." I thought a moment or two before I answered, "And how do you feel about that?" Their marriage was over before the end of the year.

Bob was very jealous and didn't want me to make trips out of town. On more than one occasion, he met me in another town when he should not have known my whereabouts. He had used his master key to enter my office and find my itinerary. I complained to the president, and Bob almost lost his job! One night when I was in Kansas City and already in bed, I picked up the phone to hear Bob's voice. He was angry and blaming me because he had "had a few too many." "If you had stayed home, this wouldn't have happened." He was obviously very upset, saying that he would tell me why when

I got home, and then added, "It's like this, you go through life thinking you are a Cadillac and find out you're nothing but a damn Chevrolet." His Aunt Gladys had told him that he was part Native American. His paternal great-grandmother was ¾ Menomonee and ¼ Chippewa. His father died of the flu during World War I when Bob was less than three years old. He grew up not knowing his father's family.

We both began seeing psychiatrists in hopes of straightening out our "muddled" lives. It seemed it was only his personal life that was muddled, since by this time he had been elected president of Provident Life. The company was growing, and his home office and field employees, as well as the janitors, loved him. He was on an equal terms with all of them.

Chapter 12

FIRST LADY OF PROVIDENT LIFE

Robert William Edick and I were married on August 19, 1963, at Detroit Lakes, Michigan, by a very reluctant Episcopalian minister, with the janitor and the cleaning lady as our attendants. Our minister at the First Presbyterian Church in Bismarck had refused to marry us because each of us had been divorced, not once but twice.

I found myself in a fishing boat near Pelican Rapids on August 20th at 5:00 am. It was a cold, rainy morning. Although I've never been an early riser, this was my new husband Bob's idea of a perfect honeymoon.

Ours had been a very stormy courtship, and there were many cloudy days in the early months of our marriage. Bob was very jealous of me and my working at a job that required travel out of town, so I agreed to resign my position with Stanley Home Products. We were in New York City when I mailed my letter of resignation to become a full-time mother, housewife and First Lady of Provident.

Moving into Bob's home on 1100 North First Street was a challenge! The kitchen cabinets held more than dishes and pots and pans; they also held tools and fishing tackle! The counters and the kitchen table were covered with fishing rods and reels. The basement held several boxes of fishing worms.

As you might have guessed, my husband Bob's favorite pastime was fishing, when he wasn't watching football. It was not unusual to see him watching one game on TV, while listening to a couple more games on the radio. He was an expert at predicting final scores.

It was about this time that the game began of trying to turn me, the uneducated country girl, into a refined lady capable of being the First Lady of Provident Life. Working with Stanley Home Products for more than ten years had opened up a whole new world for me and taught me a lot, especially how to get along with people; however, Bob saw the need for me to learn more in order to fill the role of his wife and First Lady of Provident. I remain forever grateful for Bob's constructive criticism that helped mold me into a well-rounded individual.

Bob gave me lessons to improve my grammar in an attempt to eliminate my "mid-west twang," and tried to teach me a more graceful way of walking. Most of my clothes from Penny's, Target and the thrift stores were discarded; and I was given charge accounts with the better women's clothing stores in town. Bob used to say, "A cheap handbag spoils a beautiful outfit." That's one lesson I remember, nearly fifty years later. I still splurge on designer handbags that I probably can't afford. I stopped doing my own hair and nails and made weekly trips to a beauty salon.

Bob's mother and his Aunt Gladys worked together trying to teach me the appropriate way to set a table with my newly acquired Spode china, crystal stemware and sterling silver, as well as how to properly plan a menu to entertain Bob's peers.

Mr. and Mrs. Robert Edick

CERTIFICATE OF MARRIAGE

STATE OF MINNESOTA, County of ___Becker___ ss.

I Hereby Certify, that on the ___19th___ day of ___August___, in the year of our Lord one thousand nine hundred and ___68___, at ___Detroit Lakes___ in said County, I the undersigned a ___Clergyman___ did join in the Bonds of Matrimony;

___Robert William Edick___

a resident of the County of ___Burleigh___ State of ___North Dakota___ and

___LaVera Mae Massey___

a resident of the County of ___Burleigh___ State of ___North Dakota___.

in the presence of

_____ Witness

___Emanuel M. Hansen___

P.O. ADDRESS: ___1181 Phinney___

___Detroit Lakes, Minnesota___

OFFICE OF THE PRESIDENT
AND DIRECTOR OF SALES

December 13, 1963

Dear LaVera:

I received your letter when I returned from my trip to the West Coast and though I regret, from a business standpoint, that you have decided to discontinue your service in Stanley, I wish you much happiness in your new role as a full time homemaker and wife of the President of Provident Life Insurance Company.

I do appreciate the good work you did while you were in Stanley and wish you much happiness in your new role.

The Eleventh was a HUGE SUCCESS not only in the Kansas City Area, the Southwestern Region, but throughout the Stanley world. We have what we think are GREAT PLANS for the new year of 1964.

My very best to you for a MERRY CHRISTMAS and a HAPPY AND HEALTHFUL NEW YEAR.

Best personal regards.

Sincerely,

Foster E. Goodrich
President and
Director of Sales

Mrs. LaVera Edick
P. O. Box 1474
Bismarck, N. D. 58502

It seemed I didn't quite fit in with doctors and lawyers wives, most of them college graduates. It always upset me when I was asked where I went to school. I just replied, "In Nebraska," not telling them I had graduated from the "school of hard knocks."

In Juanita Edick's eyes, I was several rungs lower on the ladder of social acceptance than Bob's first wife, Ruth. She was the North Dakota Governor's daughter, while I was the daughter of a struggling dry land farmer. I never quite took Ruth's place and was often reminded, "Ruth would never have done that," when I pulled such blunders as cracking an antique glass pitcher when I rinsed it in water that was too hot, or using a can of salmon without removing the bones when I made salmon patties.

I wasn't allowed to change the location of pictures on the wall or move furniture without his mother or his aunt's approval. I hated the duck mural on the dining room wall. A few years later, I solved that problem by buying a new, very large china cabinet to hold my Spode, crystal and Irish Belleek. The only wall the china closet would fit on was the wall with the duck mural!

A cleaning lady came in once a week to clean the house. All the re-decorating, papering and painting was done by a hired professional. I was raised to be very thrifty, and was accustomed to doing my own housework, papering, painting, gardening and even the refinishing and reupholstering of old furniture. These were habits that were difficult to break. I failed to fit into the mold of our peers. I tried playing bridge and took golf lessons, but never really enjoyed either bridge or golf or learned to play a good game. I would come home with a headache from trying.

I still loved to don a ratty old T shirt and jeans and tackle a dirty job; however, over time, I learned to be a lady when need be and dress up in my formal gowns with bouffant hair styles and wigs, mink stoles and diamonds.

Bob and I visited New York City several times in the 60's. More than the tourist attractions I had seen on my first trip with my Stanley friends, I came to love the hustle, bustle of the garment district, Wall Street, in the days of the ticker tape, and Greenwich Village. It was during the "Beatnik Era," when I could buy candles and woven tin baskets for a dime. The next year, the same woven basket was featured in the Neiman Marcus Christmas catalog for twenty-five dollars. In 2011 Sharri still had one of those baskets displayed in her kitchen. In addition to shopping, we also had our caricature portraits done. I was the "typical" housewife, eating chocolates and watching TV, while Bob was the fisherman. Today those caricatures are hanging at our lake cabin. We ate dinner at an Italian restaurant where we were entertained by "bottle playing" waiters. Bob said, "Could you just make our decision from the menu?" The meal was excellent and I'm sure the waiters were very well compensated. Bob loved good food and well-known expensive restaurants. It was on this excursion that we attended the World's Fair. More than fifty-one million visitors attended the fair during its two years in New York City. We tasted Belgian Waffles at the food booth and got the recipe. Belgian Waffles from that recipe are still being made in the homes of my children and grandchildren. Mike always requested those waffles in lieu of a birthday cake. I would like to share the recipe with you:

Belgian Waffles

Waffles

1 egg yolk	1 cup sifted flour
1 cup sour cream	2 teaspoons sugar
½ cup milk	1 teaspoon baking powder
3 tablespoons melted butter	¼ teaspoon each soda and salt
1 stiffly beaten egg white	

In a mixer blend egg yolks, sour cream, milk and butter. Stir in sifted dry ingredients. Fold in stiffly beaten egg white. (makes 2-10 inch waffles)

Serve with strawberry sauce and ice cream fluff.

Strawberry Sauce

Blend until coarsely crushed-

1 cup berries   1 tablespoon sugar

Ice Cream Fluff

Whip 1 cup whipping cream until thick but will not hold its shape. Add 1 cup vanilla ice cream by spoonful, beating just until smooth.

In the early 1960's flying was still a mode of travel for the more affluent, rather than the mass, no frills transportation it has become today. Sharri started her career as a flight attendant for American Airlines in 1964. Billboards all over Southern California featured four American flight attendants, one of them being Sharri, eating a candied apple; a pilot and a copilot telling the world that American Airlines was flying to the World's Fair several times a week. Bob and I met Sharri during one of her layovers in New York City. We ate dinner at our favorite Italian restaurant. Sharri made the day for a starving Greenwich Village street artist by having her portrait done.

I truly lived the life of a "queen for the week" when I attended an Insurance President's Convention at the Waldorf Astoria with Bob. I wore Evan Picone and Jones of New York suits and dresses, a full-length mink coat, diamonds and pearls. I shopped on Fifth Avenue, dined on filet mignon and caviar and danced in the ballroom where the Presidential Inaugural Ball was held.

Several years later, after Sharri and her family moved to Yardley, Pennsylvania, Sharri, Carolyn and I often found an excuse to see a Broadway Play in New York City. We found we could board a train, in Trenton, New Jersey, ten minutes from Sharri's Yardley home, and be in the city in time for lunch and a matinee. After the matinee, a walk through Times Square, a bit of shopping at Macy's and we could still be home in time for a late dinner. Jay, always concerned for our safety, said, "Leave your jewelry at home and don't act like a tourist; don't carry a camera or stand and gawk at the skyscrapers."

Life with Bob and with Provident was a busy time and found me devoting much time and effort trying to be a good wife and a good First Lady. I sent Christmas cards to all of the field office employees and their families, making sure to remember all the

Sharri

Sharri is third from the left.

children's names. I arranged a monthly luncheon for the wives of home office employees and recognized all the new babies by visiting them with a gift of a sterling silver piggy bank.

The annual Christmas party at our house was a huge success. I cooked for weeks ahead of time and served a gourmet buffet dinner for close to seventy-five home office employees and their spouses or significant others. One year I made an ice sculpture of Rudolph by putting water in an inflatable plastic reindeer, then removing the plastic after the water had frozen solid; of course, I put a cherry on the end of his nose! Another year, an artist friend of mine, Joyce Manolovitz, entertained our guests by doing their portraits in charcoal.

I have always loved nature, flowers and trees. I'm reminded of a line from Joyce Kilmer's poem, *Trees*: "I think that I shall never see a poem lovely as a tree." (Poems and illustrations are made by folks like me, but only God can make a flower or a tree.)

Not a flower was to be seen in the yard on First Street— when I moved there. Bob liked it simple. "Easy to mow the grass," he said. However, I soon had flowers boxes built and planted for the back yard and planted more than thirty rose bushes on the south and east sides of the house. The Bismarck Garden Club visited our yard and people stopped by to photograph my beautiful roses. Early one morning I spotted a photographer with a squirt bottle of water putting dew drops on the petals to enhance his photo! Bob bragged that I was dubbed the "Rose Lady of Bismarck" and in a few years was helping me cover the bushes with leaves for their winter nap.

The year was 1963 when my mother won a prize for her recipe for Glazed Fresh Apple Cookies. The recipe was published in Capper's Weekly along with this notation: Mrs. Minnie Woodring, Holdrege, Nebraska, writes that she has received a letter from her granddaughter in California saying she has shared the cookies with several friends who think the cookies are delicious. Carolyn was the granddaughter in California, a new bride in 1963. My mother sent cookies to her at Christmas time and to Sharri who was stationed in L.A. with American Airlines. Another well packed box of apple cookies came to Bismarck for Mike, Beckie, Bob and me to enjoy. Sharri still sends boxes of these special cookies to her siblings and to me at Christmas time and Carolyn always bakes them for her family as a special holiday treat. Grandma's cookies have been a family favorite for years!

Glazed Fresh Apple Cookies

½   cup butter
1½ cup brown sugar (packed)
1   egg unbeaten
1   cup chopped walnuts
¼   cup raisin juice or milk
1   cup raisins (plumped in water)
2¼ cups flour (or less)
1   cup apples (chopped walnut size)
1   teaspoon soda
½   teaspoon salt
1½ teaspoon cinnamon
1   teaspoon cloves

1   teaspoon vanilla

Sift together dry ingredients, (flour, soda, salt, cinnamon and cloves) cream butter and sugar until light, add egg and vanilla. Stir in half of dry ingredients; add nuts, apples and raisins. Blend in raisin juice or milk, and then add the rest of the flour mixture.

Drop by teaspoon, 2 inches apart on a greased cookie sheet. Bake 8 to 10 minutes at 400 degrees.

While hot, spread with glaze using a pastry bush.

Glaze

Blend 1 cup powdered sugar, ½ tablespoon butter and enough milk or cream to make a very thin glaze.

Beckie was eight and Mike nine when we moved into Bob's house on First Street. Bob loved the kids and showered them with gifts and goodies, such as candy and soda pop. He thought they had been deprived because I couldn't afford those luxuries. He didn't understand that I couldn't afford the dental bills that go along with too much candy and pop.

Bob was a gentleman. He always walked on the outside of the sidewalk to protect his lady. He placed my order first at a restaurant and never failed to pull my chair out and seat me at the dining table or hold the car door open for me.

A holiday never passed that he didn't send me flowers, a corsage and/or jewelry, be it Christmas, my birthday, our anniversary, Mother's Day, Valentine's Day, Easter or St. Patrick's Day. I soon had quite a collection of nice jewelry that

I am still enjoying. He must have been Knowles Jewelry's best customer!

I remember one Christmas there were two long jewelry size boxes; however, the first one I opened wasn't jewelry, it was a 6 inch railroad spike! Just Bob's subtle way of telling me I was ruining the walls by using too large a nail to hang a picture.

Bob had a photographic memory. His father died during World War I, a victim of the flu, when Bob was only three years old. Years later he drew a picture of the room his father was in when he died. He remembered the exact location of every piece of furniture, every door and every window. He never forgot his father's words from his deathbed, "Son, I am going on a long journey and won't be back; you will have to be the man of the house now and take care of your mother."

Bob didn't know his fraternal ancestors or even where his father was buried. Not long before we were married, his Aunt Gladys showed him a picture of seven young men who were his father and his fathers' brothers and told him that he was part Native American.

Bob's mother, Juanita, boasted of a royalty background. Her mother was Lady in Waiting for a Queen of England. The family was related to Lord Nelson. There were still relatives living in Ireland who exchanged letters with Juanita. When one of them died intestate in 1980, Bob inherited several thousand dollars that he invested in our lake cabin.

Bob's maternal grandfather, Robert Johnston, was a Scotch-Irish Presbyterian minister. He was one of the early ministers in Eastern North Dakota who rode horseback to officiate at funerals and weddings. I placed a copy of his date

Hawaii in 1971

book in the L.D.S. Genealogical Library in Salt Lake City. Bob remembered him as a very stern old man who didn't like kids. On one occasion, Grandpa Johnston was attempting to reach into a barrel of apples to find a choice one, while little Bobby was hanging over the edge of the barrel trying to help, when he heard his grandpa yell, "Annie, come and get this boy before I kill him." Those words the little guy never forgot!

Provident took us across country to company conventions at popular resorts. Nassau, Hawaii, Mackinaw Island, San Juan, Palm Desert, California and Scottsdale, Arizona, are only a few of the sites Bob chose to have conventions and train agents and managers of Provident Life Insurance Company.

Our convention trip to Hawaii was a lot different than my visit there with my mother in1960, when we wore muumuus and drove a jeep with a pink-striped top all over the island. Diamond Head was clearly visible from downtown Oahu in 1960. In 1971 it was hidden by high-rise resort hotels.

As part of convention activities, we cruised Pearl Harbor and visited the U.S.S. Arizona Memorial. One could see small drops of oil on the water nearby, a result of oil leaking from those tanks after 30-some years. A very solemn group of people studied the names of victims of that tragic December 7th. We were told by the guides that many of the U.S.S. Arizona survivors, who were on leave that fateful December morning, have chosen to have their ashes put to rest with their crew members.

Before our Oahu, Hawaii Convention, Bob and I entertained at a pre-Hawaii party at our house. I pulled my old ukulele out of the trunk and entertained our guests with my version of "Tiny Bubbles." Following the Oahu Convention, we met with

Regional Managers and their wives at the sparsely populated Island of Maui. I look back and remember how I picked up the handle of Maui Mae. One of the Regional Manager's wives, a blond, and I, a brunette, exchanged wigs and really let our hair down. I was not aware that Bob was putting all of this on video until it showed up at a housewarming party for one of our local employees.

It was at our Mackinaw Island Convention that we hired a palm reader to entertain the attendees. She briefly looked at my palm then made the statement, "You never look at a price tag before you buy—you obviously like nice things." I believe my white mink stole and diamonds told her more than did my palm. What made me chuckle was the fact that I was wearing a pair of heels, purchased at a garage sale for seventy-five cents.

Harold and Sheila Schaefer and Bob and I were members of a dance club that met monthly. Harold Schaefer and Bob had been friends since childhood. The dance club gave me an excuse to have a closet full of formal gowns and to wear my high heels. I loved high heeled shoes and at one time had collected over 100 pairs. Bob built a special closet in the hallway with shelves to hold all of them.

In the late sixties, Bob and I were invited to a reception at the Schaefer's for Satchel Paige, who was visiting Bismarck for the first time in more than thirty years. Satchel Paige played on the same baseball team with Bob and Harold in the mid-thirties. In 1935 African American players were comfortable living in Bismarck. "It was one of the few cities where black players were treated fairly and equally," Satchel said. It seemed that North Dakota people didn't feel they had to impress anyone.

Mackinaw Island Convention
The Edicks

Banff Convention
Front row from left—LaVera, Bob

Satchel Paige was the star of the Semi-Pro team that captured the nation's attention as one of the first integrated baseball team in history. They won the first National Semi-Pro Tournament.

In a depression era world that was very much black and white, Bismarck manager Churchill saw beyond color and filled out a team based on talent. Paige, who was playing for the Cleveland Indians when they won the 1948 World Series, said the 1935 Bismarck team was the best he ever played on.

One day, out of the blue, Bob said, "If you were to die tomorrow, no one would come to your funeral but Provident people." It was years before I realized he probably made that statement with a purpose in mind. He realized my need to reach out. I did a lot of soul searching and remembered some of the dreams I had tucked away in my attic of memories. Because one dream was to complete my education, I made plans to study for my G.E.D. exams and possibly enroll in a community college.

I started bowling in a league without using my last name. Was I able to make friends with those who didn't feel obligated to be my friend? I enrolled in a class to learn Norwegian knitting and started taking art lessons.

Bob and I were overjoyed when, in the summer of 1964, we found we were to become parents. Bob was 49, I was 38 and the baby was due in January. Now Bob would have someone to study under that pull down lamp in the kitchen.

Chapter 13

BLESSED WITH MY FIFTH BABY, ROBERT ALLAN

The wind howled and threatened snow. The thermometer registered a minus thirty-five degrees. It was midnight. I had awakened half an hour earlier with a sudden, sharp pain. I was pregnant with my fifth baby and I recognized the warning signal.

Bob, my husband, was sleeping soundly, snoring now and then. No need to disturb him until I was sure it wasn't just false labor pains. I packed a small bag with a toothbrush, comb, brush and all the things one would put in a bag for a hospital stay.

I made a pot of coffee. After a couple more pains, I began to time them—fifteen minutes apart, then ten! I shook Bob gently, "Honey, it's time to go to the hospital. How about a cup of coffee first, it's bitter cold out there?" He exploded as he started pulling on his trousers, "Why on earth do you want coffee now?" I hurriedly scribbled a note for the children, "Have gone to the hospital to get our new baby." Bob half carried, half pushed me to the car—no coffee!

Robert Allan was born in Bismarck Hospital at 3:46 a.m. His daddy was excited, then angry when the nurse jokingly told him he was the father of twins.

Little Bobby's arrival was quite an event for the Edick family. My oldest daughter, Sharri, was 21 years old and my second daughter, Carolyn, was married and had a fifteen-month-old baby, Rickie Dean. Bobby was an uncle when he was born.

Big Bob was bursting with pride. Little Bobby was very nonchalant about the whole thing and this strange new world he was in. He asked for very little, only food and dry diapers.

Little did I anticipate the reaction of Bob's employees and friends. Toys and flowers soon filled my room, including a dozen long stemmed red roses from Bob. I remarked, "Too bad they won't last, they wilt so fast." On Bob's next visit he brought a gold rose pin and earring set.

Among the toys were a baseball and several footballs for the new little Bob. He was bound to be an athlete; after all, his father played football for the University of North Dakota.

Birth announcements were sent in the form of a Provident Life Insurance policy.

Things were never quite the same after we brought Bobby home. He very quickly captured our love.

Mike was nine and letting everyone know, "I have a baby brother." Why shouldn't he be excited? He had three sisters. Mike held his little brother, changed his diapers and propped him up in the carrier seat to listen to him practice on the piano. Bobby responded with a smile and a coo.

Daddy Bob bought a movie camera to record on film each new development in his son's life. Bobby was crawling and had learned the location of every cupboard door that he could open. He scooted down the stairs on his tummy and at nine months he was walking.

Proud Parents

Bobby and Sharri

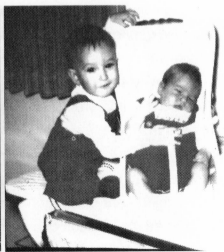

Rickie Dean and Uncle Bobby

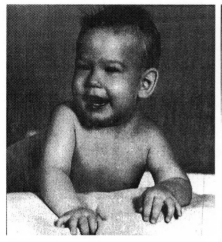

Robert Allan—6 months

Robert Allan and his mommy

Rickie Dean on Grandma's lap

I loved to rock him and sing lullabies as I had with my other four babies, but Bobby put his little hand over my mouth and said "No, mommy, no."

Bobby learned to cook while he was still in diapers. Bob liked to get up early with him and let me, the night owl, sleep in. We have movies his Dad took of Bobby in his pajamas, pulling an electric skillet from the cupboard, plugging it in, getting an egg from the refrigerator and frying it. He is a fabulous cook 46 years later.

I was so fortunate to be a stay at home mom when Bobby was little; there was time to sit on the floor and build Lincoln Log houses and Tinker Toy structures and time to read bedtime stories. I taped some of them so he could hear Mommy read when she was away from home. One night, after reading "just another chapter," I tucked him into bed, gave him a hug and kiss and whispered, "I love you, Bobby." "I know," he said, very matter of fact. Bobby was attending Sunday school at the Presbyterian Church and asked me to teach him how to say his prayers.

Bobby seldom cried. He was just a little guy when he ran into a door jamb and his left eye started puffing. Before I knew what had happened, he handed me a wash cloth and said, "Put some ice on it."

At 18 months Bobby was putting words together, such as: "That's all right, accident" and "Bobby do it carefully." At two years he was forming sentences: "Come over to his area," and "Isn't this a huge carrot?" He was full of questions, "Why does daddy have to go to work?" and "What are checks and credit cards?" He commented that the airplane was wasting gas when it idled. After a trip to the zoo he called his dog Wendy a timber wolf and his kitty a cougar.

Bobby's first dog was a schnauzer named Wendy. When she was flown to us from a kennel in Minneapolis her ears had just been clipped and were bandaged. Bobby had a bandaged thumb that needed to be soaked in Ivory soap and re-bandaged twice a day. I found little Bobby with his new puppy in his bed, scissors in one hand, gauze in the other, just in time.

Wendy was Bobby's playmate for a game of tug of war with Mom's old nylon, but his kitty was his favorite. "My kitty understands what I say," he told me. Indeed it seemed that he did.

Kitty Kim, a Siamese who was Bobby's pet, was cross-eyed and clumsy, but had a "teddy bear" personality. Kitty Kim and Beckie's cat, Candy, mated. When their first litter of kittens was born, I kept them separated thinking the male cat might hurt the babies, but after listening to him cry for a few hours, I could take it no longer. I let him join his family. Kitty Kim was the proud daddy. He groomed his babies, sat with them in their box in the basement while mommy Candy stayed upstairs, her usual proud, sophisticated self. She went to the basement only long enough to feed her babies. One day I walked into the kitchen to see Candy on the counter of the cabinet where I kept my sterling silver. She had opened the door and was grooming herself, using my silver teapot as her mirror. She sat, turning her head from side to side, brushing her fur with her paw.

Candy, also Siamese, really didn't like many of the family members and certainly not strangers! When my mother came to visit, Candy sat on the bottom stair step and challenged Mom to come upstairs until I came to the rescue. The meter man refused to come in to read the meter unless he was assured the "mean cat" had been locked up.

Although dogs have always held a special spot in my heart, one cat, Kee Kee, let me know she loved me. Kee Kee was Bobby's cat; she slept with him and ignored me until I lost my German shepherd, Czar. Since she seemed to know I needed her, she began sleeping with me and showering me with affection. When I brought a new puppy home, she went back to her Bobby.

Bobby had many toys, but would have been happy with only a few. Bobby was a preschooler when he began going to the workshop with his dad who taught him to safely handle tools. He used saws, hammers, chisels and drills with the skill of a much older boy. He made wooden cars with wheels that turned and many gifts for his mommy including an easel, a jewelry box, a flashlight that really worked, and carved plaques and clay sculptures for my art collection. I found surprise gifts from him in my suitcase when I traveled with his dad. He also entertained himself for long periods of time at the kitchen table with a sketchbook and pencil, when I was working on a painting or an art project.

Grandma Edick looked forward to Bobby's visits and he loved her chocolate chip cookies, milk and hugs. Every little boy should have a grandma to remember with love.

Bobby's playmates learned not to underestimate him. He was not a bully but even older and bigger boys knew better than to pick a fight with him. Yet he was a softy when it came to girls. Clark and Laura Woodcox were neighbors and Bobby's

BOBBY AND KITTY KIM
Art by LaVera

Beckie Jo and Candy

Bobby and Wendy

best friends. It was not unusual to see him brush a tear from little Laura's eye, put an arm around her to comfort her or stoop to tie her shoe lace. Arguments with Clark over "who had the best daddy" always ended when Bobby bragged, "My daddy is twice as old as your daddy."

Bobby was in pre-school when he remarked, "Mommy, none of the other mommies have gray hair." Most of his classmates had mommies the age of my two older girls. I was 45 and my hair was salt and pepper. It was then I started getting rid of the gray and continued for the next 40 years.

I gave up league bowling, but continued knitting long enough to knit hooded Norwegian sweaters for Bobby and my two grandchildren, Sharri's Cindy Beth and Carolyn's Rickie Dean. When I finished the last of the three, in spite of a wee mistake on one arm that I thought no one but me would notice, I wrapped it to mail. My mother's words came back to haunt me; "If it is worth doing, it is worth doing well." I unwrapped the package, unraveled the sleeve and re-knit it.

One of the few spankings Bobby's daddy gave him was when we were vacationing at Lake of the Woods. Little Bobby awakened early one morning and sneaked out of our cabin unobserved. His daddy found him at a neighbors' cabin where he had invited himself in for breakfast.

Bobby was two when he made his first long trip by car: a month-long trip, with all three children, to visit Provident agents on the west coast and his sisters, Sharri and Carolyn. It was a long trip for a two year old. We played games, read, and sculpted animals from "Sculpty," a type of clay, as we traveled down the road.

We celebrated Beckie's 10th birthday in Spokane at a Chinese restaurant. She rubbed the statue Hoti's belly for good luck.

Sharri and Jay were living at Travis Air Force Base. We were staying at a motel nearby, when Bobby threw his teddy bear in the swimming pool, then jumped in after it! Mike, then an 8-year-old, rescued his brother. I stood helplessly by, another of the times I regretted never learning to swim.

We drove through the Haight Ashbury district of San Francisco with the car doors locked. Bob had his window rolled down and shot a roll of film with his 35mm camera. It was sent to Kodak to be developed, but reported lost and never returned to us. Months later we saw the shots Bob had taken, including shots of part of our car, on "60 Minutes."

The Haight Ashbury neighborhood became the center of the "San Francisco Renaissance" and with it the rise of the drug culture and a rock and roll lifestyle. College and high school students began streaming into the Haight Ashbury area during the spring break of 1967 and during that year the area became a haven for a number of top psychedelic rock performers. The song; "Be Sure to Wear Flowers in Your Hair," written by John Phillips of the Mammas and the Papas, became a hit single.

Bob made healthy contributions to the Republican Party. In 1965 we were invited to the Lyndon Baines Johnson Presidential Inauguration. Over the years, I stuffed envelopes and campaigned door to door for our candidates. When Bismarck turned 100 years old in 1972, I volunteered to do my part in helping with the celebration.

Carolyn, Richard and their little boys Rickie Dean and Jeff came to spend Christmas with us in the early seventies. The boys, including Bobby, loved the snow and had a lot of fun building snowmen. When Jeff came back to North Dakota during the summer, he said, "Grandma, why did you get rid of all the snow?"

During their Christmas visit, Rickie Dean and Bobby shared a bedroom. After all was quiet and everyone was sound asleep, they found a pan of fudge stashed in the pantry. They ate all their little tummies could hold, and then put the pan on the floor for Wendy to polish off. It didn't hurt the boys, but Wendy was a mighty sick puppy.

A few days later, when Rickie and Bobby didn't think the fire in the basement fireplace was starting fast enough, they decided that maybe some gasoline would help! They filled a Styrofoam cup from a gas can in the garage and threw it in the fireplace! Luckily neither of the boys was hurt, and the fire outside the fireplace was quickly extinguished. Rickie Dean was upset when his daddy punished him and Bobby got by with just a warning.

I passed my G.E.D. test and enrolled in junior college. I worried that Bob might be embarrassed by my admitting to our peers that I had not finished high school or attended college; however, he encouraged me to take the steps I was taking. My years at college were most rewarding, even though I was a senior citizen in class with students just out of high school. Arnold Lahren, my instructor in the class, Telling and Writing, helped me pull out of my shell and realize I could put my feelings and thoughts down on paper.

That same year I submitted my portfolio to a two year Commercial Art School and was accepted. Commercial art was a boost to my art career. We drew from live nude models, until our work was displayed at a local mall and nude models were banned from art classes in Bismarck! I learned a bit about sign painting, photography and how to design logos. (Did you know the Mc Donald's logo, the arch, is actually two French fries?)

Mr. Jackman, our instructor, read a Ray Bradbury novel *Fahrenheit 451*, while we drew our interpretation of the story. Bradbury was an American fantasy, horror, science and mystery writer.

My journal writing began during my college years:

September 6th, 1973

As I look out my classroom window, I see rolling hills, beautiful blue sky and trees along the Missouri River. Our art class is doing a mural of a Missouri River scene at the Bismarck Roller Skating Rink. I'm pondering why it is difficult to paint something beautiful and serene. Why must we search for some famous, extraordinarily breathtaking site to feel we are painting a worthwhile subject? Is life like that? Do we overlook what really brings us happiness in search of too many material possessions? What is happiness? Is it the sound of trees rustling in the breeze, the sound of a crickets chirping, water rolling and tumbling over the rocks or is it the new snow piled high on the tree branches? Is happiness the stars in the heavens on a clear summer night, a beautiful sunset or a full moon? Is it the feel of a baby touching your face or squeezing your finger, a dog greeting you when you come home or a kitten sitting in your lap purring? No, it doesn't take a wealth of material possessions to bring happiness nor does it take a fantastic famous view to make a beautiful painting.

November 25th 1974

I made Kentucky Bourbon chocolates today, 191 of them. The recipe caught my eye, reminding me of the Kentucky Derby and the chocolates we ate on our way to the races. Or perhaps it was the mint juleps we had with breakfast that made the chocolates taste so good! The races were an unforgettable adventure. I recall the rain and the ladies fancy hats dripping wet and ruined, mint juleps glasses piled high under the bleachers and "pie eyed" betters yelling for their favorite horses. I made a collage of our losing tickets and the racing forms, the most expensive piece of art work in our home. The chocolates are great!

February 27th 1974

Bob is in Washington D.C. this week, so I have the responsibility of bringing Grandma Edick home from her stay at the hospital. I asked Mike to go along and help. "What do you think she will think of my long hair?" he asked. Possibly he doesn't visit grandma as often as he would if she didn't make remarks like, "When are you going to get your hair cut, it looks terrible that way?"

November 28th 1974

Mike and Bobby brought home a German Shepherd puppy that was listed in the giveaways. I warned my friend, "If you hear a loud explosion when Bob gets home you will know he went right through the roof!" Mike has christened the puppy Zak. He put an alarm clock in the puppy's bed, which is supposed to imitate the mother's heartbeat and keep him from crying. We stocked up on Puppy Chow. "Please, God, help Dad understand, even a teenager needs a puppy to love."

November 29th 1974

At the dinner table tonight I asked Bobby how he was going to go about selling his daddy on the idea of keeping puppy Zak, "Well," Bobby said, "I'll just tell him we paid $35.00 for him, if we have that much money invested, Dad surely won't give him away." So far—so good. Daddy said, "Well, I guess if Mommy can put up with him, O.K." Bobby had another surprise waiting for his dad tonight, a life size snowman in the back yard. His charcoal eyes winked at us and seemed to say, "I'm not a bit cold, with my stocking cap, scarf and mitts." I promised Bobby we would get a picture of him tomorrow.

December 1st 1974

One night a week is Bobby's night out. He chooses where we eat and what we do together; tonight was bowling. Daddy went to get the shoes. "What size," he asked me, "9 ½ or 10?" I wear a 7 ½. How should I expect him to remember, after all, he has only known me for 15 years! Bob is a good bowler. Bobby and I are in the same league, the "gutter ball league." Bobby was upset when his dad wouldn't stay after bowling for a game of pool. I don't think it was just playing pool, Bobby had a better chance of winning at pool and he needed to prove that he wasn't always a loser.

Daddy and Mike took care of Bobby for a week one summer, allowing Beckie and me to attend Art Camp at the International Peace Garden. It was an enjoyable time for both of us. One of the children's projects was making masks. I was working with acrylics and remember the instructor's words. "First thing is to get dirty; you can't paint well if you are worrying about getting dirty." I thought that made sense and still follow his advice; I need a roomy apron when I paint! It was a fun-filled week. We slept in bunk beds and never have peanut butter sandwiches and Kool Aid tasted so good!

I was still trying to master my Nikon when Bobby starting racing his dirt bike. I was worried on the day of his first race. His words to me, "Well, Mom, I guess you can stay home and pout or you can come to the races and take pictures." I went to the races.

I graduated in 1976 with an Associates Degrees in Art and in Applied Science (Commercial Art), and was a member of the National Honor Fraternity of the Junior College, a Phi Theta Kappa.

That same year the United States celebrated its Bicentennial. We chose to take all three children on a tour of the East Coast. It was a perfect time to learn the history of our great country, with side trips to Gettysburg, Philadelphia and Washington D.C.

Bob made sure all three of the younger children learned to fish at an early age. Family fishing trips to Westport, Washington were special. One of Bobby's best friends, Wes Winkler, often accompanied us. Deep sea fishing wasn't my thing, (I fed the fish), but shopping was. We bought treasures I found in antique shops as well as dozens of cans of smoked salmon.

An upcoming Provident Convention in San Juan, Puerto Rico, prompted Bob and me to convince Bobby's teacher that he would gain more knowledge from a ten-day excursion to Puerto Rico than from a week at school. He took his weekly

Bobby Nov 6, '73

Art by Bobby

Bobby on his bike

assignment with him and wrote an essay about the history of old San Juan. The boys spent a lot of time fishing, while I spent time learning to use my Nikon. I recall a nasty day, rain running off my head and glasses, but I was still taking pictures when a policeman stopped me with, "Senorita, the case is covering the lens."

The Puerto Ricans are a mixture of Inca Indian, Black and Spanish—or so a shop owner told me. St. Thomas, one of the Virgin Islands, only half an hour away by air, was populated by an entirely different race. They were dark English Black. They walked with a "Calypso" beat and spoke Pigeon English.

We were given free liquor with our tickets to St. Thomas. Dad and Bobby tried their luck at deep sea fishing, leaving me to pursue my favorite hobby of those days, shopping. At the end of the day, loaded down with three bottles of rum and my treasures from the shops, I was on my way to meet the boys at our hotel. An older lady with a New York accent offered to lighten my load. She asked, "Where are you from?" When I answered "North Dakota," she looked at me long and hard before saying, "But you look pretty good." North Dakota must have seemed to her the end of civilization.

Reluctantly leaving San Juan, we packed an unusual branch, or "found art" and stashed it in the trunk. I was trying to trim it to fit in our luggage when joggers came to my rescue with a pocket knife. Found art items, among them a rock with a face, helped decorate our home.

I loved our home and enjoyed decorating it. It usually had a lived in look; however, it was cleaned to perfection the weekend it was on the Easter Star Tour of Homes.

Bobby, as his siblings before him, learned at an early age to share with those less fortunate. He helped make candy and package it to send to the elderly, shut-ins and the lonely.

I treasure memories of things that were important to Bobby and to me as he was growing up: the wild crocus he dug while fishing with his dad, then carried it home in a minnow bucket; the antique overhead light shade he dug up in a field, (it now hangs in the bathroom at our cabin); the rock, with a face found in a shovel of rock at his first job; the clown figurine he bought for me from his first paycheck.

Every spring Bobby would come home with a helmet of wild asparagus found at Sibley Island, and then there was the wild horseradish that made us cry when we ground it! Bobby planted wild grape vines on the fence in the back yard. He picked the grapes, sharing them with one of his friends' dads who made jelly to share with us.

August 16th 1976 (from my journal)

(More than ten years of living the life of "First Lady of Provident" had not taken away my early training, "a penny saved is a penny earned," or perhaps it was the need during World War II rationing to not run out of food.) I have put 60 loaves of zucchini bread in the freezer as well as 30 ears of sweet corn and a bushel of green beans.

Bobby remembers going to the bakery with me and buying day old bread to freeze as well as trips to the grocery store when whole chickens were on sale. We stocked up on them and he helped me cut up and package them for the freezer. Bobby learned to economize when he was in college; he compared prices of groceries and never used prepared mixes.

He still makes his own noodles and pie crusts, and during the Juneberry season it is not unlike him to make and freeze a couple dozen pies.

Bobby must have been born an entrepreneur. He had a profitable firewood business at a very young age and began his career in construction when he and his friend Wes built a small addition, a mud room, onto our new lake cabin.

In 1980 Bob retired, after 43 years with Provident. The "Provident Beacon" dedicated an issue to him and their longtime "First Lady."

AFTER 43 YEARS . . .

FAREWELL

Robert W. (Bob) Edick, Chairman of the Board, will be retiring from the company at the end of July. Bob will have spent 43 years with Provident.

Bob was born in Deadwood, South Dakota on July 28, 1915. His father died during the flu epidemic of 1919, and he and his mother lived in Arizona and Minnesota before moving to Bismarck. Bob attended both elementary and high school in Bismarck, graduating from Bismarck High in 1932. He was an outstanding football player in high school and during the summer months was a lifeguard at the local swimming pool.

After graduating from high school, Bob attended Jamestown College, where he participated in wrestling and played on the football team, and was captain on the 1933 all-conference football team. His next three years were spent at the University of North Dakota, where Bob again displayed his expertise on the football field and on the school's wrestling team. Bob was a member of the Phi Delta Theta Fraternity. In spite of all his extra curricular activities, Bob graduated with a degree in General Industrial Engineering.

One month later he joined the ranks of Provident Life, whose offices were located on the second floor of the old First National Bank building on main street. Provident Life had been formed by a group of enterprising businessmen in 1915. When Bob joined the company, the top officers were Fred L. Conklin, President; Henry A. Jones, Vice President and Henricka Beach, Secretary. Shortly after Bob came with the company, they moved into their own office building at Second and Broadway, where the company did business until moving into their present building in October of 1954. Bob was very instrumental in seeing that the move from the old building to the new would go on schedule, and you can be sure with Bob handling the details, the move went without a hitch.

Bob started in the Auditing Department, then into the Underwriting Section, and in less than two years was named Assistant Secretary under Miss Beach. In 1942 he was named Secretary of the Company, replacing Miss Beach who had retired. Four years later he was named to the Board of Directors. In 1954 he became Vice President, and four years later was named Senior Vice President, and on April 16, 1963 Bob Edick became President of Provident Life. It was a big day in the life of this

Always active in civic affairs, he served on the Junior Chamber of Commerce, Chamber of Commerce, was a Trustee of the Presbyterian Church, a Director of the First National Bank and of the local YMCA.

Bob loves to present awards, and after he became President, he had plenty of opportunities. Going away presents, Friday noon luncheon awards, Inner Circle presentations plus all the awards that are presented at the Provident Conventions. He loved to recognize people for their many achievements.

He never missed the annual Christmas Party each year, and took an active part in most of them. I guess you would have to say the highlight of the Christmas Party was when Bob delegated "Elves" to pass out the Christmas bonuses. He also participated actively in our summer picnics. In his younger days he was always in the softball game, but in later years it was mostly heading up the chow line.

During World War II, Bob spent twenty months in Uncle Sam's Navy as an Ensign in the South Pacific. He served as a Supply Officer. Upon his discharge from the service he returned to work at Provident.

Bob and his wife LaVera have a son Bobby 15, the "apple of his daddy's eye".

It is the pleasure of the entire Beacon staff to dedicate this issue to you, Bob Edick.

Good luck Bob, it was a pleasure working with you.

Bob and LaVera

And Farewell to Our Longtime "First Lady"

LaVera Edick

The saying used to be "there's a good woman behind every successful man," but with ERA we tend to believe "alongside" would be more appropriate. And the woman who has walked "alongside" our former president we found a successful and talented lady, who along with raising a family of five, has been active in civic and cultural projects. (Paintings and a sculpture are pictured on this page and throughout the article.

Although her husband is retiring this month after 43 years with Provident Life LaVera Edick's lifestyle will change very little—at least for the next few years.

"Bob and Bobby, Jr., (15) will be spending quite a bit of time this summer renovating the cabin we bought on Lake Sakakawea," she said, "but until Bobby graduates, we'll remain here."

Not lacking for ways to spend any leisure time she may have, LaVera has in fact, made painting her prime avocation. Their tastefully decorated home at 1100 1st Street, reflects this lady's artistic talent. She is not only interested in all forms of art, but has spent a great deal of time and effort promoting cultural projects in Bismarck, and especially the E'lan Gallery.

Like the definition of the word, "e'lan": "to go forth with great exuberance," LaVera was not only instrumental in making the dream of an art gallery in our city a reality, but is an enthusiastic supporter. She is also a charter member of the Gallery, and a past president.

Her involvement in cultural organizations also includes serving as president of the Bismarck branch of the National League of American Pen Women, and membership in the Bismarck Art Association.

LaVera's interest in painting stemmed in part from her work in establishing E'lan as a public art gallery. It was about 10 years ago she began studying with Connie Gertz, a local artist and Gallery member. Later she attended art classes instructed by Rosemary Landsberger, a well-known North Dakota artist and teacher, who has gained national prominence. LaVera, who holds Associate Degrees in Art and Commercial Art from Bismarck Junior College, worked with Mr. Jackman, commercial art instructor, and Ardyce Miller (wife of Bob Miller), freelance art teacher. She has also had an opportunity to attend one of Arizona artist Zoltan Szabo's workshops.

She has exhibited and earned recognition at many art shows throughout the state, including Bismarck and Mandan art association events, besides having individual exhibits. LaVera works primarily in oils, but has used other media including acrylic and watercolor. Her subject matter ranges from portraits and still life to landscapes. One that particularly captured our hearts was a profile study of their son Bobby and one of their grandchildren, gazing out the window.

Recently she received an award at a Jamestown art exhibit for a charming view of a church steeple done in oil, which later she presented to the State Mental Hospital at Jamestown. Besides selling some of her work, she has donated several canvasses to organizations for charity benefits and to ice hockey. LaVera has picked up the knife and recently tried her hand at sculpting. The results are a beautiful impressionistic carving of hand-rubbed redwood, with intricate, flowing lines. Although her personal criticism of the results were "that I get too humanistic," we found it delightful to the eye.

She not only enjoys making new wood into things of beauty, but has long been a collector of antiques, which she has lovingly restored to their original charm. During the summer, she enjoys getting outdoors, where she grows tea roses in beds bordering their home. (Doug, our official photographer, tried to get a few shots of the colorful blossoms, but the camera does not do them justice when depicted in black and white.)

With seven grandchildren to dote on plus Bob's love of fishing and hunting, and LaVera's interest in art, the Edicks' retirement years will be full and rewarding ones.

Chapter 14

MY LOVE OF ART AND SISTERS AT HEART

Graduation from college gave me time at my easel and time to do volunteer work. Promoting the Arts in the community helped express and share my love of art. Perhaps the realization of a need to promote art appreciation began when, as First Lady of Provident, I entertained prospective employees' wives while their husbands were being interviewed. I was often asked, "Where are your art galleries?" In 1963 not even one art gallery could be found in the Bismarck-Mandan area. In the early 1940's, the Bismarck Art Association was the beginning of art appreciation in the area when a few artists began showing their work at an annual show. In 1967 the idea of a gallery was introduced by Connie Gertz when she rented space to teach art classes and charged the students a monthly fee. She suggested forming a gallery and naming it Elan, meaning to go forth with great enthusiasm! In September of 1968, when Connie moved out of town, by-laws were drawn up, the name Elan was adopted and officers were elected from the few founding members. Vi Frier was elected president, LaVera Edick, vice president, Jewel Hofmann, treasurer and Doris Asplund, secretary. Our first gallery was a church building on 11th Street and Avenue B. We solicited funds from local businesses, banks, hospitals, and, of course, Provident Life to keep our doors open. We wrote a grant application and received $500.00 from Dakota West Art's Council.

The National Endowment for the arts, created by an act of Congress in 1965, is an independent federal agency supporting artists and art organizations and bringing the arts to all Americans. Dakota West Arts Council received an annual grant through the national agency which they, in turn, granted to local artists and art galleries.

Elan Gallery changed locations a number of times before renting a two-story house near the City Library, known as the Foley Home. The house was built by James Foley in 1907. He was Poet Laureate of North Dakota in the 1930's. In 1994 the house was placed on the "Historical Homes" list and today is among other historical Bismarck buildings at Buckstop Junction, a museum park in Bismarck.

Our new gallery was badly in need of a face lift. A handful of artists rolled up their sleeves, used lots of soap and water, painted, hung wall paper and made drapes. We were proud of the end results and we were finding more and more charter members.

The first Elan Summer Art Fair and Bake Sale was held in the gallery's yard in 1974. Now known as "Capital A" Fair, it is held annually on the state capitol grounds and draws artists and crafters from across the country.

On January 1, 1983, Elan Art Gallery merged with Bismarck Art Association to become Bismarck Art and Galleries Association, (BAGA). In 1991, BAGA moved to their present location 422 East Front Street. In 1992, 300 artists displayed their work at the annual fall show.

The Board of Directors of the Bismarck Art Association awards the 1982 Honor Citation to LaVera Edick for her many contributions of time and talent to the visual arts in the Bismarck area. — Both administratively and artistically — LaVera has exemplified the importance of art in her life and therefore, in all of her endeavors. For these reasons, the Bismarck Art Association is pleased to honor Citation recipient LaVera Edick — this 2nd of October, 1982.

President

38th ANNUAL
BISMARCK ART ASSOCIATION
FALL SHOW 1982
"YOU GOTTA HAVE ART"
* SHOW LOCATION CHANGE
BJC ARMORY

LaVera Edick has been chosen by the Bismarck Art Association Board of Directors to receive the 1982 Honor Citation Award. LaVera was selected in recognition of her many contributions of time and talent to the visual arts in the Bismarck community.

LaVera served as Co-director of the Bismarck Art Association's Annual Art Exhibit in 1971 and has worked on many of their committees for the exhibits over the years. She has also been active with the Religious Arts Festival each year.

She is a Charter Member and past president of the E'lan Art Gallery and the Bismarck Branch of the National League of American Pen Women, and has served in several other offices of these organizations.

She has exhibited and received recognition for her art work in many shows throughout the state and her wood sculpture was selected for the Bismarck Art Association's First Juried Art Show "Stage One-Eighty One," at the Gannon Gallery.

LaVera has an Associate of Arts degree from BJC and has attended several art workshops and classes to further her knowledge of art. She has also taught art classes at the Senior Citizens Center on a volunteer basis.

In the past few years, LaVera has devoted much time to the study of American Indian Art. She is an exemplification of a life concerned with the arts, be it in producing or studying the many facets of art or working administratively in the art field.

Bob and LaVera

In 2011, BAGA burned the mortgage on the space they occupy. They work consistently to stimulate the study and presentation of the visual arts; they hold monthly exhibits of local, regional and national artists. It has been more than 40 years since the first gallery, the Elan, opened its doors in Bismarck-Mandan.

My personal art career was thriving. I entered shows, sold a few paintings and donated many to non-profit organizations such as the North Dakota Mental Health Association and North Dakota State Hospital. I felt it might help brighten the day for those who lived there. I also donated a painting to the "Hockey Boosters" for their fund raiser. In more recent years, several of my paintings are donated annually to the Anne Carlsen Center for Children in Jamestown, to be sold at a fundraising auction.

Volunteer work as an art teacher at the Burleigh County Senior Health Center and at the School of Hope for handicapped children was very rewarding. The children there were so loving and appreciative. Many of the seniors had always wanted to take art lessons but busy lives had kept them from it. One of my students entered her painting in an art show and won an award. It made the day for both of us!

My artist friend Jewel and I directed the fall art show in 1971. In 1982, I was chosen as artist of the year by the Bismarck Art Association. I continued entering area art shows and volunteering help at the local shows. I won a few cash awards and some of my work was selected to hang at the State Capitol during legislative sessions.

Jewel Hofmann, Ann Hayes, Bonnie Kosir and I were among the artists who painted murals of Paris' Montmartre,

The National League of American Pen Women, Inc.

PRESIDENT'S CITATION

Presented to

LaVera Edick

I, Grace Powers Hudson, President of The National League of American Pen Women, Inc. do hereby confer upon you the President's Citation for your contribution to the welfare of our organization as you have served as President of your state 1986-1988.

This certificate is an earnest expression of appreciation and a symbol for the splendid quality of service rendered.

Given under the Corporate Seal of The National League of American Pen Women, Inc. this 18th day of April, 1988 at the Biennial in Washington, D.C.

Grace Hale Hudson
National President

The National League of American Pen Women, Inc. takes pleasure in announcing the election to membership of

La Vera Edick

in the classification of

Art

Washington, D.C.
October 12, 1974

Lee M. Waldrop
National President

Virginia R. Collier
Membership Chairman

Washington D.C. Home of N.L.A.P.W.

depicting the work of Toulouse Lautrec to decorate the hall for the annual Hospital Ball fund-raiser. I was able to continue my art education by studying with local artists Rosemary Landsberger and Vern Skaug and attending workshops held by well known artists such as Zoltan Szabo and Fritz Scholder.

I applied for membership, submitted my art portfolio, and was accepted as a member of the National League of American Pen Women, (NLAPW) on October 12, 1974. Their home in Washington, D.C., the former home of President Lincoln's son, Todd Lincoln, is beautifully furnished with antiques and has sleeping rooms that are rented to visiting Pen Women for only ten dollars a night. A library holds copies of books by Pen Women authors and the walls display paintings of Pen Women artists.

Over a hundred years ago, women writers were not allowed to be members of the prestigious National Press Club in Washington, D.C. This poem by Pen Woman Licile Bogud tells the story:

Merry Century!

Near the turn of the century
    A hundred years ago
Ladies didn't mess around
    In men's affairs you know.
When men would write a column
    In Washington, D.C.
They'd form a club and meet for lunch
    And have themselves a spree.
But when women would write a column

The men folks locked the doors
"No ladies here!" the sign said
　　"We've told you that before."
A few courageous ladies
　　Who wrote as well as men
Got themselves together
　　The Women of the Pen.
Today we are still together
　　A full five thousand strong
We write, paint and make music
　　Right here where we belong.
So hats off to our founders
　　The gals who had the guts
To get in there and organize
　　No ifs or ands or buts!

The lady who wrote the inscription on the base of the refurbished Statue of Liberty was a Pen Woman. (I was invited to the dedication ceremony.) The Vietnam Memorial was designed by a Pen Woman. Dale Evans Rogers was a member of a NLAPW branch in California. Helen Keller, Taylor Caldwell, Hillary Rodham Clinton, and Medora, founder of historical Medora, North Dakota, were all honorary members of NLAPW. I was elected State President in 1986.

My husband, Bob, began collecting and appreciating Indian art, perhaps because he had some Native American genes. I refurbished the lower level of our home to be used as his den. I bought and refinished the first desk he sat at when he went to work for Provident Life and decorated the walls with a small collection of Indian art. Within a few years our collection included baskets, pottery, beadwork and even an Indian headdress. My interest led to the study of the various tribes and to presentations for the local Kiwanis Club, Bismarck Junior College Art Class, and Mrs. Stump's 5th grade class at Will-Moore Elementary, where my granddaughter was a student. The entire class wrote thank-you notes with illustrations of our Indian art display.

The 1860's was a time of tremendous change and new ideas, especially for women, a time when the country was rebuilding itself after the Civil War. It was during those years that completion of both the American Transcontinental Railroad and the Suez Canal was celebrated. The world could now be navigated in record time!

The bicycle was invented in 1861, giving personal independence and freedom. The early 60's also saw the invention of the safety pin, rayon, pasteurization of milk, the internal combustion engine, the machine gun and dynamite—all of which had an impact on daily and commercial life. The typewriter and sewing machine date from this period as does the impressionistic movement in art.

I was invited to become a member of P.E.O. and was initiated into Bismarck Chapter AA in May of 1973. P.E.O. was founded in 1869 at Iowa Wesleyan College by a group of seven young women, most of them college students. Today, P.E.O. is an international women's organization with nearly 250,000 members in the United States and Canada. It is a philanthropic organization where women motivate each other to achieve their highest aspirations. P.E.O. has provided loans and scholarships to more than two million eighty-three thousand women through five educational, financial assistance programs

My dear ⟨name⟩,

It is a pleasure to extend to you the invitation of Chapter A A State of North Dakota to become a member of the P. E. O. Sisterhood. In accepting this invitation you are required to affirm your belief in God and to state that you come voluntarily, with a desire to be of service to the Sisterhood.

The initiation fee is ten dollars which should accompany your acceptance of this invitation.

Sincerely yours,

⟨signature⟩ (Mrs T.B.)

Corresponding Secretary

OPENING ODE

We who are sisters in heart and spirit, give thanks for the star and its message.

May Purity, Justice, Faith, Truth and Love make glad and holy the secret places of our hearts.   Amen.

OBJECTS AND AIMS

The objects and aims of this Sisterhood shall be general improvement, which shall comprehend more especially the following points:

To seek growth in charity toward all with whom we associate and a just comprehension of and adherence to the qualities of Faith, Love, Purity, Justice and Truth.

To seek growth in knowledge and in culture and to obtain all possible wisdom from nature, art, books, study and society, and to radiate all light possible by conversation, by writing and by the right exercise of any talent we possess.

To aim at self-control, equipoise, and symmetry of character, and temperance in opinions, speech and habits.

It shall be the chief duty of each member to consider thoughtfully the full import of P.E.O. This will include a sincere regard for our influence in the community, a careful consideration of feeling when speaking and a determination to do all we can, at all times, and under all circumstances to express a loving concern for each sister.

and graduated more than eight thousand from P.E.O.'s Cottey College.

The educational loan fund lends money to worthy students of college age. In 1949, after World War II, an International Peace Scholarship was established after a group of P.E.O.'s, sitting around the kitchen table said, "We need to do something to help bring about world peace." This fund encourages women from all countries to pursue graduate study in the United States and Canada.

In 1971, P.E.O. explored the need for a new project enabling women, whose education had been interrupted, to return to school to support themselves and their families. (My daughter Beckie, with three children to support, received a grant from P.E.O. to help her obtain her degree in nursing.)

P.E.O.'s are extremely caring women who develop close lifelong friendships. Recognizing that the bonds of sisterhood create a source of energy for helping women, they take seriously their commitment to each other and the world.

My P.E.O. sisters often asked me to present the program at a chapter meeting. A P.E.O. sister commented, "LaVera presented a fascinating program entitled "Probing Past Times." During coffee time we were invited to browse the "Indian Room" of their home. It is quite likely that 200 years from now, some young people will be in the Bismarck area, having arrived by spaceship, checking state and local records and asking questions of the local folk about a lady, talented in painting and writing. Recounting all the things they have heard about this fabulous lady and wanting to see for themselves the place where great-great-great-great-grandmother LaVera

(Woodring) Edick lived, they may say with pride, "Do you know that she was a P.E.O., too?"

The title, "My Favorite Thing," for another presentation gave me much food for thought, a reason to review the pattern of my life. Our genes influence who and what we are, as do special people in our lives. Although my life's journey has led me in many directions, my motivating theme has been the Love of Life. Though I didn't have a biological sister, I've found many Sisters at Heart, including my P.E.O. sisters.

I was elected president of my P.E.O. chapter in 1988. I am proud of the fact that both NLSPW and P.E.O. are known for the recognition and protection of women.

Once I dreamed of visiting far-away places; however, family responsibilities came first. In 1978 when Carolyn asked me to accompany her to Spain and Morocco, I didn't hesitate in answering, "I'll apply for my passport tomorrow." We had a wonderful ten days together. I bought a toy sword for Mike in Toledo and we rode camels in Morocco. Quite by accident, we crashed a General Electric party being entertained by belly dancers, and even toured the night clubs with our handsome Moroccan guide, who had eyes for Carolyn!

A few years later, Carolyn invited me and her sisters to visit London with her. What a thoughtful, generous lady and what wonderful memories! Memories include those of a "Jack the Ripper" walking tour one cold, foggy evening, and Liz Taylor on stage in "Lil' Foxes."

In 1984, Bob and I toured Europe with my art class. We stayed an extra week to visit Alsace, the land of my Vautrin-Wotring family and I earned three college credits. Although I didn't complete my four year degree in art, I continued working toward it. In 1985, I accumulated two more credits by attending a writing workshop held in Duluth, Minnesota, by the University of Minnesota.

A few months before Bob's retirement in1980, we bought a very old, two-bedroom cabin on Lake Sakajawea. It became a weekend project. Bobby and I hauled rock from the area and built a wall and base to hold a Franklin coal-wood stove as heat for the cabin. Beckie, pregnant with Taylor, spent many hours helping make the place livable with paint, paper and elbow grease! We tore out old, worn linoleum and rented a sander. Czar, my German Shepherd, kept me company for a couple of days while I refinished the floors; the kitchen came first, with furniture piled high in one bedroom and the living room. A beautiful moon greeted Czar and me as we walked down to the lake before climbing in the second bedroom window and falling asleep on a mattress lying on the floor. The finished floors were a bit uneven, but they matched the rest of the cabin.

Bobby and his friend Wes, both teenagers, built a mud-room off the back door of the cabin. Mike and Sheryl also helped, but they were busy building their own home on the river south of Mandan.

Another of Bobby's projects was to construct a redwood hot tub. Over the years, all the little ones in the family learned to swim in that hot tub. Before the days of the hot tub or a bathroom, I used to bathe on the deck in the kids' plastic swimming pool. Of course, it was dark, after the kids were in bed and the neighbors weren't home!

There are many memories as I look around the cabin rooms today. The antique oak chairs around the kitchen table were

Our Lake Cabin

"Then"

"Now"

covered with red, green and orange paint before I refinished them and added new cane seats. The china closet, purchased at a farm auction for $14.00 also was refinished. Bobby found bentwood chairs and a coffee table in a deserted barn. The claw-foot bathtub and corner sink came from the old Patterson Hotel, at a cost of $5.00 if "you haul it away."

Bob loved the cabin and spent hours planning the addition of a lake room, bedroom, laundry room and bath. Bobby did the lion's share of the construction which was probably where his construction career actually began. The entire family has contributed to the cabin as it is today, a beautiful, modern, five bedroom, two bathroom home.

A "face make-over" by an Estee Lauder representative led to a very successful fundraiser for Dakota West Arts Counsel. It all began when Donna, from the Estee Lauder home office, was teaching me how to use their cosmetics and I was, as usual, talking about the arts. The idea of a fundraiser called "Art on a Living Canvas" was born. Co-sponsored by Estee Lauder, Herberger's Department Store and DWAC, with a planning committee that I chaired, we raised $2,500.00 for the Arts. Held at the Holiday Inn, the evening included a delicious dinner, while on stage live models from the audience were given a face make-over by Estee representatives. Easels were placed around the room where BAGA artists painted faces on canvas. Estee gave away very generous door prizes of their cosmetics and a special gift to me was the largest bottle of "Knowing" perfume—still my favorite.

The following year Herbergers and DWAC co-sponsored a Secretaries Day style show, "Spring Fling." With much help from fellow artists, I chaired the event. Local businessmen were asked to escort the models to the stage. The manager of Herbergers said to me, "If you ever want a job, let me know."

The National Assembly of Art Agencies was held in Washington, D.C. in 1988. As vice president of Dakota West Arts Council, I was sent as a delegate. We were invited to "The Gala Bash" at the prestigious National Press Club and were entertained by a satire group, "The Dirty Die," the hilarious take-off of a current political scandal. A New York Art Association reception was hosted by none other than their president, Kitty Carlisle. I recall the jam session in the hospitality room, with someone at the piano, others strumming guitars and banjos and even "washboard strings,"—a fun-loving group dedicated to promoting the arts. It was an enjoyable time, but also a big responsibility to take back the knowledge I had gained to benefit our local art community.

I was president of DWAC in 1990, and took an active part on various boards: as an advisor for Prairie Skies Art Exhibit and Auction, sponsored by the N.D. Nurses Association; on a planning committee for a Centennial Arts Conference to be held in Aberdeen, South Dakota, and as a coordinator for the "Arts Beyond Boundaries" conferences in Rapid City and Medora. I also gave a dedication speech for the Eagle Sculpture at Pioneer Park in Bismarck.

At the International Convention held in San Diego in 1990, I met a writer who taught poetry at Folsom Prison. He sent me copies of some very "tear jerking" poetry written by his students, the "lifers."

Art left the canvas when a small group of my artist friends and I started a "Crazy Quilt Club." According to folklore, "The crazy quilt was first made by pioneer women and so-called because, with all the hardships they endured, quilting kept them from 'going crazy'." I attended a Bobbin Lace class long enough to collect a few choice bobbins, make a lace-making cushion and a twelve-inch long piece of bobbin lace. My great-great-great-great-grandmother, Hannah (Hitchcock) Frost made and sold bobbin lace when she first came to America from England in the early 1800's. It was used to embellish men's shirt collars and cuffs.

I wore many different hats during the 80's and 90's. Entries in my journal tell part of the story:

January 1985:

Went to B.T.O. (Big Time Operators Investment Club) this morning. We sold 100 shares of Apache Oil stock and 100 shares of Service Master stock and bought 100 shares of Reynolds Tobacco Company. I voted against the purchase as I'm hoping tobacco companies will all go broke! However, Reynolds is so diversified that they are buying all sorts of companies, from Kentucky Fried Chicken and Oreo Cookies to Nabisco. B.T.O. is made up of eighteen women who each put $20.00 a month into the treasury. My main interest is to learn a bit more about stocks and bonds.

February 1987:

Painted Pei Pei, a little Chinese girl, to learn to paint different skin colors; I gave the painting to her mother.

June 1987:

Visited the big island of Hawaii, as a guest of Jackie and her friend Doris, to recuperate from gallbladder surgery. "Pigged" out on papaya!

December 1987:

Painted portraits of all my grandchildren as Christmas gifts for their parents.

January 1988:

Taking a series of Sunday classes at Bismarck Junior College on Eastern Religion.

February 1988:

Sold painting "Little Eskimo Girl" at St. Alexis Hospital for $175.00.

Easter 90:

As I fill my grandkids Easter baskets with twelve colorful socks holding candy and a dime in each toe, I can hear them saying, "What a goofy grandma."

August 2, 1990:

U.S. declared war on the Persian Gulf. I sat glued to the television with flashbacks to World War II. How different today, nearly fifty years have passed since 1941 when it was an announcement on radio; now it is all played out on television however, the gut feeling is still the same, the same sick feeling knowing many innocent lives will be lost.

September 10, 1990:

Bob and I spent my 65th birthday at the cabin. I sat at the kitchen table and wrote a letter to my children:

Dear Family,

An article from our church bulletin helped me understand why I feel the urge to give you some of my possessions as gifts. It is not that I plan to leave you soon, but rather a need to organize my life and my house here on earth; that being done, I'll be free to paint pictures, work on my crazy quilt and bobbin lace, and pursue genealogical research on our family. All those things one has a tendency to put off until tomorrow. Suddenly tomorrow is here and one realizes there are fewer tomorrows.

So please, feel free to let me know if there are things you would like to have. I'm not saying I'll give them to you, but then again, I might!

With love from Mother

Bobby and I first noticed Bob was having problems when he made some very costly and time consuming mistakes in the planning and construction of the addition to the cabin. Then, there was the day I found him drawing a map to help him find the way to the barber shop he had been driving to for years. Soon after that he lost the ability to safely drive his car, and one day he stacked books on the car seat and convinced ten-year-old Nickie she was old enough to drive and didn't need a license. She was caught on the way downtown by her mother and was grounded, but Grandpa wasn't. The bank called me when he put his driver's license and his credit cards in the A.T.M. machine instead of his A.T.M. card.

Both Nickie and Bobby were a lot of help watching over Bob. He spent a lot of time in his big, brown leather chair watching television and eating ice cream. Our new Westie puppy, Tina, was often in his lap. He would pet her and say, "Is she purring yet?" I answered, "She's a dog, Bob, she doesn't purr." Minutes later, "Is she purring yet?"

Nickie often came over after school and helped out when I needed to be away from the house for a few hours. She was very fond of her grandpa. She wasn't old enough to do a lot of cooking, but she knew how to make pancakes and bean burritos. Grandpa loved pancakes and would have gladly eaten them at every meal. One day Nickie found a gallon of ice cream in the dishwasher and said, "Grandpa that belongs in the freezer." "No, it doesn't," he answered, and proceeded to move things from the freezer to the dishwasher.

Bob seemed to enjoy the cabin and we spent a lot of time there. We were on our way to the cabin when I asked Bob who he used to work for. He thought a while before he answered, "Some European outfit." "What did you do for them?" I asked. "That's a good question," he said, "I had a desk job—they built bridges and things."

It was cold at the cabin and a fire in the Franklin stove would have felt good, but we were out of firewood. I found an ax and broke up an old picket fence. We needed firewood, we needed to get rid of the old fence and I needed exercise, although I got plenty of it there. I went to bed exhausted and slept like a log! Bob slept well and was perfectly content during the day sitting in the lake room looking out at the lake. If I put a "Whoopy John" record on the stereo, he would get up and dance to the music.

I felt close to my pioneer ancestors that week we spent at the cabin. I lived the life of a pioneer growing up in Nebraska. The water in the cabin had been turned off and the pipes drained. We hauled water from town and used the outhouse. It was a quiet and peaceful time, with only the birds and perhaps an animal or two to keep us company. Occasionally a deer came up into the yard, and one morning, from the kitchen window, I watched a wise old owl sitting on a nearby branch. Moving his head from side to side, he was surveying his domain. I love being close to nature where I can let my hair down and just be me.

One evening as I was refinishing a coffee table Bob said, "You are sure a handy girl to have around, would you marry me?" I answered, "Who are you married to now? I thought you were married and had a son." "No," he replied, "I've never been married or had children." It angered him when I said, "No, I think I'm too old to get married."

It was sad to see a highly intelligent man, as my Bob was, losing touch with reality. He had forgotten the life he had lived, and no longer knew his loved ones.

In spite of Bob's illness during his last years, he was able to remain at home and was not bedfast until he suffered a stroke in mid-April of 1991. He spent several days at a Bismarck hospital and would have gone into a full-time nursing home when, on April 29th, he died of a heart attack.

Bob wouldn't have minded the snow storm on the day of his funeral. He loved North Dakota, snow and all. He had a military funeral with the gun salute and I was presented with the flag. Bob had many, many friends; we received more than 175 sympathy cards and letters. My P.E.O. chapter members attended the funeral and brought food for 25 family members that evening.

Bobby found a way to ease the pain of losing his father by shutting himself in his room and designing a tombstone. The finished monument was beautiful, depicting tall North Dakota wheat, birds in flight and the statue of Sakajawea, three of the things his father loved most—North Dakota, hunting and Provident Life Insurance Company.

I am pleased that Bob and his wife, Tracee, keep Bob senior's memory alive by having his portrait displayed in their home. Nickie and her children take flowers to his grave often or just stop by to say, "We miss you, Grandpa."

From my journal—May, 1991

I have good days and bad days. I still expect to turn around and find Bob standing behind me at my desk.

July, 1991

A letter from my 80 year old friend, George Irwin:

Dear LaVera,

Just a note of things I recall from time to time—Grand Island and your home there, your family, your good work, dedication and determination. Then you were taken away, away up North, but we were happy for you and our company. They knew a good girl when they found one, and then seeing you at Kansas City meetings. You were always a beautiful person in your own way. Yes, I recall, LaVera, you had some tough breaks, but you had and have what it takes to keep on keeping on and enjoying the days ahead. I'm proud of you.

Always, George

August 3, 1991:

Garett, Amelia and I leave for Pennsylvania today. Sharri will join us for a few days in Washington, D.C. We will stay at the Pen Women house and have a key to the front door.

September, 1991

Chaperoned 20 of Nickie's teenage friends at a slumber party at the Holiday Inn. Have you ever tried sleeping in a room with wall-to-wall girls? I found myself thinking of my teen years, giggling, and of course "boy talk."

October, 1991

Met my life-long Stanley friend, Norma and her husband Pat in Minot to attend the annual "Hostfest." We saw some great shows including Red Skelton and Bill Cosby.

December, 1991

With dreams of turning the fall and winter of our lives into a long Indian Summer, Bob's cousin, Dave Edick and I, who had both lost our spouses, were married on December 14, 1991.

July, 1992

I followed Nickie to track meets throughout the years—1984 in Spearfish, South Dakota, 1986 in Casper, Wyoming and in 1992 Dave and Tina accompanied me to a Regional

Olympics Track Meet where Nickie participated. It was held in Minneapolis and many black athletes were there. They loved Tina but when I mentioned that I once had a white German Shepherd, one little black girl asked, "Why do you always have white dogs?" I pulled Tina's hair back to reveal her little tummy and said, "Look, honey, she has white hair, but her skin is dark."

I owe a debt of gratitude to my late husband, Bob. Without his emotional and financial support over the years, I would have been unable to pursue my many endeavors.

Chapter 15

MY OTHER MOTHER

Was it luck, was it destiny or was it our Guardian Angels that brought Ruth Woodring and me together again? Ruth was not only my second cousin and my friend, but in later years she became a second mother to me. Ruth and her daughter, Ana Lee, often visited us at our farm home in Nebraska when Ana Lee and I were little girls. We looked so much alike that our neighbors couldn't tell us apart and even in our pictures as adults, we could have been sisters.

It was when my daughter Sharri and her family moved to Walnut Creek, California, in 1968, that I was amazed to find Ruth living just a few blocks away. Ruth had lost her only child, Ana Lee, just months before as a result of a cerebral hemorrhage. It was a very sad time in Ruth's life and also a time when I was in need of a friend and confidante. From then on Ruth and I kept in touch by correspondence and by my frequent trips to Walnut Creek.

Early in our relationship, one of Ruth's letters to me told her story:

Dear La Vera,

In response to your last letter, I'll tell you a bit about myself. I was born January 15th, 1902, in Curtis, Nebraska. My father and your grandfather were brothers. I had two brothers, Earl and Clarence and two sisters, Bessie and Helen. Helen was just two years older than me and we were very close. I still have a letter Helen wrote to my mother in 1914. Helen was 14 and she tells of sewing a new dress for me and of baking bread. Losing Helen, much too early in her life, was a very sad time for me but somehow, I found peace. When we face difficult times in our lives, we are really never alone. A new strength comes to us. Our Guardian Angels are watching over us.

I grew up on a farm, near Stockville, Nebraska, with a beautiful grove of elm and black walnut trees overlooking Medicine Creek. I was only four when I conducted "imaginary school room classes" in a special spot in that grove of trees.

When I was fifteen the state of Nebraska granted me a credential to teach public school, grades one through eight. I taught for several years before attending State Teacher's College in Kearney, Nebraska for my teaching degree.

I was 21 and in college when I became pregnant with Ana Lee. I was in love with someone other than her father, but I married Bert Young to give Ana Lee a name. We never lived together as man and wife.

My mother died shortly after Ana Lee's birth. I returned to teach in the Stockville area and my father helped out by taking care of Ana Lee.

Ana Lee's Mother, Ruth
ca.—1935

LaVera and Ana Lee

LaVera

Ana Lee

Even as adults, we could have been sisters.

STOCKVILLE COUNTY FAIR
Art by LaVera

Ruth's Grandmother Sanders
in front of her Nebraska log home

When Ana Lee was six years old, I married Dale Corder and went to live on a farm with him for a few years. Seemed Dale loved the bottle more than either me or Ana Lee. We were divorced and I reclaimed my maiden surname, Woodring. Soon after, Ana Lee and I moved to Idaho when I found a higher salaried teaching position.

I met a soldier in Idaho who convinced me to move to San Francisco where he was stationed. Ana Lee was a teenager by this time. Everything was wonderful until I discovered "soldier boy" had a wife back in Connecticut. I may still have letters from him in the footlocker in the garage. I wouldn't want anyone but you to read them as they were "sizzlers."

Ana Lee and I both loved San Francisco. She found employment as a teen-age fashion model. I continued teaching while I pursued my own education by earning two bachelor degrees and a master's degree.

I had been teaching for forty three years and was nearing retirement age when Andy came into my life. He was twenty five years my junior. Although it is a platonic relationship, I would prefer it to be more. Age does not take away ones sexual needs or desires. Andy is a warm, loving person and a genius. He helped design the "moon buggy" for the first "walk on the moon." Neil Armstrong was the mission commander of the Apollo 11 Moon Landing on July 20, 1969.

Andy and I both bought homes in Walnut Creek and live just a few houses apart. We have dinner together whenever he is in town. He is a busy man.

We have joined an Antique Car Club and are thoroughly enjoying one another's company.

This is a real writing binge I'm on; I really didn't intend to write a book!

With love from Ruth

Ruth had lost her Ana Lee and a few years later, in 1976, I lost my mother. We needed each other. She became my "other mother" and I became her "other daughter." We could talk about anything and everything; it seemed we had a lot in common. She was also my teacher. When I made a grammatical error or misspelled a word in a letter to her she would write back, "Look it up in the dictionary." We exchanged letters for more than fifteen years. Ruth shared her life and the antics of her cat family. I told her about my busy life and my problems. She always seemed to sense when I needed a "sounding board."

Dear LaVera,

You sounded a bit sad or perhaps tired in your last letter, but I can't imagine you either tired or sad, only cheerful.

How you manage to keep up with your many activities, I'll never quite understand. Maybe it's that North Dakota climate, or perhaps a gene from your Bohemian grandmother. You come from a "Go out and do it" family. Your parents, Ray and Minnie Woodring were cut from the same mold and they no doubt inherited those characteristics, giving you an extra dose of it. Just never giving up is an important part of life, if the thing you are working for is something you really want.

Love from Ruth

Ruth with her optimistic outlook on life became a source of support during some trying times in my life.

November 8, 1982—my answer to a letter from Ruth.

Dear Ruth,

Your concern and your words of encouragement are appreciated so much. I have been doing a lot of self analysis and soul-searching. Life is becoming a bit easier than it was this past summer.

Bob, Bobby and I have been through almost three months of family therapy as outpatients at Heartview Drug and Alcohol Abuse Center. Bob is attending A.A. and I am going to Al-Anon each week. Bobby is once more the sweet kid that he has always been, his grades are improving, he is spending a lot more time at home and the line of communication between us is once again open.

Bob was an alcoholic for many years before he quit drinking on his own. What we didn't realize was how his years of alcohol abuse had affected the whole family, filling both Bobby and me with resentment that surfaced in each of us in different ways. Bob had unsolved problems because he would or could not admit that he was an alcoholic.

Bobby turned to his peers for support when he felt his family had let him down. He began experimenting with alcohol

Ruth and Andy

Ruth and Andy in "Mini"

Ruth and LaVera

and drugs and was picked up for driving while intoxicated. All this and Beckie's recent divorce proved to be too much for me. I realized I needed help, I couldn't cope by myself. Al-Anon is helping me release a lot of pent-up emotions, to really take a good look at myself and to ask God for help.

Beckie and her three children had been living with us until her father made a down payment on a house for her. She is in nurse's training and trying hard to keep up with everything. Nickie, 5, is in kindergarten, Amy, 3, in day care and Taylor,2, is with a sitter three days a week. I take care of him on Tuesdays and Thursdays.

Bob has been helping Beckie fix up her house this past month and it has been good therapy for him. Part of the problem since his retirement has been too much spare time. He follows me, in his car, every time I leave the house and even had my phone tapped so he could tape my conversations. Through therapy, he is beginning to realize that jealousy has been as much of a problem as alcoholism, all stemming from insecurity in his early years. It is going to take a lot of time and understanding but I'm more optimistic about the future than I've been in months.

My headaches are disappearing; after I broke a tooth, my dentist discovered the cause. I was gritting and grinding my teeth in my sleep as a result of tension. He fitted me with a retainer to be worn at night.

Ruth, I apologize for the long letter and for crying on your shoulder. Now it's time to count my blessings and look forward to good times in the days ahead. I admire that quality in you so much. You take time to enjoy the little things that make it all worthwhile. I feel so very fortunate to have a Ruth in my life.

                                    With love from LaVera

Ruth, always a teacher, taught me how to appreciate life and when events threw me a curve, she knew the right things to say and do to get me back on track. It seemed like God's plan. He knew we needed each other.

A quote from Ruth's letter to me:

"Thank you, LaVera, for being the sweet adorable person that you are! Our roots go back a long, long way and we still have the relationship and friendship that has followed us from those early days. I just want you to know how much I appreciate all the nice things you do for me and especially I appreciate having a LaVera in my life. You are such a good, faithful "daughter" to me. Thank you so much for your ever present help to me and for all the beautiful things you do for so many people."

Before Ruth and I became re-acquainted, my son Mike wrote a letter to Ruth asking for her help with a genealogical project at school. That sparked my interest in learning more about my family and "from whence I came." Ruth and I shared this quest and information for many years.

A note on Ruth's calendar, November 14, 1980:

Major surgery for "Lil Pinto." When she awakens she will be an electric car!

Andy built two electric cars, "Mini" and "Lil Pinto." He was probably one of the first to build and drive an electric car on California roads. He wrote, published and sold a "how to" book on how to convert a car into an electric car.

Ruth and Andy made two trips to France and Alsace searching family roots for his St. Amant family and our Woodring family. They paved the way for research Bob and I did on our trip to Europe in 1984.

Ruth and Andy were planning a third trip to France, when a heart attack took his life at a young 52 years of age.

Years later, Ruth writes:

I have been so lonely for Andy lately. I find myself with so many memories of the day he died, as if it happened yesterday. As time goes by it is supposed to get easier but it isn't. It hurts as much as ever and perhaps more; the things we used to do, his thoughtfulness in caring for me. There could never be another Andy.

Calendar note—March 31, 1981

A hint of spring, first oriole in my yard putting pep into the eyes of my cats.

Ruth enjoyed a beautiful day, a full moon, the cloud formations, a gentle breeze, a soft rain, a kitten purring on her lap, even the birds making love in the tree she could see from her kitchen window. She found enjoyment in feeding and watering the birds and learning their names. The squirrels knew they would find food as did stray cats. She adopted a family of cats. In her words: "I have something to wake up for in the morning, someone needs me, my cats are my children."

Ruth's letters to me over a period of years told the story of how love for her cats and their love for her brought joy and contentment to the senior years of her life.

Quote from my letter to Ruth, September 5, 1991

"Yes, I agree—animals are much more intelligent than we give them credit for, especially your cats, but you know what, Ruth? You are a good teacher and you are teaching your cats all the time."

Ruth stood about five feet four inches tall and weighed about 140 pounds. She wore her dyed, dark brown hair shoulder length. Her skin was smooth with few wrinkles. She had a certain "old world" beauty and charm and a twinkle in her eye. Ruth had a sense of humor and wasn't afraid to laugh at herself and her mistakes or admit that she was wrong. She said, "Keeping busy keeps us out of mischief, but I like to leave room for a bit of mischief if I see it coming along."

Ruth took good care of herself by planning nutritious meals, watching her diet and seeing the doctor regularly. She managed her money well; however, money was not a consideration when she bought gourmet food for her cat family.

Ruth stayed young in mind and spirit. She read a lot, her dictionary always handy. She kept abreast of world happenings. Six o'clock news on TV was a must. She was anxious to learn new ways and accept new ideas. She loved clothes and preferred bright colors, purples or reds and dramatic patterns. Her clothes closets were crowded with beautiful clothes, many wearing such labels as "Sax Fifth Avenue." She didn't go shopping often, only when I came to visit and we took her 1965, bright red Mustang out of mothballs.

A letter to LaVera when Ruth was 78:

Dear LaVera,

It is good to take the time to write to you. Time didn't jump at me and say "come sit," but I jumped at time saying "give me a break." I find this pen makes marks only when it is pushed, something like me, I sometimes have to be pushed.

A thought came out of the blue, one of these days I'm going to get into my study room and sort and arrange things so I can use the room again. It was a happy thought and I soon realized new for me and in keeping with the kind of person I was in the past. I'm hoping these spurts of energy will return often. This is the first time in many months I've had even a desire to make that room a habitual place to enjoy and to work on my family history.

My folks seemed to discourage my interest in genealogy, but Andy and my trips to our homeland, France, have made family history study a big part of my life in the years past. I musn't reminisce too much. After I'm rested I should be very happy. Did you know it takes energy to feel happy?

With love from Ruth

Excerpts from Ruth's letter two years later:

My right hand pains and it is difficult to grasp a pen. Previously only my left hand was affected. My ring finger and thumb are pregnant; their knuckles are extended like pregnant bellies. I am so thankful that I am able to care for my cat family, my home and myself. I try hard to keep problems and worries out of my thinking and generally I can. I have so much to be thankful for. I'm determined to snap out of any worries and let nature take its course. Just looking at the painting you did for me of a beautiful little girl with her cat relaxes me.

Part of another letter from Ruth at age 87:

I fell today trying to kill a spider. I think from now on I'll let the spiders alone, to live and multiply. My thinking has been very confused since my fall. I'm having trouble trying to keep up with the responsibility of getting things done. I can't see the light at the end of the tunnel, but I'll keep searching for it! Maybe I'm just tired today. There is so much good in the world, I should be glad to be part of it but I'm too tired to participate, which is all wrong.

When I went to visit Ruth a few weeks later, the table was covered with piles of unpaid bills and the next morning they came to turn off the electricity. It was time to grant "Power of Attorney" to me to take care of her financial responsibilities.

Ruth felt a burden lifted when her attorney drew up the papers. I ordered meals on wheels to be delivered to her each day and arranged for her to start wearing an alarm button.

A letter from Ruth only weeks later:

Dear LaVera,

I'm restless, like a cat with fleas and I'm wondering why. Neither of my Paul's, my friends across the street, approve of my getting rid of my "ball and chain" alarm button, which I detested from day one, nor the "meals on wheels," which was a godsend for a while, but I prefer being on my own. I'll miss them I'm sure, but the time has come for me to do my own thing, in my own way, as I never want to become a vegetable, maybe a fresh one, but not one that is soft and wobbly with no flavor!

There are so many things to tell you, but I can't think what they are now! What can I do to bring my thinking capacity back again? Why don't the words come to me as they used to? Of course, I know the answer, but I keep trying to believe it will return; that it will be almost okay again. Believing and having faith are good medicines. Some of my writing is almost as it used to be, I must be thinking right.

From a letter a few weeks later:

I've been trying to swat a fly which I couldn't hit if it was the size of a cow! I've been trying to write, but my thinking sometimes plays tricks on me and frankly I don't know how to handle this new problem. Of course, now that I am aware of this, I must guard against it as much as possible. I must relax more and try not to expect too much of myself.

My fingers are flying over the keys of my typewriter, unconcerned where they are going to land: it's time to quit for today. I still have much to tell you, I've only unpacked the little things on top, all the big, heavy things are underneath, but they will have to wait.

Ruth was 92 when I stayed with and cared for her for more than a month to give her caretaker a vacation. My Westie, Tina, was with me and Ruth held her in her lap by the hour. Before I left, I bought a life-sized stuffed animal, a Tina, to sit on her lap.

Ruth was living in a fantasy world. She thought no one in her family loved her because they never visited her.

I made an album for her with pictures and obituaries of her parents and sibling. We talked about it and she began to accept the fact that they were all in heaven. She was the only one left of her immediate family. She seemed less confused, her spirits improved and she laughed and joked almost like her old self.

As she aged and lost her memory, Ruth was still very aware of her appearance. She worried about the dark spots on her hands and arms. She had a crooked finger that she was going to have put in a cast, "one of these days." She noticed pretty teeth and was going to get her teeth "fixed" and wanted new, more fashionable eye glasses.

Ruth commented on what I was wearing and it bothered her when I was in my "grungies." She preferred seeing me in my better, more colorful clothes. She frequently watched TV and one evening made a remark about one man, "I like his dark shirt and light pants, they are a nice combination," then added, "I like to squeeze a man into my life once in awhile, it makes life more interesting—but after I get to know a man, I don't always find him as interesting as I thought I would."

I never failed to get a laugh from some of the things Ruth said at almost 96 years old. One morning she said, "Someone is always seeing or hearing something and going to my mother with it and then she scolds me for flirting." "Were you a flirt?" I asked, "You were a very pretty girl." With a twinkle in her eye and a mischievous look she answered, "Yes, I was a flirt and I knew how to do this, too," as she took a few awkward steps with a pronounced swing of her hips.

During those years Ruth seldom knew where she was. Much of the time she was in Stockville, while at other times she was traveling and needed to get back to her teaching job before school started.

One night at the dinner table Ruth said, "This is a good place to stop and eat; the food is always good here." When we left the table she was upset because she couldn't find her handbag.

Another evening I was in the kitchen preparing dinner when Ruth called from her recliner in the den, "Mother, could us kids just fix us some cereal, we are getting hungry?" I related this story to our insurance adjuster the next day. Her reply gave me food for thought. "You should be pleased that Ruth is with her mother, in her mind, as that was, no doubt, one of the happiest times of her life."

During Ruth's last years, Dave and I bought a mobile home in Mesa, Arizona, and had plans to become "snow birds." I had hopes of spending some time in my "rocker." That was not to be.

I spent six weeks with 96-year-old Ruth, allowing her caretaker to visit family in the Philippines. It was then I realized, as her Power of Attorney, that the time had come to find better care for my Ruth, and to put her house on the market to give her the extra money she would need in the days ahead.

She purchased her home more than thirty years ago for $25,000. Over the years it had become what real estate agents call a "fixer upper" and would sell at a "buyers market" price; however, Ruth needed money to live on! Again, I got out of my rocker, rolled up my sleeves and went to work.

I hired the house repainted, inside and out, had a new front door installed and tore out old, worn carpeting to find beautiful oak floors underneath! I refinished the kitchen cabinets, had new appliances installed and replaced the thirty year old drapes with modern blinds.

The back yard was a maze of overgrown trees and shrubs. A small building, that had been a "cat house" in days gone by, got a new roof and paint job. I trimmed trees and shrubs to the best of my ability, then, professionals came in to open up a beautiful sunny yard by taking out a few trees. Rock was put in the front area and some cacti transplanted from the back.

Although Ruth hadn't noticed all that was being done to the house, she obviously would have approved. One morning she said, "When I buy a house I would like to buy one just like this one."

Now it was time to list Ruth's house for sale. It sold the first day on the market for $239,000.

In the meantime, I had found a new home for Ruth, a group home with only four residents.

Spending time with Ruth, caring for her and getting her house ready for market, was a sad experience I would long remember. It was saying good-bye to the Ruth I used to know and praying God would not prolong calling her home. Her life was not what she would have wanted it to be.

My involvement with Ruth's aging process enabled me to realize that I might someday travel down this same path and that I needed to continue using my arms, legs and brain. Without exercise the brain will deteriorate, just as will the body. Being there with Ruth prompted me to "count my blessings," sort out my priorities, be happy for the simple things in life and to count each and every day as a gift from God.

For the past few years I had been putting together a memory book of Ruth's life. I knew that I was approaching the final chapter in Ruth's book, just as she was nearing the final chapter in her life.

Ruth celebrated her 97th birthday in the hospital. She had a dozen red roses by her bed and a card that played "Happy Birthday." Although she hadn't known me for several months, she recognized me that day. I put my head close to hers and said, "Ruth, this is LaVera." She gave me a big smile and a kiss and said, "LaVera, I love you."

Ruth kept asking for "Baby." It wasn't until Josie, the manager of the group home Ruth was living in, told me, "Baby sits in Ruth's wheelchair with her, all day, every day." Baby was the life-sized stuffed Westie dog I had given her.

Ruth passed away on July 23, 2000, at 98. Her "Baby" was buried with her. At her graveside service the minister touched my shoulder and said, "Someday soon she will come to comfort you."

*This charming Walnut Creek home has been all "gussied up"
for new owners with new hardwood floor entry, new appliances,
new carpets, new front door, and freshly painted interior and
exterior. There are three generous bedrooms and two baths(the
Master Bath has new tile) a spacious living room with hardwood
floors and fireplace, and a family room adjoining the kitchen.
There is also a large yard and plenty of room to expand if desired.
Shopping, schools, and good commute access are near-by.
A great home awaits you..*

Listed Price: $239.000

LaVera and Tina

Chapter 16

INDIAN SUMMER

The Indians believed that Indian summer was a period when their God from the Southwest would send a breeze to warm the atmosphere.

Webster defines Indian summer as a brief period of unusually mild weather, in late October or early November, when the sky is clear and cloudless and the atmosphere smoky in appearance.

I like to think of Indian summer as a long, beautiful season that shortens the winter of our lives.

In the early spring of our lives we dream. I used to sit on the porch of our farm house in Nebraska, watch the clouds roll by and dream of what it would be like when I grew up. Are all children as I was, so anxious to fit into the shoes of the elders they admire the most? We dream of what we will do, and all the great things we will accomplish.

Early in the spring of my life, I dreamed of being a teacher, probably because I admired my first teacher so much. She was my teacher for grades one through four and we kept in touch for more than forty years. A few years later I dreamed of being an actress and an artist like my mother. I dreamed of a house with a white picket fence, ruffled curtains and flower boxes at the windows. I dreamed of a prince charming to make it all come true.

I met my prince, Frank Elmer Miles, and married at age seventeen. Many of my dreams were pushed into the subconscious as I struggled to be a good wife and mother and help support the two little girls who came along before I was twenty one. I was very proud of those two little girls, and still am.

The summer of my life was a long summer and many times a hot, uncomfortable summer. I was twenty-seven, recovering from a divorce, when I met Floyd Leroy Massey, prince number two. Five more years passed without my dreams coming true. Do they ever? Or is it that person in the mirror we must look to for the fulfillment of our dreams? No, our cottages didn't have white picket fences, but they did have ruffled curtains at the windows, flowers boxes, and they were clean and cozy. My children, numbering four by now, made any house a home and it was a happy summer when we worked, played, laughed and learned together.

My sales work career with Stanley Home Products took me away from my home and my children much of the time, but my dream of acting did become a reality as I entertained groups of ladies through the Stanley Home party plan.

My dream of teaching came true as I taught my Stanley dealers the art of selling. And yes, my dreams of teaching came true as I taught my little ones to fly on their own.

Prince number three, Robert William Edick, came along in the summer of my life and my fifth baby was born. I retired from work, had time to spend with my husband and time to play with and read to my children; time to try my skill as an artist and time once again to dream! I dreamed of going back to school and getting a degree.

I found time in the summer of my life to get my G.E.D. (General Educational Development), and enroll at Bismarck Junior College. The following year I was accepted into a Commercial Art School. My dream of becoming an artist was being fulfilled. I was a busy lady, studying, traveling with my husband and tackling new projects and hobbies.

We stay young by continuing to grow. We insure a long Indian summer by taking inspiration from the young in spirit who remain active throughout their lives. Grandma Moses started painting at age 90 in the Indian summer of her life. Edison was busy in his laboratory at eighty-four. Benjamin Franklin helped frame the American Constitution at eighty years of age.

A sign on my work room wall reads, "It's never too late to have a happy childhood." We stay young by keeping our hearts young—it can be done. Poet Carl Sandberg said, "It is not bad for a man of many years to die with a boy's heart, or a woman of many years to die with a girl's heart."

We are not born all at once, but by bits; the body first and the spirit later. Some events in life are faded and distorted. Distancing is often deliberate to avoid painful memories in the computer of our brains.

There are natural experiences of learning, and then there is programming or what others feed into us to get us to do what they want us to do, think or feel.

The stories written of my childhood, the stories of the spring and summer of my life are written as an older woman remembering, not as a child or young woman speaking.

The world we arrive in at birth molds part of us. We finish the job of ordering our lives with God's help. When the pieces come together a mosaic appears. Sometimes, out of a life of seeming chaos, the end product is a thing of beauty. It takes both sad and happy days, both light and dark, to form a beautiful mosaic.

Every life has a purpose, a plan, a meaning of its own, whether you believe it's your own doing, karmic destiny, socially imposed or by divine plan.

We grow up, bit by bit sometimes, other times by leaps and bounds. Psychologists who study death and dying tell us that we don't die all at once either, we die many little deaths as we go through life. We learn we cannot be everything, do everything, or have everything. We should stop for a moment before we do whatever we think is so important and ask ourselves, "Is this important?" Who says this is important? Our peers, or is it a fear of the eyes of the world upon us?

At age 65, when I lost my Prince Bob, I found myself asking, who am I, where have I been and where am I going? There had been clouds in my life, but they were clearing away. The computer of the mind seems to have a way of recalling the pleasantries of life and leaving unpleasant events in a haze.

I received a long letter from my dear friend, George Irwin, now 92 years old, urging me to keep busy. "You're not the type to sit in a rocker," he wrote.

I had a dream of Bob just after his death. He was small, child-like, walking with a woman, but as he turned toward me his face was as I remembered him before his illness. He smiled, waved, again turned his head, and disappeared into the distance. It seemed like a message to me, "I am safe, well and happy here with my mother."

A few years before Bob's death a palm reader had told me, "Your husband is ill; he will pass on and you will remarry a man you know; I see trees, many trees."

Dave Edick, Bob's first cousin and his wife, Betty, who lived in New Ulm, Minnesota, had visited us in Bismarck several times with their two adopted children, Greg and Tammi. Betty and I kept in touch by letter. When Betty passed away, Dave sold the New Ulm home and moved into their hunting cabin on 40 acres of forest land near Lena, Wisconsin.

The first time I saw Dave's home was when Bobby and I accompanied Dave to the 100th birthday party for their Uncle George, who lived in Indiana. It was a chance for Dave and me to become re-acquainted. The morning we left our hotel in Oconto Falls to return to Bismarck, Dave came to have breakfast with us and brought me a bouquet of wild flowers and a bowl of strawberries from his garden. It was such little things that endeared him to me. On the way home, we drove past his home and I saw trees, many trees! I invited him to visit us in Bismarck.

Later, when I visited Dave at his home, my gut impulse was to turn and run! One could hardly call the three-room hunting cabin a home. There were only paths from room to room between the packed boxes. The bedroom was furnished with only a mattress on the floor. The kitchen was a disaster with many cabinet doors hanging by one hinge. Mice were having a banquet, and now and then a bat flew into the hallway, sending me screeching to the other end of the house! There was a bathroom, but no water. Dave had tapped into a natural spring and installed a faucet in the basement. As he said, "We have running water when we run to the basement to get it."

Even the yard had piles of "treasures" covered with tarps held down with bricks. I later found those piles of treasures to hold everything from junk to diamond jewelry.

Why did I again return to Dave's home in Wisconsin? Perhaps it was destiny, a part of God's plan. I tried to understand! Dave had worked for Kraft when an accident at work nearly blinded him, putting him on disability pay. Was his handicap an excuse? Did he need my help?

Dave became prince number four, and sang "Amazing Grace" when we were married at the First Presbyterian Church in Bismarck. Since David Edick and Robert Edick were first cousins, my surname stayed the same.

Dave was a strong man, a tall man with white hair and beard, a "look alike" for Colonel Sanders. He loved nature and gardening and took time to feed and identify the birds. He encouraged me to learn the names of wild flowers he picked for me and to watch the squirrels and chipmunks at play.

We spent hours getting to know one another. I wanted to know about his dreams of the past and future. What was he like as a child, a young man, an adoptive father to his two children? I wanted him to know where I came from and what my dreams had been through the spring and summer of my life. I dreamed of enjoying a long, warm Indian summer with prince number four by my side.

I soon started looking for my "lemonade recipe." I hadn't used it in awhile. I rolled up my sleeves, got out of my rocker, took my credit card out of my wallet and attempted to make a home out of chaos.

My brother, Harold, his wife Dee and my cousins, Neomia and her husband Delmar, from Nebraska, were planning to visit

Certificate of Marriage

This Certifies that

La Vera M. Edick

and

David J. Edick

were by me united in

Holy Matrimony

at FIRST PRESBYTERIAN CHURCH, BISMARCK

on the 14TH day of DECEMBER

in the year of our Lord 19 91 according

to the ordinance of God and the laws

of NORTH DAKOTA

Rev. Mark A. Bavert

Witness CINDY SHANE

Witness ROBERT EDICK

LaVera Edick
and
David Edick

with the blessings of their children and grandchildren,
wish to announce their marriage
on
December 14, 1991
at the
First Presbyterian Church
in Bismarck, North Dakota at 4:30 p.m.

Please join us for this happy occasion
when two persons and two families become one.
LaVera and David feel their newly found,
but very deep love for one another will turn
the Autumn and Winter of their lives into
a beautiful, never ending Indian Summer.

A reception and dinner will be held at
the bride's home 1100 North First Street,
following the ceremony.

Please no, gifts, just let us know
by December 7th if you will be
able to attend.

Our Wedding Day

us. I found an excuse not to be home. I was ashamed for them to see how I was living!

A second floor was added to the cabin, walls were covered with knotty pine, new kitchen cabinets and appliances, including a washer and dryer, were installed. The old wooden floors were sanded and finished. We turned a dilapidated old cabin into a "mansion." My home in Bismarck sold and we moved most of my furniture into our new home.

Dave had a beautiful voice and sang in a barbershop quartet. It was when the quartet presented a performance of "Circus, Circus" at Wisconsin State University, that Dave volunteered me to paint clown's faces. Unlike his cousin Bob, Dave didn't have a jealous bone in his body! I spent two evenings in the men's dressing room painting faces.

Prince number four and I were married for almost ten years. We found time to travel a lot, first a trip to Hawaii and then a week in Jamaica. I did genealogical research on the Edick family, as this Wisconsin area had been their home since before the Civil War. Edick ancestors, the Tourtilotts, founded Green Bay.

We had lived in our new home only a few years when the highway department decided to build a road through the middle of the living room and we were forced to sell. It was after our Wisconsin home sold that we bought a mobile home in Mesa, Arizona. Several years earlier I had purchased a single wide trailer in Bismarck.

From my journal:

November 11, 1998:

I'm at our trailer in Bismarck; Dave is in Minnesota with his son. It is Veterans Day and I am ill with a virus. I've been feeling just a bit sorry for myself that I'm not basking in the Arizona sun, but as I sit with my first cup of coffee, I realize, perhaps God creates these situations for me with a purpose in mind. My children, Sharri, Carolyn, Mike, Beckie, and Bob are always so thoughtful to call and see if I need anything. Bob brought groceries to me yesterday and shoveled a path to my front door. My children are all busy with their lives, their families and that is as it should be. But again, perhaps God creates situations such as my being snowbound and ill to let me know how much love is in their hearts for me. It is a good feeling!

Dave and I spent more and more time apart during the next few years. I spent time in Bismarck and California caring for my "other mother" and getting her home ready for market. Dave could have gone with me to help, but it seemed he was finding it more and more difficult to be away from his former home state; however, we planned to spend summers in North Dakota and at the first hint of snow, become "snow birds" in Mesa.

It was in early November of 2000 when we hit a sudden detour on the path of life.

Chapter 17

IT CHANGED MY LIFE

After I lost my "other mother," Ruth, in July, of 2000, I returned to Bismarck and tried to catch up with chores that had been neglected at my Bismarck trailer and lake cabin located seventy miles north of Bismarck. The family and I tackled repainting the cabin and that is how I spent my seventy-fifth birthday on September 10, 2000.

In early November, Dave and I were on our way to Arizona for the winter. On November 6th, we met with Ruth's family in Stockville, Nebraska, in memory of Ruth and to donate a chair to the Cambridge Museum. The chair had a buffalo hide seat and was hand carved by Ruth's maternal grandfather Sanders, who was a pioneer in that area.

The following day, Monday, November 7th, we were on our way to meet my Forster cousins for dinner. Dave and I were riding with my cousin Neomia and her husband, Delmar, who was driving the vehicle. Ironically, we were on a county road just a mile from my birthplace. It was dusk and beginning to snow when we hit a farmer's tractor that was parked in the middle of the road without warning flares. The front seat passengers were protected by air bags and were not seriously injured; Neomia and I were in the back seat without our seat belts fastened. The emergency crew worked nearly an hour to rescue us from the mangled vehicle. Among my injuries were my left femur bone, which was broken in five places, and a deep gash in my forehead that just missed my left eye.

As soon as I arrived at the hospital emergency room, my family was in touch with nurses and doctors caring for me, checking on my status. I remember very little about the next few days; however, I do recall seeing all five of my children at my bedside. Surgery for my broken leg was not done for several days, while my overall status was evaluated.

Good Samaritan Hospital in Kearney, Nebraska, was my home for the next six weeks. I recall one night, early in my stay at the hospital that I felt so hot that I wanted to kick off the blanket covering me, but I couldn't move. The room suddenly became icy cold. I felt pressure on my right shoulder—I was alone in the room—then it was hot again! Was it Ruth there to comfort me and urge me not to give up?

As soon as I was able to be out of my hospital bed and into a wheelchair part of the day, I asked for a table to be placed at the end of my bed. I needed a writing desk. There was work to be done, letters to write and checks to be sent to Ruth's heirs. I was executrix of her estate.

Kent Bonar, one of Ruth's heirs, wrote a letter of thanks, telling me a bit about himself. He had walked twenty-five miles to cash his inheritance check. We have continued corresponding over the years and I have come to know and appreciate Kent. He is a well-educated man, a graduate of the University of Missouri. In his last year of college he was in an accident, costing him an eye. It was then that he chose the style of living he embraces today.

Kent is a naturalist, living close to God with his five coon dogs, without electricity, plumbing, telephone or car. He spends much of his time finding, sketching and recording endangered species of wild life, birds and insects as well as trees, flowers and plants. He is often referred to as the "John Muir" of the Ozarks. He has written text books for the University of Missouri and his story has been recorded on film. With his eye patch, battered straw hat and worn clothing, Bonar seems an unlikely hero. His cabin bordering the upper Buffalo River wilderness in the Ozarks of Northwest Arkansas is "slapdash" functional. The film shows several of his coon dogs sleeping in the shade of the porch. I value his many letters to me, written in calligraphy with a quill pen, including illustrations of rare, endangered species of birds, insects, flowers and plants he found in the wilderness. Kent himself is an endangered species. He possesses a very special gift. I have sent Kent copies of my paintings and poems and shared genealogical information about our family. A quote from one of his letters: "Just as I advocate preservation of wildlife and nature, you preserve the history of our family."

I spent part of each day at the hospital visiting patients in nearby rooms who needed encouragement, my cousin Neomia being one of them. She was not responding well to therapy and was very depressed.

Chaplain Willis deserves a lot of credit for keeping my thinking positive and assuring me "God is with you." "When God solves your problems you have faith in his abilities; when God doesn't solve your problems, He has faith in your ability to help yourself."

I was learning to use a walker but still in the wheelchair much of the time when I convinced the doctors I was able to return to the home of my granddaughter, Nickie, in Mesa. I wanted so much to be home by Christmas! I had hopes of being mobile, without the aid of a wheelchair or walker, one day soon. In the meantime God had left me with one good leg, two good arms and a good brain. I believe He expected me to make good use of what I had. Somehow He granted me the serenity to accept things as they were and to enjoy life.

A few dark threads in the weaving of my life are shown by the journal I kept, at the request of my lawyer, to be used as evidence in a pending lawsuit.

November 7, 2000, found me in Good Samaritan Hospital, Kearney, Nebraska, where I was a patient for the next six weeks. I returned to Mesa, Arizona, on December 20th, just in time for Christmas without my usual Christmas spirit! My granddaughter, Nickie, cared for me in her home for the next two months as I was unable to care for myself.

February 20, 2001, I moved back to our Mesa mobile home with my husband Dave and tried to learn to cope with my disability.

A typical day:

I was usually in bed by 10:00 P.M. A very annoying bladder incontinence problem that developed during my hospital stay got me up every two or three hours. I would awaken between 6 and 7:00 A.M. feeling that I'd had no sleep. If I took a pain killer and tried to position my left leg in a more comfortable way, I might sleep another hour or so.

I did my bed exercises first and then I hobbled to the kitchen on one leg! (My left leg had not healed enough to bear weight.)

Thank God for my aluminum legs, my walker. Have I mentioned that I thank God every day for being alive? I love life.

9:30 A.M.: I took my medication and vitamins and prepared breakfast. The "carry pack" on my walker was a way to carry eggs to the stove, milk to the table and bread to the toaster. I learned to balance myself with my walker, slide hot dishes from the stove to the counter across from the table, then by standing halfway between and making use of both my arms, I could pick the dish up with one hand, and very carefully set it on the table. It was slow (I wasn't used to that), but in half an hour breakfast was ready.

10:15 A.M.: Another half hour putting food away and washing dishes.

10:45A.M.: Time for chair therapy exercise that needed to be done three times a day, in an attempt to keep my joints from stiffening.

11:00A.M.: Time to get dressed, and maybe a shower. (I didn't have energy enough for a shower every day.) I usually did some laundry before time for my noon exercise. I put my dirty laundry in the bath tub. I couldn't use it for bubble baths anymore because I was unable to climb in and out. I missed that. Reaching from the toilet stool to the bathtub, I put dirty clothes in a shopping bag; by tossing the bag ahead of my walker a few times, I got it to the laundry room. The same bag carried the clean clothes to my bed to be folded.

12:30P.M.: Another round of bed exercises, maybe time to write a few letters; pay a few bills and record medical bills before preparing lunch. I tried to accomplish as much as possible during the morning hours, because by afternoon I was worn out and retired to my recliner. I would prop my leg up to reduce the edema and try to read a bit before evening exercises, dinner and bed.

April 10, 2001: Often I just sat there looking at things I wanted to do, but couldn't. That loosened wallpaper needed to be pasted down; I couldn't climb up to do it; six months ago I could! The kitchen light bulb needed to be changed; I couldn't climb up to change it! Six months ago I could. My "reacher" would do some things, but it couldn't do it all!

My walker would take me some places but it couldn't help me pick the grapefruit or trim the bougainvillea. Six months ago I could take care of the yard, now I couldn't.

Six months ago I could reach the dishes in the high cupboard by standing on a stool, and the pots and pans in the bottom cupboard by leaning on my knees, now I couldn't.

The orthopedic surgeon in Mesa was not painting a pretty picture; it seems that the area of shattered femur bone was not growing back together. Six months after surgery, I could not put full weight on that leg for fear of breaking the titanium rod that holds the bone in place. They told me that I might never be able to use that leg. I was given three options:

Option one: Wearing an electronic bone stimulator (EBI) for 10 hours a day for up to 400 days.

Option two: Surgery to remove a screw that might help mesh the two ends of the femur bone together by allowing the rod to drop a bit. I understood this would give me a shorter left leg.

Option three: Surgery for a bone graft, taking the graft bone from my right hip. Even with that, there was no guarantee that the bone would heal, enabling me to walk again. I had days when I fought depression.

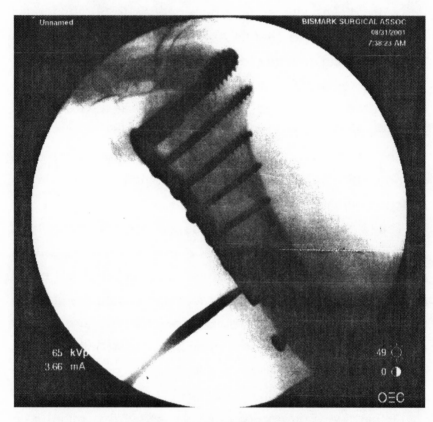

An x-ray of my left femur.
Thanks for Dr. Adamson of Good Samaritan Hospital, I still have a
leg, albeit one that does a lot of complaining!

May 16, 2001: My husband Dave left for Wisconsin via North Dakota to spend the summer fixing up a trailer on his land as a hunting retreat for his son, Greg and himself. I somehow felt God was testing me. I didn't realize it then, but the trailer was actually Dave's future home. It was the beginning of the end of our marriage. Our divorce was final less than two years later.

May 21, 2001: I was fitted with the bone stimulator and wore it faithfully, ten hours a day. I got along okay, although it was a challenge to prepare meals, do dishes, laundry and take care of myself and my Westie, Tina.

My granddaughter, Nickie, was a godsend. She did my grocery shopping, vacuuming, floor scrubbing, bathroom cleaning, bed linen changing, garbage detail, and took me to all of my doctor appointments. I couldn't have managed without her. Her daily visits always brought a smile to my face. Her son, Justin, less than two years old, helped take care of his great-grandma. He brought me a pillow to elevate my leg, helped me to the bathroom by following my walker and he always knew which leg he could sit on when we read and drew pictures. He was a ray of sunshine and always had hugs and kisses.

My children, grandchildren, great-grandchildren, brothers, nieces, nephews and many friends were wonderful morale boosters with their many calls, letters and cards. My oldest brother, Harold, was 85 and not a day went by that he didn't call to see how I was doing and tell me that he loved me.

June 13, 2001: I had reconstructive surgery on my face to repair the damage done to my left eyelid and eyebrow in the accident. After the surgery, Nickie took me to her home for a few days to recover. The pain medication helped, but I was still in a lot of pain, not only from my eye, but also my leg. A trip to the emergency room and X-Rays a few days later showed that I had a broken screw in my leg.

September 15, 2001: I had been wearing the growth stimulator (EBI), ten hours a day for three months. (I continued wearing it for several years.) I saw an orthopedic surgeon in Bismarck and two weeks later had surgery to remove two screws from my leg and replace them with two shorter ones.

I kept my fingers crossed and said a lot of prayers that the bone would start healing. It didn't, and months later bone graft surgery failed to help. (I still have the rod in my leg.) I did a lot of complaining about my problems in those days and had a tendency to tell anyone who would listen. I have always disliked it when other people do that.

Perhaps tragedies happen because tragedies are a part of life—just as death is a part of life. One cannot have life without death and one cannot have happiness without sadness.

I learned not to look at what I had lost, but at what I had left and believe that God left me here for a purpose. I hadn't completed all He had planned for me. I seemed to have an inner peace that was missing a few years before. Someone up there was helping me make the right choices. "Thank you, God."

I learned to focus on what I could do rather than what I couldn't do and to count my blessings. In a few years, I was able to care for myself, my home, my dog and to drive my car. I had to give up my love for high heeled shoes and settle for sensible flats.

I spend many hours with oils and pastels, creating portraits of my grandchildren and recording genealogical history on canvas.

From my journal, September 25, 2004:

What a pleasant surprise! The phone rang this morning and I picked it up to hear the voice of my very good friend, 93-year-old George Irwin. He had been on my mind lately as I worked on my memory books, rereading the cards and letters from him, always encouraging me to do my best! He reminded me to keep busy, to have activities to keep me fresh and mindful. He said, "Do something, don't just sit, and I'm hoping you have this already worked out." I followed George's advice. In my 80th year, five years after the accident that changed my life, I held a one-man art show at BAGA. I have continued working on my memory books and doing research on our family tree. In addition, I travel to important family events, such as family reunions and weddings. I also continue to maintain contact with my family and friends via letter, phone calls, and sometimes even visits. I am always ready for a new adventure.

Artist's Statement

LaVera Edick is a local resident who has been active in promoting visual arts in the Bismarck community for many years. I now spend my winters in Arizona and enjoy teaching art to family members.

My interest in art began as a little girl. A new box of crayons, once a year, was a hi-light in my childhood.

I recall visiting the school at Rosebud Indian Reservation as a pre-schooler and how fascinated I was with a display of the student's art work. In elementary school I learned to carve animals from Ivory soap and do reverse painting on glass.

The years rolled by——I kept busy with five children, and not until my youngest was in school did I pursue my ambition to learn more about art. I enrolled at BJC and graduated in 1967 with Associate degrees in Art and Commercial Art.

I am a charter member and past president of Elan Art Gallery founded in 1967 and now known as BAGA since they merged with Bismarck Art Association. Rosemary Landsberger was one of my first art teachers. I learned a lot about composition and color in her classes.

I started taking art lessons from Vern Skaug over thirty years ago and continue to attend his workshops whenever possible. Portraits are his specialty. He is a great teacher. I have worked in oils and watercolor but my favorite medium is pastel.

My five children, thirteen grandchildren and thirteen great grand-children give me a multitude of inspiration for family portraits. My Midwest background and many endeavors throughout my life, including travel and genealogical research, has impacted the subject matter I have chosen to portray.

Past & Present
by
LaVera Edick

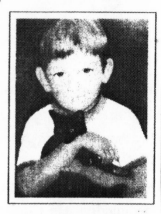

Exhibit Dates:
July 5-30, 2005

Justin and Grandma
BAGA Art Show

Title

Carla and His Boy
Extra, Extra
Mother and Child
Mom Likes Me Best
Morona
Jacob
Laguna Beach
Blue Velvet
McBurney's Sheep
Vautrin's Mill
Playmates
Training For The Race
Lattig Immigrants
The Dirty Thirties
Grandma Bertha
Mitchell's Masterpiece
Kitty Kim
The Kid's Breakfast
Mischief In The Making
A Morocco Street
Buddies
Little Miss Curiosity
Daddy's Hat
Poor Cat
Homestead
Mary and Her Lamb
Bye, Bye, Grandma
Bobby and Skelly
Baby Sister
Clate's Image

Chapter 18

MY FAMILY—MY LEGACY

My nest has been empty for many years, giving me time to look back at what my life has been. My children have always been the most important part of my life; it was not easy to let them go. But our children are loaned to us only for a few years, and then we must let go, as it should be. We teach them to fly and then let them try their wings, perhaps making some of the same mistakes we made. My children are all individuals, as I urged them to be, and are very special people. They have high moral values, an excellent work ethic and a strong pioneer spirit. Both the men and the women in our family are strong-minded and follow in the footsteps of their Woodring ancestors in doing whatever it takes to accomplish the goals they set for themselves.

My life would be very shallow without my children and their families. I hope they think of me not only as a mother, grandmother and great-grandmother but also as a friend. God gives us a mother, grandmother and great-grandmother, but we are free to choose our friends. My mind travels back in time and recalls the joy of being the mom of five beautiful children and now I am reliving those days as grandma and great-grandma.

I recall many happy, fun-filled, adventurous and sometimes sad days with my family. In my kaleidoscopic memory I see many pictures, among them: Sharllyn and me with baby Carolyn in the buggy and our dog Spotty tagging along behind on our way to the grocery store. That was before I learned to drive. Little Mike at 15 months old climbing upon the bed and giving me and his new baby sister Beckie a big kiss the day we came home from the hospital. Beckie, as a toddler, dancing on the top of the coffee table. And baby Bobby, sitting on the floor with his mommy, building Lincoln Log houses when I was forty years old and a stay at home mom.

Sharri, my oldest daughter, was 21 years old the same year Bobby, my youngest child, was born. Sharri was a flight attendant for American Airlines when she came home to visit her new baby brother.

Carolyn was married and the mother of little Rickie Dean. They stayed at our house in Bismarck for a few months while Rickie's daddy was in Vietnam. When Bobby was born, he was already Uncle Bobby to Rickie Dean, who was 15 months old. Rickie Dean was my first grandson and his stay at our house as a baby created a strong bond between us. I couldn't wash the pencil scribbles off the laundry room door for months after he moved to San Diego with his parents.

We gave our two older girls almost twin names, Sharllyn Faye and Carolyn Kaye, without realizing it at the time we named them. I often dressed them alike, until they objected to it. They were individuals growing up, but as they became adults, they discovered they had more and more similar characteristics, however, Sharllyn was a blond and Carolyn had dark hair. It is not unusual, although living across the

United States from one another, for them to buy the same furniture and fabric for drapes or to send me identical greeting cards. They anticipate when one or the other has a problem, is ill, or needs help and will often call to ask, "Is everything okay?"

Sharri attended college at Arizona State University in Tempe and was active in water ballet and drama. In 1963 she was runner-up for Miss Arizona. In that same year she met Jay. Jay loves to tell the story of how he won Sharri on the toss of a coin. He and a friend tossed a coin to determine who would first ask her for a date and Jay won.

After her college years, Sharri became a flight attendant for American Airlines and was stationed in Los Angeles. Rioting and looting broke out in the Watts area of L.A. on August 11, 1965, after police arrested a black man accused of drunk driving. The riot lasted a week with 34 persons killed and more than 1,000 injured. I worried about Sharri driving through that area on her way home from work. More than one night I called to make sure she had made it home safely.

Jay joined the Air Force. He was stationed at Travis Air Force Base in northern California and was a navigator on a C-141 Starlifter aircraft flying in and out of Vietnam. The U.S. was involved in the Vietnam War in an attempt to prevent the spread of communism throughout Southeast Asia. U.S. ground troops were deployed to Vietnam in 1965. They fought a jungle war against the Viet Cong, who would attack in ambushes, set up booby traps and then escape through a network of underground tunnels. For U.S. forces to even find the enemy was difficult. Our forces couldn't determine which of the villagers were enemies, as some of them, even

328 | LaVera Edick

women and children, helped build booby traps and housed and fed the Viet Cong. The Viet Cong hid in dense brush and our forces cleared those areas by dropping agent-orange, causing the leaves to burn or drop off. Many of our soldiers became frustrated with the fighting conditions. They suffered from low morale, became angry and some used drugs. U.S. leaders lost the American public's support of the war.

Sharri and Jay were married in 1966 while she was based in San Francisco and he was at Travis Air Force Base. She continued flying until she became pregnant with Cindy. In those days American Airline attendants were very carefully chosen and expected to walk a straight line. They wore skirts, heels and caps, were told what color nail polish to wear, how their hair should be styled and were subject to random weight checks, making sure they were always trim and attractive. Both Cindy and Brent were born at Travis Air Force Base Hospital.

Jay worked in the Northern California area as a stock broker before moving to Colorado in 1972 and becoming involved in the tennis industry. Sharri went back to college, the University of Boulder, and then became a buyer for a large sporting goods chain based out of Denver. In 1979 they moved to Pennsylvania and started their own business, "Guardian Alarm Systems." Sharri helped her husband run that business for many years. Now, in their retirement years, Jay is an avid bicyclist and has taken a few art lessons. Sharri is taking piano lessons on her new baby grand and becoming quite an accomplished pianist. They are both enjoying life with their family, including their four grandsons.

Carolyn was always one to help others. As a teenager she was a "candy striper" at a local hospital. A candy striper is a volunteer who wears a cute little red and white uniform and apron and helps the nursing staff by doing little things to make the patients more comfortable. Candy stripers originated as a high school class project in East Orange, New Jersey, in 1944. This experience no doubt influenced her career choice as a nurse. After the birth of her two boys, Carolyn pursued her education, first getting an Associate of Science degree in nursing and becoming a Registered Nurse and then completing her Bachelor of Science degree. Carolyn worked diligently to keep up with everything—starting her career as a nurse, mothering her two little boys and helping support the family; however, she always had time to attend Jeff's basketball games and track meets, help Rickie with his projects and help both of them with their homework.

Carolyn was hired right out of nursing school by a local hospital and was employed by them for more than thirty six years. She started on the night shift working in several different units, but found her niche in Labor and Delivery. Over the years, her career evolved from staff nurse to assistant head nurse, head nurse, lead nurse, operations coordinator and manager of several units.

After college, her husband Richard devoted much of his time, energy and money into starting a new business. Today the business, after being bought out by their son Rick, has emerged from waterbed stores to full-line furniture stores.

Carolyn became a grandma when Rickie's twins, Madelyn and Nathan were born. Today all six of her grandchildren have happy memories of time spent at Grandma's house—playing games, making cookies, reading, singing and playing in the pool. Carolyn has retired, but keeps busy in her role of a loving grandma.

Mike missed having a daddy figure in the early years of his life and often asked about his daddy. As a teenager he spent several summers with his dad on the farm in Nebraska, resulting from a telephone conversation when I said, "Ike, it would be a pity if you didn't get to know your son. He is so much like you—he looks like you, walks like you and even talks like you."

Mike took a year off to work after graduating from Bismarck High. He was working on the construction of a power line in the Dakotas during the winter months when he decided college wasn't such a bad idea. Mike was always an adventurous lad; he loved snowmobiling and drove both the snowmobile and his car a bit too fast. (He may have learned that from his mother.) I could understand when he decided to major in aviation and minor in business. He liked the thrill of flying. I realized what an excellent pilot he was when he flew me back to Nebraska in a small plane, before his instrument rating and during an ice storm, at the time of my mother's death.

After graduating from Mary College, Mike met and married Sheryl, the love of his life. He worked for Commander Aviation for a few years; however, a problem with color blindness kept him from achieving the goals he wished for in aviation. He started working for Basin Electric and was eventually given the position of Project Manager for the Dry Forks Station, a Basin Electric Power Cooperative project in Gillette, Wyoming, where coal is converted into electricity. Groundbreaking was November 2, 2007, and the estimated cost of the project was more than one billion dollars. The plant was dedicated

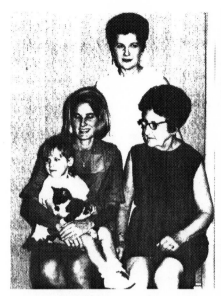

From right—Grandma Minnie, Grandma LaVera, mother Sharri, and baby Cindy Beth.

From left—Grandma Minnie, Grandma LaVera, mother Carolyn and baby Rickie Dean.

Cindy Beth in her great-great grandmother Anna's rocker.

Rickie Dean's twins—from left Nathan and Madelyn.

Bobby with Mom and Dad

Mike

Caitlyn One year old

Beckett One day old

(The two youngest of
my twenty great-
grandchildren)

Beckie and her family,
from left—Nicole, Taylor
and Amelia

on August 11, 2011, and is in full operation at this time. Mike recently accepted a new position with Basin Electric Power Cooperative as Contract Manager. Mike is a busy man, but does manage to find some free time to work in the yard during the summer and to build furniture in the winter. He has built some beautiful pieces of furniture for his wife, his children and grandchildren, many of the furniture designs are from copies of pictures in a 1918 Sears Roebuck catalog.

As a little girl, Beckie liked to carry her "briefcase" around and play office. She seldom played with dolls until she was given a Barbie doll. She spent hours with her Barbie and Ken collection and even had a house and car for them. As a teenager she was one of the prettiest and best dressed girls in school.

Beckie had been married and had three children when she went back to college and acquired her Bachelor of Science degree in nursing. She bought a house, a fixer upper, with the help of a down payment from her dad, Ike. She was the "fixer upper." She did an amazing job of redoing that house, putting in new kitchen cupboards, moving the location of the sink, changing walls and refinishing woodwork from paint to original varnish. She lived in that house many years during the time her family was growing up and she was developing her career as a nurse. It takes a very special, caring person to do the type of work she has done and continues to do as a nurse in the Psychiatric Unit of the Veterans Hospital in Phoenix, Arizona.

Bobby was born on a very cold day, 35 degrees below zero. He has never let the cold weather stop him. As a little boy, he would cry when I made him come in from play when his ears started to freeze. He followed in his big brother's footsteps of loving adventure. As a young boy, he would rather work in his dad's workshop building things than play with his toys. I was upset when his dad bought a dirt bike for him and when at age eleven he decided, with his dad's permission, to enter races. Just as Sharllyn, as a little girl, invited the neighbor kids over when I made a batch of animal cookies, Bobby invited friends over when I made a crock pot of soup. One friend, who wasn't getting along well at home, stayed a couple of years. From a very early age Bobby was an entrepreneur with a firewood business. He designed and built a log splitter that is still being used thirty one years later.

Bobby graduated from college with a Psychology Major and a Business Minor. The last semester he carried a load of 27 credits in order to get his minor in business. He talked the dean into letting him carry that many credits, as the max to be carried was 24. Although psychology has not been his career choice over the years, he uses that talent every day in getting along with and helping people. He is now known as Bob. He is married to Tracee and has a Bobby of his own and a Mayla. He is still a builder, of houses that is, as a Construction Manager for Edgewood Development Group.

It was 2011, when Bob received a phone call from a man who identified himself as Jeffrey from Greeley, Colorado. He indicated that they were related. He was the half-brother Bob had been trying to find for the past twenty years. Bob, Sr. would be so happy that his two sons have found one another. I welcome Jeffrey and his children with open arms to our family.

My five children and their families are:

Sharllyn Faye married Jay and they have two children, Cindy Beth and Brent David. Cindy married Bill and they are the parents of Tyler Brandon, Jacob Ryan and Tristan Matthew. Brent married Catherine and they have a son Aaron Grant.

Carolyn Kaye was married to Richard and has two sons, Richard Dean and Jeffrey Todd. Richard Dean is married to Janine and has three children from a former marriage: the twins Nathan Andrew and Madelyn Richelle, and Elissa Christine. Jeffrey and Evi have two boys, Zachary James and Luke Richard. Jeffrey has an older son, Ryan Mitchell from a former marriage.

Michael Ray is married to Sheryl Raye. They are the parents of three, Garett Ray, Jessica Raye and Mitchell Ray. (The whole family has the middle name of Ray or Raye.) Garett and his wife Rebecca have a son Jameson Joseph and a daughter Caitlyn Grace. Jessica and her husband Boe have a son Gannon Michael and a new baby boy Beckett Boe. Mitchell is in college.

Beckie Jo has four children, Nicole Jo, Amelia Mae, Taylor Adam and Leesha Madisson. Nicole is married to Nate and has two children, Justin Thomas and Brooke Marie. Amelia and her husband Mike have two daughters, Stevie Jo and Madisson Mae. Taylor has a daughter Atlanta Jesse and a son Jace Adam. Taylor's significant other is Brandy, and is the mother of Jace. Leesha is in college.

Robert Allan married Tracee and they have two children, Robert Patrick and Mayla Marie. (Mayla's name is derived from my name, La Vera Mae.) Robert and Mayla are still in school.

I am the grandmother of 13 and the great-grandmother of 20. Caitlyn, whose baptism I attended quite recently, is the youngest of the great-granddaughters. The oldest are the twins, Nathan and Madelyn, who are 24 years old. I'm hoping to be a great, great-grandmother in the near future. Madelyn was married on June 29, 2012.

I answer to many different "grandma names." Jeff called me "Dwams" when he was little and still does, as do his three boys. Cindy's children call me "Grambea," Amy's Stevie Jo calls me "Grandma Tousie." Brent's Aaron is the only one who calls me "Great-Grandma La Vera."

My family is scattered far and wide from the East Coast, Pennsylvania and Florida, through the Midwest from North Dakota, Wyoming, Colorado, on to Arizona and the West Coast of California. No matter how far away my family may be, or what their ages, I never stop wanting to keep a protective arm around them.

It is most interesting to watch them grow up and to observe how their personality, environment, attitude and very likely their genes affect the choices they make in life.

Rickie Dean is the oldest of my seven grandsons. He used to call me his "pretty little grandma." Rickie is a successful businessman who has a special way of working with people and utilizes this skill each day in his furniture business.

Jeff has always loved sports and in his youth was a very competitive athlete; he graduated from California State University and then obtained his CPA. He is currently launching a new internet-based marketing business. Rickie and Jeff both reside in California.

Garett lives in Gillette, Wyoming, and has just started his own business. With two babies under two, he spends a lot of time changing diapers and helping his wife, Becca, who is an RN.

I used to watch Brent fly model airplanes as a little boy. He is now an International Pilot for Continental Airlines and lives with his family in Florida. He and his son, Aaron, enjoy assembling and launching rockets.

Taylor continues to explore different employment opportunities in search of his career path. His words, "I want most of all to be a good daddy."

Mitchell is in his second year of college, majoring in horticulture, at North Dakota State in Fargo. In his spare time you will find him strumming his guitar. I enjoy listening to him play and I'm hoping he will pursue his interest in art.

Robert Patrick, a seventh grader, is a straight A student. He is a very intelligent, polite, well-mannered young man and I'm sure he has a bright future ahead of him. He is currently 8th in the state in his category of wrestling.

Of my 13 great-grandsons, Nathan is the oldest. He is going to college and working with his dad in the furniture business. He loves camping and riding his dirt bike in the desert.

Ryan, Jeff's son, has been attending Arizona State University with a focus on business. His new interest is body building.

Tyler, Cindy's son, is in his first year of college at Kunztown University, majoring in business. In his spare time he is an avid snowboarder. Tyler always has time for his Great-Grandma LaVera. Our conversations mean a lot to me.

Justin has always been a Great-Grandma LaVera's boy. Justin has a very nurturing spirit. He loves animals, enjoys year-round hunting and fishing and follows in his mother's footsteps in being an outstanding athlete. He plays soccer for school as well as being on a travelling team. His mother Nicole has been one of his coaches. You might say she is a "Soccer Mom." Justin also plays the drums and is taking piano lessons.

Zachary is a very outgoing young man who enters into conversations with adults very easily and always has a big hug for his Great-Grandma LaVera. He loves spending time on the computer and playing video games.

Luke is an athlete like his dad. He plays soccer, basketball, is a junior lifeguard and is on two baseball teams, one a traveling team. In 2011 he threw the first baseball at the beginning of a professional baseball game. Grandma Carolyn seldom misses one of Luke's games.

Jacob is interested in art and theater and has taken classes in "Improv." He has performed in the play "Alice in Wonderland." Both he and his younger brother Tristan love to spend time with Grandpa "Pop" and Grandma Sharri.

Tristan is interested in science and airplanes. He is working toward his pilot's license at age eleven and already flying, taking off and landing without assistance.

Aaron, influenced and encouraged by his dad Brent, is involved in rocketry and has earned his black belt in martial arts.

Gannon is an athlete, active in both hockey and T-ball. He also loves animals and like his Grandpa Mike has an aquarium. He named one of his fish "Tuna" after his paternal Grandpa and he calls his crab "Crabby Patty."

Jace looks like a little football player and is a carbon copy of his dad Taylor in looks. Like most little boys, he loves and collects toy trucks, especially monster trucks.

Jameson is a very active toddler, who at our family reunion recently chased his little cousin Madisson, also a toddler, trying to give her a hug.

I have six granddaughters and seven great-granddaughters:

Cindy, the oldest, has always loved horses and has owned horses for more than twenty years. She and her horse, "Talk of the Town," won multiple championships in the "Hunter Show World." Cindy is an entrepreneur and is currently running "Viva La Bean," an espresso bar catering company.

Nickie has a Bachelor of Science degree in Criminal Law and a minor in psychology. She is currently working part time as she has a full time job caring for her home and children while her husband is in Afghanistan. Nickie is very devoted to her family and most thoughtful of others.

Amy has a Bachelor of Science in Nursing and is currently working at the Veteran's Hospital in Phoenix, Arizona. She is a devoted mother and very competent in her chosen profession.

Jessica is an RN in Neonatal Intensive Care and is pursuing a degree as a Doctor of Nursing Practice, specializing in pediatrics.

Leesha is entering her junior year of college at North Dakota University, with a major in the medical field.

Mayla, a sixth grader is the youngest of my granddaughters and right now is majoring in "pretty clothes and boys." She sings in the school choir.

Dear
grandmatousie
and tousie
I love you.
Are you
doing good?

Someday are
you comin to
are has?→
My mom is
have a BaBy!
And I
test for my
Belt that is
yellow! love
Stevie!

Guramutose
wut are
you going
to Ryt
BAK
to me?
And
I am
doina
gud too!
are you
haveing
fun?

A letter from my pen pal—six year old Stevie Jo.

Madelyn, the oldest of my great-granddaughters has a Master's Degree in Accounting and is a CPA working in Denver. She keeps very busy with her job, her husband Danny and their two Great Danes.

Madelyn's sister, Elissa, lives in Colorado, on a horse ranch. She, like her cousin Cindy, has always loved horses. One of my paintings is of Elissa and her horse, Princess. Elissa has a Bachelor's Degree in Psychology and is currently working on a Master's Degree in Forensic Psychology.

I saw Taylor's daughter Atlanta only a few times when she was just a baby and she resembled her daddy. Unfortunately, I have not had a chance to get acquainted with her, until recently when she moved in with her daddy.

Stevie Jo, as a preschooler, is my pen-pal. Her letters to me are precious.

Brooke is taking dance lessons and loves books. She is a tender hearted little girl, very active, very talkative, has a lot of determination and certainly has a mind of her own.

Madisson and Caitlyn are my two youngest great-granddaughters. They are both beautiful babies. Madisson is a toddler and Caitlyn was only a few months old when I attended her baptism.

The days of having Mike and his family and Beckie and her family close by gave me the opportunity to see their children often. They spent a lot of time at our house and at the cabin. Nickie loved to dress up in my jewelry and my shoes and now Brooke is following in her mother's footsteps, in my shoes!

Annual "Woodring-Forster" family reunions give me an opportunity to get better acquainted with my family as well as the families of my brothers Harold and Willis. (My older brother

Harold passed away three years ago, at age 92. And in 2011, my oldest nephew, Gary, was taken from us by cancer, at age 73.) An auction is the highlight of the reunion. Each family brings an item, preferably with family sentimental value. The proceeds are used to help defray the costs of the next year's reunion. Willis is the auctioneer, and his daughter Brenda is the highlight of the auction with her rendition of the "Auctioneer's Song." I can remember when, as a little girl, she sang that song at her daddy's auctions. Now she is a grandma!

In spite of living hundreds of miles apart, Harold, Willis and I always found ways to be together. During my years with Stanley, I recall both of my brothers meeting me in Kansas City, where we sat in a restaurant and talked most of the night. (I nearly fell asleep at our Kansas City area board meeting the next day.)

Harold helped many, including me, his sister, on the road to success by letting them know he believed in them and their ability to succeed.

Willis is one of the most generous, soft-hearted individuals I've ever known, who has helped many find a better way of life. It was while Willis was in the army, stationed at Fort Sill, Oklahoma, that he went to auctioneer school. A man by the name of Charles Gannon influenced Willis to start his own auctioneering business. Willis made progress by leaps and bounds in the auctioneering and "close-out" business. I was always amazed that he could walk through a store, any store, be it furniture, tools or jewelry, and evaluate what he could offer, to be sold at "auction close-out" for a profit. Willis put in long hours and much hard work to become the owner of Omaha Distributing. At one time he also owned "Debranice Lamp Company" (named for his three daughters, Debra,

Brenda and Denice). Although Willis is no longer an active auctioneer, our annual reunion auction gives him a chance to practice his "auctioneer cry"—and I think he has fun doing it.

I guess, in my mind, I will always be my daddy's little girl! I like to wear yellow because one day he said, "LaVera Mae, you should always wear yellow; you look so pretty in yellow."

My dad was on his death bed in Omaha. I had driven all night from Bismarck to tell him goodbye. He opened his eyes as I walked to his bedside and said, "LaVera Mae, you look so tired." Those were his last words. He died on October 29, 1963, at age 69.

It was a few days before Christmas, 1976, when I last talked to my mother. In a phone conversation I said, "I won't be able to spend Christmas with you, but I'll be there to help you celebrate your 80th birthday." She replied, "I don't think I'll be here." She passed away the day after Christmas, at age 79.

Time marches on and more and more I find that little things mean a lot. Material possessions are less valuable to me than they once were, but there are those sentimental keepsakes that money couldn't buy that mean so much: the rock with the face that Bobby brought to me from his first construction job and the clown figurine he bought with his first paycheck; the little box Beckie bought with her pennies and left on my pillow with the "I'm sorry, Mommy" note; the little blue tray Nickie made in class; the beads little Rickie strung for me; the miniature wishing well Mike and Sheryl made from a tin can and stones; the dressmaker's collage from Cindy; the quilt made by Sheryl with Czar's picture embroidered on it and the many, many letters and drawings from my grand-and great-grand kids.

Me and my children—back row—Mike,
center from left—me, Carolyn, Bobby,
from left—Beckie and Sharri

My brothers, from left—
Willis and Harold

DO I HEAR TEN?
Art by LaVera

The possessions most treasured by me are those that bring memories of a special person, time or place in my life. I believe those special treasures are to be passed down, not passed away. When a loved one passes away, their possessions, property and prayers do not die with them. Like the ancient oak tree bearing acorns generation after generation, long after the person who planted the tree has passed on, many descendants from our ancestors are still alive, sprouting new branches.

Our lives, yours and mine, are answers to more prayers than we will ever know, many that were prayed before we were born by our ancestors. It has been said, "God has a plan for all of us and He hears our prayers. He keeps the family prayer files open long after we are gone." Are many of our ancestors' prayers still alive, blessing generation after generation?

I remember my maternal great-grandmother saying her prayers with her rosary and patting me on the head while saying "Good girl." Was I included in her prayers? By reading my paternal grandmother's poetry, I can imagine the prayers she said for her children and grandchildren. It was she who instilled in my father the belief that God has a plan for each of us.

I thank God every day for the gift of life. Life is a gift to all of us and the way we live that life is our gift to others. Leaving behind a legacy on life's lessons, wishes and dreams may last longer than any gift of money ever could.

Chapter 19

WHAT'S IN A DASH?

Genealogy has become one of the nation's most popular hobbies. In 1790 when Edmund Burke wrote *Reflections of the Revolution in France,* he included the thought, "People who never look forward to prosperity will never look backward to their ancestors." More and more we Americans are asking, "Where did I come from? Why did my ancestors come to America? What part did they play in shaping the future of this wonderful country we Americans call home?" And probably the most interesting question of all, "What traits of my ancestors are showing up in me? Why am I like I am? What traits of my ancestors can I see in my children and grandchildren?"

Over the years my genealogical research has taken me to many cemeteries in the United States as well as in Europe. The headstones vary from a hand-poured marker, with name and address carved in cement, to monuments with eulogies, but always a name and dates, such as John Doe, 1850-1930. I have often wondered, "What's in the 'dash'?" "What were those 80 years like for Joe Doe? What made him tick?"

I've researched to find stories and photos of many of my ancestors. What I may be attempting to do is answer: "What's in the dash of my own life, LaVera Edick, 1925—?"

I've recorded just a bit of my "dash" information, attempting to help you, my family, know who our ancestors were and what they were like. Photos push the "I remember" buttons: those aged faces, once young, now gone, finding a grandson resembling his great-grandfather or a daughter with the same facial features as her great-great-Aunt Jeanette. I have found photos of four generations: family reunions, weddings, babies in long baptismal gowns, ladies with cinched in waist-lines and mile-high hats, horses hitched to wagons or buggies and the first black Ford cars.

My son Michael had not seen his father since he was two; however, as a young man not only did he look like his father, but he had the same mannerisms, the same gait to his walk and a similar voice. I am much like my father: my philosophy on life and religion was also his, as a result of environment, (he was raised by a Quaker mother) or was it? How much is heredity or in the genes? Why am I like I am and why is Michael a carbon copy of his father?

I realized a strong personal desire to know more about the history of the land of our forefathers and foremothers and more about them as human beings.

This is a story of our family. There are many unwritten pages in our history books. We learn about the early explorers, the law makers, presidents, V.I.P.'s, but what about the other builders of America? What about the millers, weavers, shoemakers, the farmer and his pioneer wife? This story is of them, their struggle to survive, their determination and contributions.

Over the past forty years, I have traveled the trails of pioneers along the Delaware River in Pennsylvania, routes of covered wagons from the east to the "wild west" in the early 1800's and walked in the paths of our forefathers and foremothers in Europe.

The Vautrins in France were French Huguenots. More than four hundred years before World War II and the Nazi Holocaust, another horrifying holocaust took place in France, beginning with the St. Bartholomew's Day Massacre of the Protestants, known as French Huguenots.

The reformation which began in Germany in 1517, spread to France, bringing about a great change among the people. Industry and learning flourished, and over one-third of the population began to embrace the Reformed Protestant faith. (Our Vautrin family was included in that number.) The French Protestant Huguenot uprising was based on anti-feudalism; however, the Huguenots were also striking against the established Catholic Church, as it was a part of the feudal system. Since almost half of the real estate in France was owned by the church at that time, the Huguenots were definitely a threat. A Jesuit priest and spiritual advisor to the King's Court urged the massacre of the Protestants as penance for their many sins.

The Catholics believed that the Huguenots had to be exterminated, or at least humiliated, dishonored and shamed as the inhuman beasts they were perceived to be. They found teachings in the Bible to substantiate their beliefs. Many Protestant homes were burned and many victims were thrown into the Seine River.

August 24, 1572, was the date of the Bartholomew's Day Massacre and the beginning of the murder of more than 100,000 Protestant Huguenots in one week. Ordinary lay Catholics were involved in the mass killings; there is overwhelming evidence that they believed they were executing the wishes of the King and of God. The Siege of La Rochelle began soon after 1572, and the massacre continued for centuries. Many surviving Huguenots were imprisoned or used as slave laborers. Those able to escape took their manufacturing skills with them, creating a poverty-stricken France and eventually resulting in the French Revolution.

Our Vautrins escaped to Alsace-Lorraine. The German region of Alsace held villages that were nearly deserted as a result of a plague known as the "Black Death," and killing an estimated 30 to 60 percent of Europe's population. A French tour guide told us, "It was during the "Plague Era" when the phrase, Bless You, was born—if someone sneezed, it meant almost certain death from the plague."

The German Alsace region that became home to the Protestant Huguenot families lies in a small area between the Vosges Mountains and the Rhine River with boundaries of not more than 30 miles apart. The region of French Lorraine is located in the north-east of France and borders German Alsace to the east. A series of wars ravaged the area and Lorraine went from French rule to German rule and Alsace from German rule to French rule a number of times. In the late 1500s, Alsace-Lorraine was a mosaic of French Catholic and German Protestant villages; a language evolved from the two nationalities, known as "Alsatian." The name Vautrin had two spellings and two pronunciations. In France it was Vautrin, pronounced Wautrin (since there is not a W in the French vocabulary). In German, the name soon became Wotring.

The 30-years war (1618-1648), a religious and political war, affected Alsace and Lorraine and killed 90 percent of the

Our Family Tree

population. It took many years after the end of the war for immigration to overcome the lack of population. Among the immigrants were the Vautrins from France, Samuel Vautrin's wife's family, the Beckers from Switzerland, and the Balliets.

Many of the founders of America had Huguenot ancestors, among them George Washington and Theodore Roosevelt. A Huguenot refugee named Apollos de Revoir settled in Boston and had a son who signed his name Paul Revere! Huguenot descendants realized that armed citizenry in France would have prevented the Huguenots Massacre from happening. As a result, they gave us the First and Second Amendments to the Constitution, in part giving us freedom of religion and speech and the right to keep and bear arms.

Vautrin is one of the most ancient French names and appears as early as 1227 on the Bann Rolls of Metz, in the Duchy of Lorraine, and again in 1245 and 1262 on the same rolls, in which bearers are shown to be persons of substance and position. That the Vautrins were people of consequence is shown in frequent ennoblement of Vautrins by the Duke of Lorraine as early as 1540 and as late as 1720.

When the Huguenots of the Duchy of Lorraine were driven into exile, many were deprived of their possessions and their wealth and compelled to work for a living in their place of refuge. Among the exiles were gentlemen and noblemen who were unaccustomed to manual labor. The Vautrins chose milling as their vocation. For generations they owned and operated grist mills on the River Saar and on creeks flowing into the river. The early grist mills were water-powered. A "sluice gate" was opened to allow water to flow from the river or creek, onto or under a "water wheel" making it turn and furnish power for the grinding process.

The townspeople were dependent upon the local mill, as bread was a staple part of their diet. The farmers brought their grain to be milled and in exchange received ground mill or flour, minus a percentage called the "miller's toll."

In many cases the Vautrins were the only ones in the small Alsatian villages who were literate; as a result, they were most often chosen as burgermiesters or mayors of the village.

Paulus Vautrin, born in 1570 in the Metz area of France, was the first known Vautrin in Kirrberg, a German-held village in Alsace-Lorraine. In the early 1600s during the 30 year's war, France gained control of the village and Paulus and his family were forced into exile in Barbelroth, Germany. Paulus and his wife are buried there. (Ironically my maternal ancestors, the Forsters, were also living in that same village during those years.) The Kirrberg mill is still standing. In 1984 I enjoyed a glass of wine with the resident of that mill-home, a Woodring descendant by the name of Erma Frey. Paulus Vautrin had a son, Hans Jean Vautrin, born at Kirrberg in 1605, before the family went into exile. As an adult, he returned to Kirrberg and the mill-house of his birth. He became mayor of the village, married Judith Dufour, and they became the parents of Jean Pierre Vautrin, born February 26, 1643, at the Kirrberg mill-home. Jean Pierre Vautrin married Marie Simon, daughter of the mayor of the predominately Jewish town of Lexheim. Their son, Abraham, born in 1674, married Catherine Brodt, also of Lexheim, in 1697. Abraham Wotring, Sr. built the mill-home in Finstinger, now known as Fenetrange. Many of the villages had two names, depending upon which country

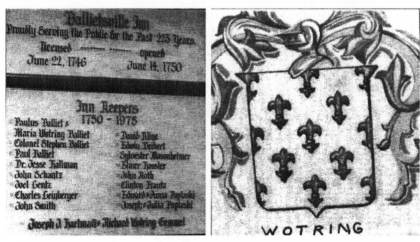

Ballietsville Inn

Built and managed by Paulus Balliet and his wife Maria (Wotring)
Balliet before the revoluntary war. An Indian fort was located under
the kitchen of the inn.

was in control. The families living in those villages had neither churches nor pastors of their own. They were of the Reformed Church and were secretly visited by pastors in the "Desert," as they called their places of hiding, the moors, valleys, quarries and hollow riverbeds in which they assembled to worship God. Abraham, Sr.'s son, Abraham, Jr., was born July 11, 1700, and Samuel in 1714, both at the Finstinger (Fenetrange) mill-home.

America must have seemed a possible haven, a place where they could enjoy freedom of worship. In Alsace, they were serving God in the fire; in America they could honor Him in the sunshine!

The Abraham, Jr. and Balliet families left their Alsatian homes as immigrants to America, arriving in Philadelphia in 1733. The long and perilous trip in a sailing vessel on the stormy Atlantic and the crowded conditions were a sure way, if not the pleasantest way, to bring out the good and bad qualities in fellow voyagers. In many instances, acquaintances formed on ship, ripened into firm and enduring friendships, resulting in the founding of homes in the same area of the "wilds" of the new world, and on occasion in the subsequent marriages of their children. Such was the case of Paulus Balliet and Mary Magdalena Wotring.

It was, indeed, "wild country" with the presence of wild beasts and venomous reptiles, a roadless, pathless wilderness, with the ever-present dread of savage Indians lurking in concealment.

Ballietsville is the oldest of the villages in North Whitehill township of Lehigh County, Pennsylvania. The village was named for Paulus Balliet and Mary Magdalena (Wotring)

Walking Purchase Plaques

By the Lenapes

By Pennsylvania Historical Society

Balliet. Balliet built a log cabin trading post in the village in the mid-1700s. It served as the church, school, town hall and a place for Indians to trade their furs for supplies. The log cabin was eventually replaced by a stone structure, known as the Whitehall Hotel. Later, the hotel name changed to Ballietsville Hotel and became a post station, where stage coach drivers changed horses. (Two of my daughters and I enjoyed dinner at the hotel's Five Star dining room in the mid-eighties, when it was still owned by Wotring descendants.)

Paulus and Mary Magdalena (Wotring) Balliet were the parents of Stephen Balliet, a colonel in the Revolutionary War, who was noted for his participation in the "Battle of the Brandywine," (now the area of one of my favorite art galleries, "The Andrew Wyeth Gallery.") According to tradition, Colonel Stephen Balliet helped save the Liberty Bell. The famous bell was hidden in a load of hay as part of a baggage train of the Army. Colonel Balliet assisted in the planning and delivery of the Liberty Bell to Allentown, Pennsylvania, where it was buried beneath the floor of a church.

In 1680, King Charles of England granted over 45,000 square miles of land, south of New Jersey and north of Maryland, now known as Pennsylvania, to William Penn. Relations with the native Lenape Indians was one where natives and colonists could walk amongst one another as brothers and friends. Although, due to the grant from the King, Penn was already in possession of the land, he made a point of purchasing it from the natives. After William Penn's death in 1718, charge of Pennsylvania fell to his three sons.

The "Walking Purchase" of 1737 was among the most devastating betrayals ever dealt to the native Lenape Indians.

The enactment of the infamous "Walking Purchase," by doctoring, or perhaps entirely forging, a document dated 1686 took many square miles of land from the Lenape. The document, were it valid, extended Penn's land north of a 1682 purchase to a distance of "as far as a man could walk in a day and a half." Penn's "hired runners" covered many times the distance of the 40 miles the Lenape had assumed to be the largest area that could be covered in a day and a half. Nearly 1,100 square miles of land was taken from them. (Could this be where the phrase "crooked as a Philadelphia Lawyer" came from?) Today monuments may be found commemorating the purchase, one being a Lenape monument citing the injustice done to them.

The Lenape Indians held deep resentment toward the men who had tricked them. They sided with the French during the French and Indian War—and bloodshed did not end there. The Indians, when wronged by a white man, took revenge on their enemies without regard to age or sex. It therefore frequently happened that the innocent suffered many times for the deeds of the guilty. Indian raids and massacres were their way of revenge. During those troubled times, the settlers would leave their homes and seek refuge in forts. In the Lehigh Valley area that was the Ballietsville Fort, which could be found beneath the kitchen of the Ballietsville Hotel.

A number of captives were taken by the Indians during that time. Those who looked more native, with dark hair and eyes, were generally adopted and not killed. A dark haired girl, whose surname was Frantz, was washing flax in a creek near Ballietsville when she was captured by the Lenape. They pricked a mark, resembling a hen's foot, on her right wrist.

She lived with an Indian as his wife and had two children that she was allowed to keep when she was returned to the whites after seven years of captivity. Two years after her return from captivity, on the 9th of May, 1769, she married Nicholas Wotring, the son of my ancestral grandfather, Samuel Wotring. She became noted for her knowledge of herbal medicines and healing traditions which she had acquired from the Indians. Her services were in great demand. She traveled by horseback throughout the valley, caring for the ill.

My ancestral grandfather, Samuel Wotring, brother of Abraham, sold his mill in Bischtroff, Alsace, and with a new bride and his four children left for America to join his brother. They embarked on the Saar River for their journey down the Rhine to Amsterdam, where they boarded the ship, Phoenix, arriving in Philadelphia on September 15, 1749. He settled near Abraham in the Lehigh County area of Pennsylvania.

On the 8th day of October, 1763, a clear, delightful fall day, a band of twelve Indians, whose fur pelts had been stolen from them the night before, crossed the Lehigh River near the Ballietsville trading post. Mistaking the Mackley home for the Balliet home, they murdered two of the children and burned their house. They proceeded to the homes of the Marks and the Schneider's. (Mrs. Schneider was Abraham Wotring's daughter.) The Marks escaped, but both homes were burned after the murder of Schneider, his wife and three children. Two more daughters were scalped and left for dead. This was the last Indian massacre in Lehigh County.

In 1763, the Samuel Wotring mill on Copley Creek, near Schnecksville, Pennsylvania, was built from logs contributed by the neighbors. This log mill was in operation until 1837,

Phillip and Maria Elizabeth Woodring are buried at Hay Cemetery in Easton, PA. Phillip was a Revolutionary War veteran.

Phillip Woodring's Blacksmith shop at Easton PA.

Joseph Woodring, grandson of Phillip—father of Cyrus Woodring.

when a two-story, stone mill (still standing in 1981) was built to replace it by Samuel's son, Samuel, Jr. Sand Springs Park, in Schnecksville, was the site of Wotring, Woodring family reunions, beginning in 1904, for nearly 100 years.

Samuel's oldest son Philip left home in his late teens to become an apprentice blacksmith to Peter Lattig of Easton, Pennsylvania, and became known as Philip Woodring. There were and still are Wotrings in the Lehigh County area, 30 miles to the west, and Woodrings in Easton, all of the same Samuel Wotring family.

Both Philip Woodring and Peter Lattig, who emigrated from Holland, were Revolutionary War veterans and both were elders in the Reformed Church of Easton, which was used as a military hospital during the war. Philip and his wife, Elizabeth (Wagner) Woodring are both buried in the Hay Cemetery at Easton.

The hereditary traits of the Vautrins, Wotrings, and Woodrings showed extraordinary strength and persistence in religious matters as well as in their vocation. They were not only devout Reformed Protestants, but they followed the milling profession through many generations for more than three hundred years—on both hemispheres, in the old world and the new.

Philip Woodring's son John married Peter Lattig's daughter Elizabeth. John and Elizabeth were farmers and had a son Joseph, born March 15, 1813 and nicknamed Josh, he married Anna Maria Fenstermacher in February of 1836. Maria was the youngest child of a large family. Her father died in 1815 shortly before she was born. Little Cyrus, my great-grandfather, was born on May 31, 1836, and after that a baby a year was born, or almost. Maria tried to nurse her babies as long as she could, believing that by using that method she could prevent another pregnancy. She really didn't want a large family like her mother, Anna Maria (Wuchter) Fenstermacher, but what choice was there? Josh was a hot-blooded American male and it was her "wifely duty." Of course, some of that "amour" could have been a result of his French heritage. Josh's early male Vautrin ancestors were very well educated—Jean Pierre Vautrin was fluent in both German and French, but only two generations later, when Jean's grandson Samuel came to America, he could only make his mark ^^. It was an impressive mark, but Josh could never figure out what it meant—Vautrin, Wotring, Woodring or Wotring Mills? Josh's father John gave land for the first school in Cedarville, a little village near Easton, and he and his brothers learned the three R's.

Josh would no doubt have been called an entrepreneur. It wasn't long before Esq. was being used after his name in the Easton Press. The first land he bought just happened to be rich in iron ore and the Glendon Iron Mine prospered. Josh bought land and more land as well as shares in the Easton North Hampton County National Bank. He planted apple orchards and built a beautiful brick home nearby in Cedarville.

Josh and Maria's son, Cyrus, married Mary Hannah Horn on July 9, 1857, and brought her home to live with his parents. Cyrus' bride was the daughter of Elijah and Elizabeth (Frost) Horn. Elizabeth's parents, Thomas and Hannah Frost, came to Lambertville, New Jersey, from England in 1825. Mary Hannah's mother was a strong willed woman with a show of determination that helped her cope with life. Because there

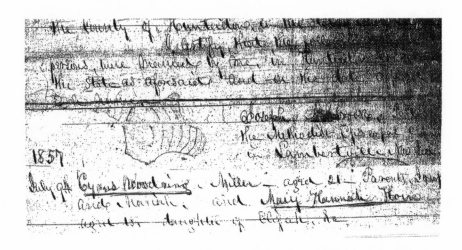

Cyrus and Mary (Horn) Woodring
and their son, Hubert.

NEBRASKA GRIST MILL
Art by LaVera

was never enough money for food and rent, she became a dressmaker and a bobbin lace maker, skills she had been taught by her mother. Elijah was a door-to-door shoemaker. It was Julia Horn, sister of my great-grandmother Mary Hannah, who told Ruth Woodring's brother, Earl, that her grandfather was a great law-maker. I have searched in vain to find proof that our famous lawmaker grandfather was James Wilson, signer of the Declaration of Independence.

Both the James Wilson family and the Horn family lived in New Jersey in the early 1800s. Two of the Wilson children were named Mary and Elijah. Mary Wilson married Benjamin Horn in 1809 and Elijah Wilson Horn was born in1810. One of Mary and Elijah Wilson Horn's sons was given the name of Wilson and Wilson was the middle name of several other sons. Their oldest daughter was named Mary Hannah. The first female child born into the family was traditionally named for both grandmothers. Mary Hannah's maternal grandmother's name was Hannah. Could Mary be for her paternal grandmother Mary Wilson? My grandfather, son of Cyrus Woodring and Mary Hannah (Horn), was named Charles Wilson Woodring. The middle name of Wilson continued in that family for several generations. I am still searching for proof of Elijah Horn's birth to Mary Wilson and Benjamin Horn and our relationship to James Wilson, but might word of mouth be good enough?

Mary Hannah went to her parents' home in Lambertville when the first two babies were born, William and my grandfather, Charles Wilson Woodring. Cyrus insisted on the babies being baptized at the Reformed Church in Easton,

Pennsylvania, the church of the Woodrings since before the Revolutionary War.

Cyrus worked at his Uncle Williams' grist mill near Easton. He developed a bad cough and lung problems probably as a result of dust from the mill. Because of Cyrus' health, his father Joseph helped him buy a farm and he moved his family to Illinois. The farm was swamp land and it seemed Cyrus really wasn't cut out to be a farmer. The farm was sold and he went to work at a mill in Rockton, Illinois. Cyrus and his family moved from mill to mill. When his wife saw him looking at a map, she and the kids started packing. His father Joseph loaned him money now and then to help support a family of thirteen and always sent a barrel of apples at Christmas time. I'm not sure why Grandpa Cyrus went from mill to mill so often, but I've been told he kept moving to mills using stone burrs and the old method of grinding. As soon as the mill owner modernized to steel rollers, he left. (He would have been a "sought after" miller today. Stone ground flour is preferred by many bakers and natural food advocates because of better texture, nutty flavor and the belief that it is nutritionally superior and has better baking qualities.) In 1873, he moved his family to Milledgeville, Illinois, where he was proprietor of a mill for several years. He was a miller in Salem, Nebraska, when he died at age 63.

My father must have been a lot like his namesake, Cyrus, whose granddaughter described as a gentle, hard working man perfectly willing to be a foil to his dominant, fiery, English wife. However, with his German determination, when he felt something deeply, he held his ground. His wife, Mary Hannah, was known to be strong-willed with

Our Yetter Family in Freckenfeld

Our Forsters in Rulfenrod

a mind of her own. Cyrus often left his wife at home and pregnant. She gave birth to 13 children in 23 years, an average of 13 months between babies. She probably nursed the babies as long as she could, as that, other than abstinence, was the only known birth control in those days, and even that was uncertain. She was pregnant almost half of her childbearing years. Apparently she wasn't strong willed enough to say "no." Cyrus had gone to a farm sale in the neighborhood and left her home pregnant. A neighbor and his wife came along and she asked if she could climb in their wagon and go to the sale with them. (When her husband sighted her, she just stuck her nose in the air and looked the other way.)

In 2006, my niece Karen, her son Kevin and I traveled to Europe in search of descendants of our maternal ancestors: the Yetters and the Forsters in Germany and the Tomaseks in Bohemia, now a part of the Czech Republic.

Our guardian angels surely must have been with us. We found Yetters, as owners of a catering business in Freckenfeld, Germany, and Forsters, who were organic farmers in Rulfenrod, Germany. I had researched both of these villages years ago and found church records from the 1600s, where birth, baptism and death records were recorded in Latin.

We visited the town of Neider-Gemunden, Germany, where my great-grandfather, Henry David Forster, was born on October 25, 1829. He was only six years old when his father, Ernst Forster, was killed by a gunshot in a careless way (according to church records). The Forsters were foresters, who, at that time, were the only citizens of Germany allowed to carry guns. Henry David migrated from the Port of Bremen, Germany, on June 29, 1849, landing in New York City on August 22ⁿᵈ of the same year.

Our next stop was Vollmersweiler, Bavaria, Germany, the birthplace of Elizabeth Yetter who migrated to America at age 20.

Henry Forster and Elizabeth Yetter met and married in Putman County, Illinois, on April 7, 1856. I have a copy of a page from the family Bible listing the names and birthdates of their fourteen children, written in German.

Our next stop was Fenetrange, the Alsace area of France, and the former home and mill site of my paternal ancestors, Abraham Wotring, Sr., father of Abraham, Jr. and Samuel. We knew that the ruins of the mill were on Little Mill Road, but neither Ruth nor I were successful in finding the site on our trips to Europe in the 80s. Kevin used his German vocabulary and his quest for knowledge of our family in finding the present owner of the old mill building. We were invited to a nearby restaurant for conversation and refreshments. (I later did a painting of the restaurant building, an old hotel, a tower nearby and an archway that was a gate to the city in olden days.) We walked through that archway down Little Mill Road to the site of Abraham, Sr.'s mill, built in late 1600 to the early 1700s. I was trusting my memory to find other Vautrin, Wotring mill homes; it had been 22 years since my last visit there. We were successful in finding the early Vautrin mill-home built in the 1600s in Kirrberg and the Samuel Wotring home in Bischtroff; however, both homes had deteriorated since I saw them in 1984.

Henry D. Forster
Migrated from Germany
in 1849.

Elizabeth Yetter
was 20 when she came
to America from Bavaria.

Henry and Elizabeth met in Putman County, Illinois
and were married on April 7, 1856

Samuel Wotring's Mill in Alsace—ca. 1740

FENETRANGE
Art by LaVera

Site of Samuel's father Abraham's mill.

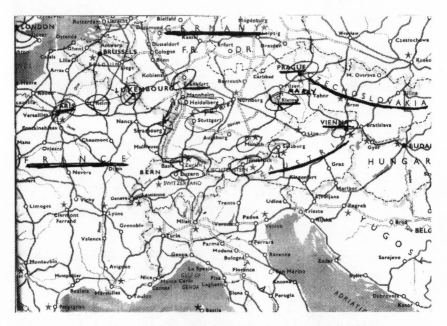

We found our Tomasek family in Makov, now Czech Republic, near
Klatovy. Our Woodring, Wotring family is from Alsace, France,
North of Strasbourg.

Our Tomasek family, Jacob and Tereza and their six children, including my grandmother Anna, came to America on the ship "Moravia," arriving in New York City on April 2, 1886. They homesteaded five miles north of Smithfield in Gosper County, Nebraska.

Near Klatory, in the Czech Republic, in the small village of Makov, we found Tomaseks. Our guardian angels were still with us! The first door we knocked on turned out to be the site of the first Tomasek home in the area in the early 1500s. It was there that we met a young girl, Jaroslava Tomaskova, a descendant of the family who could speak English. She was a godsend in searching local archives in the months ahead. We still correspond. She has married, and has two children, whose pictures are in my refrigerator gallery. In the same village of Makov, we found more Tomasek descendants living on a farm that had been a Tomasek Brick Factory hundreds of years ago. How could I refuse an antique, hexagon shaped brick from the Tomasek farm? What made my suitcase so heavy? Why, a brick of course!

The desire to learn from whence I came, led me to trace my Woodring family back to "Pre-Revolutionary War Days," and to become a member of Daughters of the American Revolution, (D.A.R.). I applied for membership through the records of Philip Woodring. Becoming a D.A.R. member made me more appreciative of our flag and what it stands for. I wanted to learn how my ancestors participated in building our country, the United States of America.

The study of Western Civilization in college and our art class tour of Europe in 1984 was a start. Working as an assistant librarian at the L.D.S. Genealogical Library in

1776 *1890*

THE NATIONAL SOCIETY OF THE

Daughters of the American Revolution

This certifies that

LaVera Woodring Edick

is a regularly approved member of the National Society of the Daughters of the American Revolution, having been admitted by the National Board of Management by virtue of her descent from a patriot who with unfailing loyalty rendered material aid to the cause of American Independence during the Revolutionary War

Given under our hands and the seal of the National Society this seventh *day of* December *1983*

National No 678558
Admitted December 7th 1983

I became a member of D.A.R. in 1983

1776 *1890*

THE NATIONAL SOCIETY OF THE

Daughters of the American Revolution

To all to whom these presents shall come, Greeting:

Know ye, that reposing special trust and confidence in the fidelity, diligence and discretion of La Vera Woodring Edick

We, the Daughters of the American Revolution, at the Ninety-eighth Continental Congress *have confirmed her* State Vice Regent of North Dakota

Therefore, she is hereby authorized and empowered to execute and fulfill the duties of said office, according to the By-laws of said National Society until her successor is elected.

In witness whereof, the President General, the Recording Secretary General and the Organizing Secretary General have hereunto set their hands and caused the Seal of the National Society to be affixed, at Washington, D.C. this twenty-first day of April 1989.

Ann D. Fleck
President General

Yvonne S. Boone
Organizing Secretary General

Dorla E. Kemper
Recording Secretary General

Bismarck was also good training. The head librarian, Beth Bauman, was a good teacher.

I became a member of the Bismarck-Mandan Genealogical Society and in 1987 became its president. During the same year, I met Steve Barthel from the L.D.S. Library in Salt Lake City, Utah. He taught a class at our workshop on European research and I taught "Beginning Genealogy." (Teaching teaches the teacher.) Steve invited me to visit him and his wife in Salt Lake City and offered to help me do research in the library. I owe much of my success in genealogical research to my good friend, Steve.

I became regent for our local D.A.R. Chapter and two years later was elected as State Regent. I resigned that position due to a change in my lifestyle during the Indian summer of my life.

Recently, we Americans found ourselves in what was called, not the Great Depression, but the Great Recession. Terrorism and an anti-Islamic backlash brought questions of religion. The Islamic poet, Rumi, said, "God is like an ocean and religions are like the rivers that all flow into the same ocean, our origins are the same, our destinations are the same; it is our paths that are different."

From 2007 to 2010 American households are said to have lost eleven trillion dollars in real estate savings and stocks. More than half of U.S. workers either lost their jobs or were forced to take cuts in hours and pay. Bankruptcies were reported to be at a sixty-five-year high.

We reshaped how we lived, worked and spent, even the way we thought about our future. Many of life's big decisions, such as whether to marry, have children or even to divorce are said to have been postponed, awaiting better times. We learned to separate our wants from our needs and found ourselves spending less on unnecessary clothing, restaurant meals, vacations and all the frills the average family had splurged on in the past. We rolled up our sleeves and did what needed to be done when our nation faced a crisis. We, as Americans, have a history of working together and recognizing the value of people over things.

Chapter 20

THEN IT'S WINTER

The winter of my life is near. "Indian Summer" and fall drifting into winter becomes more evident each day. I feel a reluctance to arise early in the morning, and I'm aware of the extra effort it takes to get up from my recliner. Although my body is saying, "It's winter," my mind is saying, "But I still have a lot of entries on my (to do) list."

Winter has always been a time for me to sit back, reminisce and catch up on all those things I've put on the "back burner" during the earlier, busier seasons.

The school of life is going well; however, year after year I seem to get the lowest grade in "Weight Loss." I have followed, or attempted to follow, Dr. Gott's "no flour no sugar diet." I am addicted to sugar and chocolate and just like fighting any addiction it is very difficult. I backslide far too often. When I read that dark chocolate was actually good for you, I resolved to eat just one Dove Chocolate a day! That resolution was soon broken! Have you noticed that grocers put the candy bar display right by the check-out counter? Some days, especially if its mealtime, I just can't resist; however, I no longer buy the little Halloween candy bars, the ones I like best, for trick or treaters.

I'm finding a trip to the grocery store is a real challenge for the day. I don't walk well, but I do walk, and I use the grocery cart to make it easier. I find my days are shorter and I need more sleep. My steps are slower and it takes longer to do what needs to be done. I still have 24 hours of time to spend each day; however, my energy is being rationed and I need to find ways to conserve it. Taking a nap is not just a treat anymore, it is a necessity, 'cause if I don't I just might fall asleep in my recliner.

I'm attempting to make both of my homes more adaptable to the winter season of my life. I've cleared out top shelves to eliminate the need of a step stool, and I've weeded out many unused, unneeded items from my closets, cupboards and décor, making it easier to clean and dust. I do my own housework; however, I've discovered the furniture doesn't need to be dusted each week and the bed sleeps just as well if the sheets are changed every ten days instead of each week.

I cook more than one meal at a time and freeze the extra. I rinse dishes after each meal, but load the dishwasher and clean counters while I'm standing at the stove cooking. If I sit down, I'm apt to let something on the stove burn.

In Bismarck I use a little red wagon to help me move things, such as flower pots, from place to place in the yard, and to carry groceries from the car to the house.

I keep an extra gallon of milk, loaf of bread and meat in the freezer, so some weeks I only need to shop for fresh fruits and vegetables.

I often refer to the steps I have taken as my self-designed "Assisted Living Program."

Even though I spend a lot of time in my chair, I can still work on genealogy, paint portraits of my grandkids, do memory scrap books, write stories and improve my skills at the computer.

My faithful companion, a West Highland Terrier named Tousie, takes good care of me and loves me unconditionally. I realize Tousie has me very well trained, as did the two before her, Czar and Tina. Tousie is always so happy to see me when I return from even a short shopping trip, and I know she thinks I am just about perfect.

When I lost Tina when she was 12, I did not plan to get another dog. It was right after my accident and I couldn't walk without the aid of a walker or cane. Destiny played a part! I opened the Bismarck Tribune one morning to see an ad for West Highland Terrier puppies for sale. I called the phone number given and asked, "Do you have a female puppy?" My heart fell when she answered, "I'm sorry, we only had one female and she has been sold." I took the liberty of asking, "Could I ask you how much you charged for her?" When she answered, "$300.00," I replied, "I would have given you $500.00." A few days later Mrs. McDonald called back, "If you still want a female puppy, I have one available." I went to see the puppy, paid $500.00 for her and two weeks later brought Tousie home with me. I can't imagine my life now without her.

I would use my cane to let her off her leash at the back door and then drop it by my chair when I sat down. Tousie would pick it up and carry it away, forcing me to walk in order to retrieve it. In that way, she helped me learn to walk without a cane.

CZAR

TINA

Art by LaVera

TOUSIE

If I get too involved in a project, Tousie reminds me it is time to eat or time to go to bed. I am a "night owl" and oft-times just can't wait until morning to see how a book ends! Tousie will stand in front of me and give me a, "Don't you know its bedtime?" look and then toddle off to bed and our pillow. Tousie shares half the pillow with me. We play a few games of tug of war at bedtime and she rolls onto her back for her nightly "tummy massage" before saying "aah" and cuddling up on our pillow. When we get up very early in the morning for "potty breaks" and it is chilly, she often climbs under the blankets and my feet get a thorough washing. I awaken a few hours later with her little black nose snuggled in my hair, assuring me all is well and that we can catch a "few more winks." Some nights are short, almost sleepless, unlike those nights when dreams carry me back to places and people I've known over years past, albeit in very different and sometimes very weird scenarios! My mother would cringe if she could see me let Tousie clean off my plate at the end of a meal! Mealtime is special to Tousie. She waits to eat her dog food until she smells what we are having for dinner. Of course she loves meat, but cooked carrots and egg yolks are a special treat! Do you suppose they will improve her eyesight as she ages? Tousie has a pet door, but she was house trained to use the back door and she still insists I put her on her leash for that purpose; the front yard is her play area! As an added item on my "Assisted Living Program" and as it becomes more difficult for me to walk, I'm attempting to teach her to use only the pet door.

I live in my twin home in Mesa, Arizona, during the winter months to avoid the risk of falling on ice and snow; however, summer finds me back in my mobile home in Bismarck, where I enjoy my yard, flowers, family and many friends. Tousie flies with me from Bismarck to Mesa in November and back to Bismarck in May. She travels in a small flexible kennel that is placed under the seat in front of me. She is a good little traveler. I put my bare foot on the mesh part of the kennel; she puts her little nose on my foot and sleeps for the entire two-and-a-half-hour trip. My one way fare last fall was $90.00, while her fare was $100.00. Shouldn't she have a seat? Tousie loves both of her homes and adapts easily. Our Bismarck home has a lot of trees and a fenced yard accessible through her pet door. She loves to get a squirrel trapped in a tree, then dance around the tree on her hind legs barking at it.

The winter years of my life are a time to reminisce and a time to remember dear friends and acquaintances who have influenced my outlook and acceptance of this season of my life. Ida Lee Prokop, my artist friend, slept on a wooden slab in lieu of a soft bed, and at age 86 she had the initials L.O.L.O.T.G. printed on her business cards. The initials stood for "Little Old Lady on the Go." Ida did a sculpture for the 50th Anniversary of North Dakota, "Daughters of Dakota," depicting a pioneer woman holding a Bible, walking through prairie grasses with her daughters. She did sculptures of nine Indian busts, representing each North Dakota tribe and donated them to the State Historical Society.

I remember a very spry, 91-year-old Morton County pioneer, Nancy Hendrickson. When my friend Jewel and I visited her on her Heart River Valley homestead farm she was wearing a green visor cap, kept from the days of her motorcycle riding. She was the first woman in North Dakota to get a license to

The reason why I am a snow bird!

My winter home in Mesa

My summer home in Bismarck

drive a motorcycle. Nancy was well known for her animal photography during World War I. She photographed farmstead pets dressed to resemble people. By using doll-sized clothing and miniature props, she set them in poses imitating human activities. She gained national attention and many of her photographs were used on the penny postcards of that era.

My other mother, Ruth, at 98-years-young was still making statements such as, "Just look at those beautiful clouds," and noticing the jewelry or a pretty sweater her nurse was wearing. Her nurses commented on her outlook on life and her positive attitude.

Winter is a time to remember some of my dreams and fulfill a few of them; a time to sleep in if I want to; a time to stay up until 2:00 a.m. working on my projects; a time to wear purple and red and walk around the house in my pajamas and bare feet.

I have a beautiful family and many friends, both near and far. I thank God every day for all the little things that make life so special: the doves cooing in my Mesa yard; the frisky squirrels in the trees in Bismarck; the bunnies who seem to have made friends with Tousie; the couple who helped me find my "lost" car in a crowded Walmart parking lot.

I'm trying to sort out priorities, trying to make more time for the things that are really important to me. I'm also realizing that time is our most valuable commodity; if not used, it is lost.

Yes, life is good and the winter years of my life are special years. It has been soul-searching and very rewarding to record "What's in the Dash" of my life. Time marches on and there are many, many aspects of my life waiting to be fulfilled before the last snowflake falls.